I Hate Purdue

Why Hoosier Fans Hate the Old Gold and Black

I Hate Purdue

Why Hoosier Fans Hate the Old Gold and Black

Joe Drozda

BLUE RIVER PRESS

Indianapolis, Indiana

Contents

Introduction

The Purdue–Indiana rivalry is a rivalry between the Purdue University (Boilermakers) and the Indiana University (Hoosiers). These are the two largest schools in the state of Indiana. Although Purdue students and alumni won't admit it, IU is larger than Purdue by 2,000 undergrads, IU is 49 years older than Purdue, and IU is the more popular of the two schools. When IU has winning teams, IU sweatshirts crop up around the state, even among people that didn't attend college. Even when the Hoosier teams are not winning, merchants that sell licensed college merchandise have learned that they need to stock more IU stuff than that of Purdue. After all, IU is named for the state. Purdue is named for a businessman buried on campus.

Students from these respective schools are usually somewhat vulgar in their taunts and chants during athletic competitions. Alumni, locally and nationwide, chide alums from the other school regularly before and after games between the two schools. During "Rivalry Week" the days preceding the Old Oaken Bucket game, the good-natured fun gets more visual. The local IU Varsity Club chairman once received a presentation at his Lafayette Rotary club of a mini-replica of the Old Oaken Bucket filled with Green Slime, a Mattel kid's craft gunk. Another IU alumnus was awarded, at a sales award banquet, a package in front of more than a hundred associates and their spouses. As he unwrapped the package, he discovered it was

a Purdue sweatshirt. He promptly dropped the sweatshirt onto the floor behind the podium and pretended to wipe his feet on it. Later it was discovered that he didn't actually wipe his feet on it and had preserved it to wear, inside-out, when he worked on his car. Another Indiana alumnus and I-Man, an executive at an insurance company in Ohio, flew home from a business trip to find one of those vinyl wall hangings of a Purdue Boilermaker player on his office wall.

Many Indiana University fans smilingly tolerate these good-natured taunts by Purdue students and alumni. Of course, these things go both ways, but that's for another book another time.

IU fans don't really hate Purdue, the Boilermaker players, or the students that attend Purdue. After all, many of them are neighbors. But they do find pleasure when watching Purdue lose. This is evidenced in a statement common to IU fans, "My two favorite teams are IU and whoever is playing Purdue."

We Hate Losing to Purdue

1943: Purdue 7, Indiana 0—
Final Drive Stalls on Six

After three straight Old Oaken Bucket victories over Purdue by a combined 30–0, Hoosier fans were expecting another "I" to be placed on the Bucket on this beautiful fall Saturday. But it was the Boilermakers who got to celebrate with a 7–0 victory and a tie with Michigan for the Beg Ten championship.

Purdue broke a three-year IU Old Bucket winning streak in 1943 when they narrowly won to take back the Bucket.

The Hoosiers won everything but the final score as they bested Purdue in first downs 13–9, rushing 132–116, and passing 118–67.

The game started with the Hoosier defense dominating Purdue from the beginning. Purdue took the opening kick-off and went three and out. Then they muffed a punt kicking to their own 47-yard line. IU then drove down to the Boiler 17 and gave up an interception to Vacanti to kill the drive. After another Purdue punt and an IU drive to the Boilermaker 5-yard line, Purdue's Chalmers Elliott intercepted a Hoernschemeyer pass and took it out to the 25-yard line. Later in that drive, Sam Vacanti lobbed a pass down the sidelines to Frank Bauman, who ran on to score the game's only touchdown.

Late in the first half, Pete Pihos brought the crowd to their feet when he intercepted a Purdue pass and raced it back to the Boilermakers' 15-yard line as the first half ended. There were time management issues on the Indiana sideline. If the Hoosiers would have called a time-out, there could have been one more play.

To open the third quarter, Purdue kicked off to IU and the Hoosiers got a return to the 32, however IU stalled and punted it to the Purdue 19-yard line. Then Pete Pihos fell on a Purdue fumble. Mangold circled the end for 21 yards, and the Hoosiers were about to make a touchdown. A pass to Pihos was completed, and it was first down and nine yards to "payoff dirt." A line buck yielded a yard, a pass over the line was grounded, a third attempt caught Bob Hoernschemeyer behind the line of scrimmage, and on the fourth Vacanti intercepted for the Boilermakers. Indiana had blown its golden opportunity.

Late in the fourth quarter, Hoernschemeyer was trapped way behind the line and managed a scramble for a nine-yard gain. IU got the first down on a plunge-off tackle, then Hoernschemeyer threw a pass to Frank Hoppe for first-and-ten at the Purdue 22-yard line with two minutes left on the clock. Hoernschemeyer hit John McDonnell with a pass for first-and-goal at the six.

IU ran to the one as Purdue fans dreaded another time they failed against IU. But after two runs, the IU hopes ended on an incomplete Hoosier pass. Purdue ran out the last six seconds on the clock to seal the win.

1968: Purdue 38, Indiana 35— Decided By Referees?

As 63,294 spectators watched, Indiana's second-straight Old Oaken Bucket victory was snatched away by a call of the referees— at least, if you ask the IU coaches, it was—after the final Purdue score with 1:35 to go. Indiana had a last, flickering chance. IU driving referee Remy Meyer signaled that Indiana had made the line to gain on a critical fourth down. A Purdue player asked for a remeasurement. The chain was stretched out tight, and this time, the man in the striped shirt pointed the other way: Purdue's ball. The Hoosier's hopes for a win and a huge upset were gone.

Coach John Pont was very upset about the officials signaling an Indiana first down, then reversing themselves with a new measurement that gave Purdue possession. Pont ran onto the field for only the second time in his life. "No one can convince me an official can signal a first down, have the chains lifted up and removed from the ball, then allow someone to ask for a remeasurement and change the decision," he said with burning conviction and visible anger. "The ball was moved. This I firmly believe. But, even if it wasn't, you just can't move the chains and remeasure after once giving a signal. You live with that call or die with it. The officials were glassy-eyed. I told them the ball must have been moved but they said it wasn't, and that was the only reply I got. I'm not proud of going onto the field like that. But there comes a time when you have to fight for your players and that was it. If it comes again, I'd do the same thing. It's a downright shame that some officials can't have the same courage as the ball players in a game like this. You can't say that call beat us. But we had been moving the ball, and we had momentum, so who knows what would have happened?"

As the day began, Bob Pernell took off on a 64-yard run to give IU the first score and a lead, 7–0, after Don Warner's extra point. Then Leroy Keys, probably the greatest back ever to play for Purdue, evened the score with a 42-yard run and Jones kick. IU got back in charge when Jade Butcher scored on a four-yard pass from Harry Gonzo. The first quarter ended with IU in the lead, 14–7.

In the second period, both teams scored as Eric Stolberg caught a 26-yard Gonzo Pass that, coupled with a Warner kick, made the score 21–7. Purdue added a Jones, 30-yard field goal to cut IU's halftime lead to 21–10.

After the half, the Hoosiers made it 28–10 on a 29-yard pass from Gonzo to Butcher. Then Perry Williams, who fumbled away the previous year's Bucket at IU, scored from the one-yard line. The score was 28–17.

In the final stanza, Jade Butcher continued his mastery of the Purdue pass defenders by scoring on a 29-yard pass from Gonzo. IU spread the lead to 35–17.

Then Mike Phipps took charge of the game, completing 11 passes as Purdue scored on a 56-yard heave to Keys, then another Keys touchdown from the one on a Phipps-led drive. The final was 38–35.

1969: Purdue 96, Indiana 95— Charity from the Hoosiers

On a cold (30-degree) Tuesday night in February in Bloomington, Indiana, IU made eight more field goals than Purdue and outrebounded them by a 57–44 margin. So why did Purdue win? They hit 32 free throws when it counted, down-the-stretch.

Purdue jumped out to a commanding lead in the first half as Rick Mount, the Big Ten's leading scorer hit seven field goals in 11 tries. Purdue cashed in on 18 of their first 32 shots in the half. At the same time, IU was struggling to score. IU hit only 16 of 48 shots before the break. The halftime score was 53–39, Purdue.

As had been the case all season, the Hoosiers turned things around in the second half. They scored 56 points by banging the boards and getting tip-ins and shorter shots. IU coach Lou Watson said, "We're making a career of second-half comebacks, but this was the best one yet." The Hoosiers clawed their way back into the game and tied the score at 77, 83, and 85.

In the waning minutes, IU's Kenny Johnson made a basket to tie the score at 87. Purdue's Jerry Johnson (no relation) got the Boilermakers back in front on a rebound basket and a Bill DeHeer foul. He made the free throw and Purdue was up 90–87. Then Rick Mount made two free throws to give the Boilers a 92–87 lead. Joe Cooke and Kenny Johnson both scored to get IU back to 91 points with 1:43 on the clock. At this time, the 9,326 fans packed into the 17th Street Fieldhouse roared! But Purdue cashed four more free throws, the last two by Gilliam to take a 96–93 lead with just four seconds left. Joe Cooke made one last long-jumper before the buzzer to make the final score 96–95.

Purdue's men in double figures were Mount with 32, Gilliam 21, Bavis 13, and Weatherford 11. These four made 27 of 28 free throws. IU had Kenny Johnson with 29, DeHeer 21, Cooke 20, and Noland 17. The free throw figures for the game were Purdue 32 of 37 and Indiana 15 of 25. Obviously, the way to win a rivalry game is to shoot more free throws and make them.

1973: Purdue 72, Indiana 69— A Hiccup On the Way to the Final Four

Figuring that the Boilermakers needed to cool off IU's leading scorers—six-foot, nine-inch center Steve Downing and John Ritter, a forward/guard—Purdue's coach Fred Schaus had Jovan Price and Jerry Nichols work the whole week to prepare for Ritter. They succeeded by holding him to no field goals and only two points. Preparing John Garrett for IU's center was a different story. Garrett fouled out, and Downing got 25 points.

Coach Knight shook up the IU lineup by starting Freshman Tom Abernethy instead of Jim Crews at guard. This didn't work well, and the Hoosiers fell behind 23–16. Then Crews came in and IU got a five-point burst as Crews hit three free throws (one for a Purdue technical). John Laskowski made a basket, Quinn Buckner scored, and IU had a 28–27 lead. Purdue went back on top 31–30 at the half. IU, the conference's second-best shooting team, was held to a 31 shooting-percentage in the half. Purdue shot even worse at 29 percent.

As the second half developed, the Boilermakers went on a run-and-gun spree, taking a 53–45 lead with 10:30 left on the clock. By this time, Garrett was in foul trouble and Downing and Steve Green cashed in to bring IU back to 66–65 with 3:13 to play. Down the stretch, IU held the ball for one last shot, but this failed as Steve Green was called for charging. Bruce Parkinson cashed two free tosses, and the game ended with two meaningless Jerry Nichols free throws to bring the Boiler total to 72.

Dennis Gamauf (much maligned all season) led Purdue by making nine of 13 shots and 22 points. Bruce Parkinson scored 14 points with six free throws down the stretch in the second half. John Garrett had 14. Both Garrett and Frank Kendrick fouled out for Purdue, as did Quinn Buckner for IU. The Hoosier scoring was led by Downing with 25 points and 10 rebounds. Steve Green had 14 points and Buckner, 12.

At the end of this season, IU won the Big Ten and made it to the final four of the NCAA.

1975: Purdue 9, Indiana 7— Fumble Costs a Bucket

On the Saturday before Thanksgiving, 43,455 fans were a witness to a tragic loss of the Old Oaken Bucket by Lee Corso's Hoosiers that only lacked a Frank Stavroff chip shot field goal to register a win. Instead, a fumble in the waning seconds gave the ball back to Purdue on their own six-yard line.

The first half of the game was scoreless until Purdue's Steve Schmidt kicked a 22-yard field goal. The final for the half was just 3–0.

In the third quarter, the Hoosiers took charge as strong line play gave them excellent field position at their 49-yard line seven minutes into the period. IU charged straight down the field on the back of Courtney Snyder, who slashed for 36 yards in seven carries. This six-and-one-half-minute drive ended when Snyder slammed across from the four-yard line. The Hoosiers took the lead, 7–3, on Frank Stavroff's extra point.

Purdue's final drive began in the last quarter starting from their 18-yard line. It began as they began using fullback Mike Pruitt almost exclusively due to star halfback Scott Dierking's ankle injury. There was, however, one big pass on the drive on a key second down. Quarterback Mark Vitali hit wide receiver Jesse Townsend for 28 yards to Purdue's 46-yard line. Pruitt took charge, gaining 36-yards on nine plays ending, on the IU two-yard line. Then Paul Beery went around the end for the score and a 9–7 Boilermaker lead with only an extra point necessary to make it three-point game. A high center snap caused Schmidt to miss the extra point, giving the Hoosier crowd hope.

IU only needed a field goal to win, but in the last eight minutes the Hoosiers coughed up possession three times. Two of these turnovers were when the Crimson were well within kicker Frank Stavroff's range. The killer came with 17 seconds left as quarterback Dobby Grossman dropped back and fired a completion over the middle to flanker Keith Calvin for 24 yards to the Purdue 7-yard line. IU already had used all of its timeouts, but there were still enough seconds left for Stavroff to swing into action. That is, except for one thing, they had to hold on to the ball. Purdue defenders swarmed Calvin, causing a fumble recovered by Boilermaker senior Dave Guthrie. Purdue ran out the clock and got to put a "P" on the Bucket, the last one they would win for a few years.

It was a tragic loss and a devastating blow to the Hoosiers, especially to Keith Calvin—who had been separated from the ball after a nice gain to the six-yard line—and to Lee Corso, who had yet to beat Purdue.

After the game, Corso said, "I believe very strongly that His will be done. That's all I've got to go on. This may be the hardest thing I've ever had to accept. I guess you just have to have faith in God. That's what I told Calvin after the fumble. We may have lost the game, but I think it was the turnaround for us. It proved we've established a football program where we can go out and be competitive Saturday after Saturday.

"We've got nothing to be ashamed of: the players, the coaches, and the IU alumni." IU President, John Ryan agreed. Corso's Hoosiers beat Purdue the next two years to prove his point.

1983: Indiana 30, Purdue 31— Two-Point Conversion Fails

Five days before Thanksgiving, Purdue visited IU's Memorial Stadium to play in front of a near sell-out crowd of 52,038 fans for the Old Oaken Bucket. The Boilermakers were logical favorites with their two great running backs, Mel Gray and Lloyd Hawthorne.

The first quarter ended with a tie, 0–0. Purdue had the ball on the IU one-yard line. The Boilers then scored on the first play of the second quarter on Gray's one-yard plunge. The Hoosiers tied it, 7–7, driving 63 yards on six plays with Orlando Brown scoring from the eight-yard line. Then Purdue came right back, driving 80 yards in 10 plays. Campbell threw 13 yards to Jeff Price for the touchdown and a 14–7 score. Purdue followed with another 10-play, 80-yard drive, scoring on quarterback Scott Campbell's bootleg from the one-yard line.

The Hoosiers managed another score in the last minute of the half. Quarterback Steve Bradley completed four passes, covering 80 yards—the last for 22 yards and a touchdown—to Kenebrew with one second on the clock. The halftime score was Purdue, 21–14.

Purdue's running game dominated the entire third quarter and some of the fourth. During that time, the Boilermakers ran 27 offensive plays to IU's six and outgained the Hoosiers 156 yards to 17. But all it produced was a 34-yard field goal by Tim Clark and a

24–14 margin. One drive ended as Campbell fumbled at the IU 21-yard line, and a missed field goal ended another. The Hoosiers closed the score, 24–17, with eight minutes left. Going south with the wind at his back, Bradley hit Gunn with two passes covering 52 yards to set up a Doug-Smith, 43-yard field goal.

Many of the red-clad were starting to head back toward Indy as the Boilermakers performed their third 80-yard drive from the two-yard line. Purdue had what looked to be an insurmountable lead of 31–17.

Bradley took just 62 seconds after Purdue scored its final touchdown to take IU 71 yards. He completed three passes for 54 yards to get Indiana to the 18-yard line. From there, tailback Bobby Howard did the rest, 11 yards to the seven-yard line. Then he went the final seven yards for a touchdown. Doug Smith's PAT made it 31–24 with 3:04 left, and there was little doubt about what IU would do next: onside kick. Chuck Razmic squibbed one straight ahead and fell on it himself as the Purdue forward wall mysteriously retreated. That gave Indiana possession at the Boiler 47-yard line. Two plays later, Bradley launched a pass to Duane Gunn, who caught it at the 23-yard line, juked a falling defensive back, and raced into the end zone to complete a 45-yard scoring play. It was now Purdue, 31–30, with 2:18 remaining. A simple extra-point, and IU would get a come-from-behind tie, keep the Bucket, and send Purdue home emptyhanded.

In this rivalry, a tie isn't really an option. Coach Sam Wyche decided to go for the two-point conversion. Bradley rolled right and threw to Kenebrew, who made a leaping reception in the back of the end zone. However, an official ruled that Kenebrew's foot was out of bounds when he returned to the turf. Purdue recovered Indiana's onside kick and ran out the clock.

1986: Purdue 17, Indiana 15—Blocked Kicks

The Hoosiers came into Ross–Ade Stadium on a sunny, 50-degree afternoon as an 11-point favorite, a position that they were not accustomed to. Many years in the history of the Old Oaken Bucket, the Hoosiers would be hard-pressed to score 11 points. But IU was

riding a 6–4 record and a sure bowl game. A sell-out crowd of 69,784, many dressed in red, saw an exciting game where a blocked field goal allowed Purdue to escape with their fourth-straight Bucket victory.

To motivate his players, Purdue coach Leon Burtnett surprised his team with Old Gold jerseys, a color not worn since 1940. Then he asked Rob Woodson, his great All-American, to play both ways to boost the team's spirit and level of play. All this worked as the Boilermakers pulled the big upset and allowed Burnett, who resigned under pressure three weeks earlier, to be a winner.

In the first period, Purdue opened the scoring 7–0 on a 51-yard, eight–play drive ending in a one-yard plunge by James Medlock and a Johnathon-Briggs kick. Later, Briggs made a 43-yard field goal, and the Boilermakers led 10–0 after one quarter. Neither team scored in the second period.

After the half, IU got on the board on their first possession of the third quarter as quarterback Dave Kramme and tailback Anthony Thompson led IU on an 85-yard drive culminating in Thompson's touchdown, two-yard run. That made it 10–7

Purdue scored first in the fourth quarter as Jeff George eluded a Hoosier blitz and threw for 37 yards to Rick Brunner, who made a diving catch at the Indiana four-yard line. They scored on a reverse by Calvin Williams and, with 14:10 left, the Boilermakers led, 17–7.

Back came the Hoosiers as Kramme hit tight end Dave Lilja for 23 yards on third down to keep a drive alive. They then unloaded a 45-yard scoring bomb to Stacey Dawsey, who made a great catch in front of Woodson and sped into the end zone. With 7:34 left, IU went for the two-point conversion and made it as Kramme hit Lilja in the right corner of the end zone. That made it 17–15, and things were to become dramatic to say the least. Purdue was trying to milk its two-point lead and the clock, with 2:23 remaining, and had a fourth-and-inch at the Indiana 43-yard line. The Boilermakers' James Medlock fumbled, and the Hoosiers recovered. Six plays later, IU was perched on the Purdue 17-yard line with a fourth down. Field goal kicker Pete Stoyanovich came on to line up for the winning points. The ball

was smack in the center of the field, and 1:07 remained. It was just a matter of execution. But with the snap of the ball, the Boilermakers poured through. This time, Scott Schult arrived almost at the instant of Stoyanovich's kick. He blocked it with his arms, saving the victory for Purdue.

Rob Woodson was a tremendous part of the Boilermaker victory. He played all 80 plays in the game on both defense as a corner and offense as a tailback. He led the team in rushing with 93 yards and receiving with 67. Purdue blocked three kicks on the day. Two were punts, and the last was the possible winning field goal.

1989: Purdue 15, Indiana 14— Cost AT the Heisman

It was a shocking day for 47,402 Hoosier fans in more ways than one as Purdue pulled off a 15–14-upset in the Old Oaken Bucket game. The Boilermakers gave Coach Fred Akers his first Bucket win and gave the Hoosiers their first losing season in four years. They dealt a fatal blow to the Heisman trophy chances of IU's All-American Anthony Thompson (AT).

Purdue held Thompson to 97 yards on 28 carries. They also kept him from scoring a touchdown for the first time in 12 games. But all this should have been forgotten because IU had an easy chance to win the game.

IU entered the game a 15-point favorite. And scored as expected, first. Scott Bonnell hit a 26-yard field goal after a 12-play, 71-yard drive in which IU quarterback Dave Schnell took off for eight yards on a fourth-and-one to move the sticks. Then Purdue had a long drive of their own as they went 83 yards on 13 plays. That led to a 24-yard, Larry-Sullivan field goal. Now the game was tied, 3–3.

From here, it was all IU until the last quarter. Dave Schnell ended the next drive with a three-yard run. The kick failed and the score became 9–3. IU made up for the extra point with a safety in the Purdue end zone as the Boilermaker long-snapper snapped the ball over the punter's head. At the half, IU had an 11–3 lead.

The Hoosiers again scored on a Bonnell field goal after a 66-yard drive in the third quarter. Schnell kept the drive alive when he took off on a third-and-one and rolled to an 18-yard gain.

From this point, everything went downhill for the Hoosiers. Purdue had a Calvin Williams touchdown to open the fourth quarter on 20-yard pass from Erick Hunter. The Boilermakers filed the extra point, making the score 14–9. Then Sullivan kicked two field goals (29-yards and 32-yards) to put the Boilermakers up 15–14.

Now the Hoosier faithful were feeling sick to their stomachs. How could this happen? Purdue had the lead with only minutes left in the game. But maybe there was hope after all, as the amazed crowd saw Anthony Thompson going out to be a kick returner. That was just not done, but heck, it was the Old Oaken Bucket game. Purdue kicked off with a high one to avoid a run-back. The IU fans started their traditional yell of "ooooh" as the kicker approached the ball. Then they gave a long "go" yell as the ball came down to AT at the 22-yard line. He went left, avoiding an onslaught of Purdue tacklers. Then he cut right and broke through the line and had a race to the end zone with Jarrett Scales, one of Purdue's fast safety men. At this point, the crowd was so loud you could have heard them in Martinsville, 20 miles away. AT had the longest run of his career (63 yards) and took the ball to the 15-yard line, setting up IU for the winning field goal.

The heartbreak of the day, week, month, and season came next. Scott Bonnell lined up for a 26-yard field goal from the left hash mark. The snap was good, and the kick was true, then hooked left and missed the crossbar by inches. The crowd was in shock.

Underdog Purdue team had ruined the season and the storybook ending to AT's college football career. The Heisman voting in 1989 was Andre Ware first with 1,073 points, Anthony Thompson second with 1,003. The margin was one of the ten closest votes ever.

If the field goal would have been good and IU had won the game, all the day's highlights probably would have been of the big run-back by AT. Surely that would have influenced the voters for the Heisman Trophy.

1990: Purdue 81, Indiana 79 in OT—Believe It

Reporters came into the Purdue dressing room after the game and read the message written on the chalk board before the team left to go out for the second half. It read "Believe." Purdue center, Stephen Scheffler, believed in his Boilermakers, especially after they beat IU 81–79 on Saturday, January 13, 1992. And Chucky White, who led the Purdue second-half comeback, believed too.

White said "Nobody respects us. They'll just say Purdue won. You can see it when they come into Mackey Arena. They are smug and going to beat little Purdue."

IU dominated the first half by starting fast, making 14 of 20 points from the field to boom out a 36–20 lead. Strong play by Eric Anderson and a technical foul on Purdue Coach Gene Keady were factors. At the half, IU led, 42–29.

In the second half, Chucky White took over for Purdue with a personal 7–0 run. He made 11 of Purdue's first 13 points, and the Boilers cut the IU lead to 47–42. The game was tied 54–54 with a 12:19 left. Then Anderson and IU regained some momentum to jump to a 69–62 lead with 5:55 on the clock. At 1:36, Purdue closed it to 73–71, then Ryan Berning hit a 15-foot jumper to send the game into overtime.

The Hoosiers went cold in the extra period, missing their first five shots. They seemed to have trouble getting good shots. Tony Jones's free throw and a Berning jumper gave Purdue a lead they would keep the remainder of the game. Lyndon Jones had a chance but missed a whirling try in the lane before Berning hit two free throws.

At the games end, Eric Anderson was the only Hoosier in double figures with 30 points. Purdue players in double figures were Tony Jones, 21; Chucky White, 19; Stephen Scheffler, 14; and Berning, 11. Scheffler went five-for-five from the field and four-for-four from the free-throw line.

s

IU's recruiting class of future stars—Chris Reynolds, Matt Nover, Greg Graham, Calbert Cheaney, Pat Graham, and Todd Leary—only contributed a total of only 29 points, one less than Anderson.

1992: Purdue 13, Indiana 10— Interception Brings Down Greased Poles

It was a typical cold and overcast fall day in West Lafayette as 58,692 fans came to Ross–Ade Stadium to see another Old Oaken Bucket battle. The crowd, usually dressed drearily in black, was unusually more colorful as a lot of red-clad IU fans—glowing from three straight bowl appearances, three straight winning seasons, and three straight Bucket wins—traveled north to Purdue.

The Boilermaker athletic department decided to dissuade the IU or Purdue students from tearing down the goal posts. Thus, they coated the uprights with some type of lard. The joke after a field goal was, "there goes a Crisco Kick."

The whole first period was scoreless, and the offenses didn't seem to click in the second quarter either. The only score occurred when Terry Samuel blocked a Jim-DiGuillo punt giving the Boilers the ball on the IU 14-yard line. It took Purdue six more plays to move the ball just 15 yards and finally score a Joe-O'Leary field goal. The halftime score was only 3–0!

The Hoosiers tied the game, 3–3, in the third period with a 27-yard drive in seven plays, leading to a 33-yard field goal. The short drive was because of a horrible, 16-yard Boilermaker punt to the Purdue 43-yard line. Purdue, however, bounced right back with a nine-play drive of 40-yards and an O'Leary field goal of 36 yards. The kicked ball hit the cross-bar and slid over. Maybe it was the Crisco? The score after three periods was only 6–3.

IU finally took the lead in the last quarter as quarterback Trent Green led a 59-yard drive of eight plays. The highlight of the drive was Green's 30-yard pass to Thomas Lewis to the Purdue five-yard line. Green scored on the ground from the two-yard line. IU was now leading the score, 10–6. Purdue scored next on an Eric-Hunter

21- yard scramble, capping a 69-yard drive that took 12 plays and was aided by a Lance-Brown personal foul tackling Hunter out of bounds. Purdue had also gotten flagged on the play for holding and would have had a third-and-37 but, after the foul, had the ball first-and-10. Now Purdue had the lead back, 13–10, late in the game.

The IU fans, getting used to beating Purdue, still felt that the Hoosiers could pull out the win as quarterback Green drove the team to the six-yard line. A simple chip-shot field goal would tie it. So, the next play was a pass into the end zone. The problem was that the receiver cut his route short and Green threw the ball to Purdue's Jimmy Young, who couldn't believe he got the ball. Young took off, and Green pulled him down by his face mask. Of course, a fight ensued. After all, that's how Bucket games usually end, right?

The Purdue students then rushed the field and climbed the greased goal posts and tore them down.

1996: Purdue 74, Indiana 72— They Danced On the "I"

The seventh-ranked Purdue Boilermakers came to Assembly hall and used the three-point shot to beat the Hoosiers and sweep the season series, taking a huge step toward winning their third-straight Big Ten crown. Purdue hit 10 of 20 threes, while IU only hit two of 10. These 24 extra points for Purdue obviously made a difference in the two-point game (74–72).

Purdue players—feeling that their last trip to Assembly Hall was beset by the lack of shooting practice on the floor and cold, slippery practice balls—came to town earlier that year. In past years, they would always spend the night in Indianapolis and come down to Bloomington on game day. At all other schools, the Boilermakers went to the campus the day before and spent plenty of time shooting on the baskets and court of their opponent. For the past three seasons, the Boilermakers maintained a great road-record (20–6) using this travel and practice routine.

The extra practice seemed to give the Boilermakers all the confidence they needed to dominate as they built a first-half lead, 51–41. The only lull in the first half for Purdue came in the first four minutes, when the IU rim was bent from Hoosier dunks. All play stopped while the rim was replaced.

In the second half, IU went on a 19–3 tear to take a five-point lead and control of the game until the last four minutes of the game when Purdue regained their shooting eye as Porter Roberts and Todd Foster connected. Chad Austin connected on a three with 13.7 seconds left to give the Boilers 74 points. IU had one last shot that rimmed out.

Scoring for Purdue was led by Austin with 18, Foster with 15, and Brad Miller with 14. IU was led by Todd Lindeman, who had 21 points. He brushed his head against the backboard on a play, and wound up with a game-high 10 rebounds. The conference-leading scorer Brian Evans was held to 17 points.

After the win, Purdue players celebrated and drew boos from the 17,371 fans as Porter Roberts kicked the basketball off the scoreboard, and Todd Foster ran out to center court and danced on the red "I." IU assistant coach Norm Ellenberger, when asked to comment on the Purdue celebration, said that he felt it was a great compliment to Indiana basketball when an opponent felt that good about beating the Hoosiers.

1997: Purdue 89, Indiana 87— Only Six Tenths of A Second Left

It's pretty rare that a basketball player repeats a shot, with an identical outcome, in a season. But when a player does the same thing, with the same result, in two consecutive seasons, it blows one's mind! That's exactly what happened in Assembly Hall on Tuesday night, February 18, 1979. Chad Austin made an 18-foot corner jump-shot to beat the Hoosiers with the clock winding down. When the ball swished, 17,367 Hoosier fans couldn't believe that he did it again. Just one year before, Austin made an 18-foot corner-jumper to beat the Hoosiers at the end of the game at Assembly Hall. Austin's basket came with only six-tenths of a second left of one of the hardest-fought battles

between Purdue and IU in the history of this great rivalry.

This was a game of hard-fought battles. Purdue opened the game with a lead, 9–2. IU came back to lead, 35–32, late in the opening half, and the score was tied, 37–37, after the first 20 minutes. The contest was even hard-fought by the IU bench as Bob Knight was whistled for a technical foul for protesting a hand-check call on Charlie Miller. Austin went to the line and proceed to hit three free throws for the foul and then the technical. The IU bench screamed at the officials that they had the wrong man on the line. The refs had a lengthy discussion and then agreed with IU. Austin's three free throws were wiped off the scoreboard and Mike Robinson, the person fouled by Miller, had to shoot. He bricked the first of a one-and-one, and Austin hit the one for a technical.

The second half was just as hard-fought, with IU taking a lead, 53–49, on A. J. Guyton's 21st and 22nd points. Purdue tied the score, 59–59, on a Jaraan Cornell bucket. Just before the end of regulation, A. J. Guyton missed a runner, and Jason Collier missed a tip that both could have provided a win for IU. When the clock hit zero, the score was tied, 77–77. So, after 40 minutes of hard-fought competition, there was a new overtime clock showing 5:00.

Finally, the evening of excitement seemed to be coming down to a well-deserved Hoosier victory as A. J. Guyton made a three-point shot for the lead with only 26 seconds left. But then Austin poured cold water on the crowd with his corner jumper. This crushing IU defeat was Coach Gene Keady's 400th win. This was also Purdue's fourth straight win over IU.

A. J. Guyton was IU's leading scorer with 31 points. Talk about déjà vu, this was the second straight game where he scored 31 points. Purdue's four freshmen all scored in double figures. Brian Cardinal had 25; Mike Robinson, 15; Jaraan Cornell, 11; and Gary McQuay, 10. IU hit 16 of 19 free throws, and Purdue made 16 of 21, with 11 of 12 in the second half. Chad Austin made only two of his first 12 shots, but, in crunch time, he went three for his last four.

2017: Purdue 31, Indiana 24— Tricks and Turnovers

After a four-year drought, the Boilermakers took back the Old Oaken Bucket—the first time since 2012. It was a game that could have been won by the Hoosiers, if not for a few plays. It was a poor start from the Hoosiers as Richard Lagow's first pass of the game, on IU's first offensive play of the day, was intercepted by Purdue. The pick was returned to the IU five-yard line. Then a touchdown was scored, giving the Boilermakers a lead, 7–0.

Later in the opening period, Purdue tried a sweep and fumbled. Tegray Scales scooped-up the ball to change the momentum. The Hoosiers then drove to the Purdue one-yard line, and Simmie Cobbs Jr. hauled in his eighth touchdown of the season, making the score 7–7 to end the period.

After a long offensive lull in the game's second quarter, Purdue pulled off a fake punt pass to get inside the IU 25-yard line. The Purdue's punter hit a cornerback on a 22-yard pass, when the Boilermakers were facing fourth-and-three from the Hoosier 43-yard line. Two plays later, Purdue scored their second touchdown on a jet sweep, and the Boilermakers led 14–7. Then at 0:53 left in the second quarter, Purdue struck again on a 49-yard touchdown pass to make it 21–7. IU's explosive offense wasn't daunted and got a big 64-yard run from Ricky Brookins moving the ball inside the Purdue red zone. Eventually Griffin Oakes converted a 22-yard field goal, making the score at the half 21–10.

In the third quarter, Purdue got a 26-yard field goal to make the score 24–10. The IU defense had made a great stop, forcing the kick.

Purdue scored first in the fourth quarter with a four-yard touchdown reception, putting IU down three touchdowns, 31–10. Then IU came back as Taysir Mack caught his third touchdown grab of the season from four yards out. The Hoosiers were still trailing Purdue, 31–17. But IU went right back to work mounting an epic comeback. Whop Philyor scored on a nine-yard touchdown reception,

and the Hoosiers now only trailed 31–24.

In the final minute of the game, Purdue recovered an onside kick from Griffin Oakes and, with no timeouts left, the Hoosiers got to watch the clock run out. The Hoosiers wound up outgaining Purdue, 497–453. Richard Lagow, in what could be his final game for IU, threw the ball 60 times and finished with 373 passing yards and three touchdowns. Junior wide receiver Simmie Cobbs Jr. and freshman wideout Taysir Mack each had more than 100 yards and one receiving touchdown, but IU's ground game couldn't muster much aside from a 64-yard run by Ricky Brookins.

Typically, the Purdue hometown press referred to IU's closing rally in the negative writing, "Thanks to a couple garbage-time drives that the Hoosiers used to make things close."

Players We Hate

Charles "Stretch" Murphy: Led Scoring Against the Hoosiers

Charles C. "Stretch" Murphy was one of the game's first big men at six-foot, six-inches and played at Marion High School (1922–26). As an All-State player, during his senior year in 1926, he led his school to the Indiana state championship. He was recruited by Purdue's Ward "Piggy" Lambert, and played four seasons for Purdue (1926–1930). Teaming with fellow Hall-of-Famer John Wooden and co-captain Glen Harmeson, Murphy led the Boilers to the Big 10 championship in 1930 after an undefeated season in conference play (10–0). He set a new Big-10 scoring record for a season in 1929 with 143 points and led Purdue to a 53–13 overall record during his tenure.

In the 1929 season, the Boilermakers beat IU, 29–23, January 19th, with Murphy scoring the game-high 14 points. At first, the Hoosier's Carl Scheid held Murphy to little scoring, but he collected three fouls by half time. Early in the second half, Scheid fouled out and Murphy took charge. The victory left Purdue atop the Big Ten with a 5–0 record.

Murphy was named a consensus All-American in both his junior and senior years and to the All-Time All-American team.

Murphy was one of the game's first true big men. At six fee, six inches, he was an insurmountable force on both ends of the court. He was inducted into the Basketball Hall of Fame in 1960 and the Indiana Basketball Hall of Fame in 1963.

John Wooden: Lived Thirteen Miles from Branch

John Wooden's family moved to Martinsville when he was 14, Wooden led his high school team to a state-tournament title in 1927. He was a three-time All-State selection.

After graduating from high school in 1928, he attended Purdue University and was coached by Piggy Lambert. John Wooden was named All–Big Ten and All-Midwestern (1930–32) while at Purdue, and he was the first player ever to be named a three-time consensus All-American. Wooden was nicknamed "The Indiana Rubber Man" for his suicidal dives on the hardcourt.

On Monday night, February 22, 1932, Wooden was personally responsible for a Purdue win in Bloomington. On this cold winter night, IU started very hot and grabbed a 25–22 halftime lead over the highly favored Boilermakers. Jay Campbell was guarding Wooden very tightly, but alas, Campbell fouled out in the second half, and Wooden destroyed the Hoosiers. He ended up with a game-leading 17 points on five field goals and seven free throws.

Wooden's teams won three times against IU and never lost. Hoosier fans were also not happy with Wooden because he lived so close to IU's campus (Martinsville) and grew-up 13 miles from Monrovia, where Branch McCracken was a high-school star. It would have been great to have John join Branch at IU.

Wooden graduated from Purdue in 1932 with a degree in English. After college, Wooden spent several years playing professional basketball in the NBL (forerunner to the NBA) while he taught and coached in the high school ranks. During one 46-game stretch, he made 134 consecutive free throws. He was named to the NBL's first team for the 1937–38 season.

Norman Cottom: Led the League in Scoring

Norman Cottom was a star player for Terre Haute Wiley High School, earning four varsity letters playing for the basketball team. He led the team to three IHSAA Sectionals and one Regional crown. They reached the state semi-finals in 1931. He was also an all-state performer in football.

After high school, Cottom was recruited to play basketball at Purdue under Piggy Lambert. He played on the varsity team for three seasons, and, as a junior in the season 1933–34, Cottom led the Western (Big Ten) Conference in scoring. He was named a consensus All-American at the end of the season. In the two seasons that Purdue played IU during Cottom's career, the Boilermakers won two games and lost one. On March 3, 1934, he led the Boilermakers to a 55–28 rout over the Hoosiers in West Lafayette. Hoosier fans felt that Purdue had run-up the score.

After college, Cottom played in the NBL (NBA) for two seasons and one season with the US Navy Pre-Flight team. He then moved into high school coaching at Alexandria, Terre Haute, Gerstmeyer, and Wiley High schools.

Duane Purvis: Never lost to IU

Duane Purvis was recruited to Purdue from Mattoon, Illinois by Nobel Kiser in 1931. He played halfback and fullback for the Boilermakers from 1932 to 1934. He was selected as an All-American in 1933 and 1934. Considered an all-around player, Purvis averaged five yards-per-carry in 1934 with touchdown runs of 80 and 73 yards. He was also considered to be an excellent defensive player and "without peer" as a long passer, using a strong right arm that also made him a world-class javelin thrower.

In the 1932 Old Oaken Bucket game, Purvis showed his accuracy and strength by tossing two touchdown passes. Purdue won 25–7. The next year, he further frustrated IU with a 40-yard run in a 19–3

victory in Bloomington. When Purvis played, the Boilermakers were 3–0 versus the Hoosiers.

He played in the 1935 East–West Shrine Game and suffered a knee injury in the game. During his hospitalization in California, the Oakland Tribune published a profile on Purvis describing him as a "brown-eyed, fair-haired, firm-jawed chap" who was considered "the finest back ever to pack a pigskin for the Boilermakers' eleven."

When asked if he intended to play professional football, Purvis replied, "I should say not. I've had just about enough football. It's a great game when you're in college and the best game to forget about when you're out. I'm going to get to work as soon as they hand me that old A.B. at Purdue." After graduation, Purvis taught in the Purdue physical education department.

For more than 30 years, Purvis held the career-rushing record at Purdue with 1,802 yards. In track and field, Purvis won All-American recognition three times; winning the National Collegiate Athletic Association javelin championship in 1933 and 1934. Purvis was also ranked third in the world in the javelin during 1933; that same year, in a poll conducted by the Associated Press, Duane Purvis was selected as the top athlete in the Big Ten Conference.

Robert L. Kessler: One-Man Fast Break

Dr. Robert L. Kessler was standout basketball player at Anderson High School. Piggy Lambert recruited Kessler to Purdue, where he became a two-time All-American (1935–36), and, as a senior, he became Purdue's first-ever consensus All-American.

Just one example of Kessler's ability to frustrate the Hoosiers came on February 18, 1935 at Lafayette Jefferson High School's big gym on north 9th Street, across the Wabash River from Purdue. Prior to building their new fieldhouse, the Boilermakers played many home games at Jeff's gym, which held more people than any venue on the

Purdue campus. That night, Kessler made 10 field goals and went 3–3 at the foul line to lead all scorers with 23 points. He dazzled the home fans by numerous high-speed, court-length dribbles and quick baskets. Purdue won the game 44–38.

After Purdue, Kessler played professionally in the NBL (NBA) for three seasons. He was named the league's Rookie of the Year in 1937–38, even though his teams never once qualified for the postseason. In his later life, Kessler worked at General Motors, where he eventually became a vice president.

Jewell Young: Led a Scoring Spree

Jewell Young was a local boy who played at Lafayette Jefferson High School and just traveled across the Wabash River to play for Piggy Lambert. Young was a two-time consensus All-American at Purdue in 1937 and 1938. He led the Western (Big Ten) Conference both years at averages of 14.3 and 15.3 points per game respectively. Young's teams at Purdue beat the Hoosiers five of six time they met.

On February 5th, 1938, just two seasons from an IU NCAA Championship, Young led the Boilermakers to a 38–36 victory in front of an overflow crowd at the Fieldhouse in West Lafayette. Even though Young opened the scoring for the game, IU kept him bottled up and built a 21–16 halftime advantage. In the second half, while trailing 26–19, Young led the Boilermakers on a scoring spree to tie it at 32-all. A 36–36 tie was broken by the Boilermakers with only a few seconds left.

Following the completion of his collegiate career, Young played professionally with the National Basketball League (forerunner to the NBA) for five seasons. He averaged 7.8 points per game. He was the league Rookie of the Year in the 1938–39 season and was an NBL All-Star in the 1938–39 and 1941–42 seasons. He later became a high school coach for 17 years for Southport High School in Indianapolis.

Terry Dischinger: "Tonight We Were the Best Team in The Country"

Dischinger, a highly-recruited six-foot, seven-inch high-school player from Terre Haute, came to Purdue, the alma mater of his parents, to play for Coach Ray Eddy.

As a sophomore (freshmen weren't allowed to play varsity by the NCAA in his era), he was named a second-team All-American, leading the 11–12 Boilermakers and averaging 26.3 points and 14.3 rebounds. He made the 1960 Olympic Team after his sophomore season.

On January 11, 1960 was the day of the first conference game of the 1959–60 season, and the Hoosiers were favored to win the Big Ten crown. Dischinger broke the hearts of IU fans by playing against the Hoosiers in Bloomington. The day before, he was reported to be doubtful due to a severe case of influenza. Instead, he not only played, but he beat the Hoosiers almost singlehandedly. He drove through the Hoosier defense time and again, scoring 11 of 20 shots from the field. He also got fouled enough to shoot 12 free throws, making eight. Dischinger's 30 points led all players. At one point in the last seven minutes, he went on a nine-point, unanswered, scoring spree to put the game away with 3:00 left on the clock. After the game, in the Purdue locker room, Dischinger said, "Tonight we were the best team in the country!" Purdue won 79–76.

During his junior season (1960–1961), Purdue finished 16–7. Dischinger was named a first-team All-American and led the conference in scoring with averages of 28.2 points and 13.4 rebounds a game. He made a single-game school-record 21 free throws against Iowa on February 27, 1961.

Purdue finished 17–7 in Dischinger's senior season. On Christmas Day in 1961, Dischinger scored a career-high 52 points against Michigan State on 19 field goals and 14 free throws. The 52 points broke Jerry Lucas's prior Big-Ten-Conference record of 48.

His 459 total points in his senior season led the conference in scoring for a third consecutive season. He was named a second-straight first-team All-American while leading the Big Ten Conference in both scoring average, (30.3 points) and rebounding average (13.4). He attempted a single-season Purdue-record 350 free throws in his senior season. Overall, he averaged a double-double of 28.3 points and 13.7 rebounds, shooting 55.3 percent from the floor, and 81.9 percent from the line in 70 career games at Purdue.

Bob Griese: Did Everything

Bob Griese came from Evansville's Rex Mundi High School where he was a three sport star. In American Legion baseball as a pitcher, he led his team to the American Legion Baseball World Series in the summer of 1963. He also starred in basketball and football. He earned 12 varsity letters. He led the basketball team to the number-one ranking in Indiana during the 1962–63 season and a record of 19–3. He scored 900 points in his high school career.

After being recruited by several colleges for football, Bob chose Purdue, where he majored in business management and again became a three-sport star. He pitched for the baseball team, going 12–1 one season, played guard on the basketball team, and played quarterback, kicker, and punter for the football team. There were many football games where Griese scored every one of Purdue's points. In his junior year, at game against the top-ranked Notre Dame, Griese completed 19 of 22 passes as he led the Boilermakers to an upset win.

Griese was a two-time All-American at Purdue, finishing eighth in the 1965 Heisman Trophy race and was the runner-up to Steve Spurrier for the 1966 Heisman Trophy. Purdue finished second in the Big Ten in 1966, and Griese led the school's first appearance in the Rose Bowl, where they defeated USC 14–13. He was inducted into the Rose Bowl Hall of Fame in 1992. He was also awarded the Big Ten Medal of Honor for excellence in athletics and academics.

In football, Griese was 2–1 against the Hoosiers. In basketball, he was 2–2. In baseball, during Griese's time, Purdue languished near the bottom of the conference.

Dave Schellhase: All-American and Academic All-American

Dave Schellhase was recruited to Purdue out of North High School in Evansville. He led the state in scoring during his senior year, averaging 30.5 points a game, with a total of 1,325 points in his high school career. He was a member of the Indiana All-Star team.

At Purdue, Schellhase was a natural small forward. In his senior year, he led the Boilermakers in scoring with 32.5 points per game while being named a consensus All-American and Academic All-American and receiving his third straight first-team All–Big Ten selection. He was a second-team All-American following his junior season. Dave scored a career-high 57 points on February 19, 1966 against Michigan.

In two consecutive seasons' late-February games, Schellhase lit up the Hoosiers with game-high scoring. On February 22, 1965, he scored 32 points, of which 20 came in the second half, shutting off any Hoosier attempts to regain control of the contest. Then on February 21, 1966, he scored 29 points. The frustrating thing was that, again, he was hot in the second half with 18 points. Both these wins were in West Lafayette, where Schellhase never lost to IU.

Leroy Keyes: Won the Bucket with Four Touchdowns

Leroy Keyes came to Purdue as a highly-recruited athlete from George Washington Carver High School in Newport News, Virginia. In his very first collegiate game, played on national television against eventual national champion Notre Dame, Keyes made his presence known by returning a fumble 94 yards for a touchdown.

He was a megastar for the Boilermakers from 1966 to 1968. In 1967, he ran for 986 yards with 13 touchdowns and had 45 catches for 758 yards and six touchdowns. He played in the January 1967 Rose Bowl game, which Purdue won 14–13 over USC.

As a senior in 1968, he followed it up by running for 1,003 yards and 14 touchdowns while catching 33 passes for 428 yards and one touchdown. With IU in town for the '68 Old Oaken Bucket battle, Keyes put the ball in the end zone four times to produce Purdue's eighth victory in ten games. He carried 28 times for 140 yards and caught six passes for another 149 yards. He had two running touchdowns and two pass-reception touchdowns. He was an All-American in both 1967 and 1968 as a runner and pass-catcher. Keyes was invited to New York for the Heisman Trophy ceremonies in 1967 and 1968 where he finished third and second consecutively. He was a consensus All-American in both years.

After college Keyes was drafted by the Eagles as the third pick in the NFL draft. He played running back and safety in the for the Philadelphia Eagles from 1969 through 1972. In 1973 he was traded to the Kansas City Chiefs where his career was ended by injury that season.

In 1990 Leroy Keyes was inducted into the College Football Hall of Fame and was in the inaugural class of the Purdue Athletics Hall of Fame in 1994.

Rick Mount: The Rocket

Rick "the Rocket" Mount graduated from Lebanon High, where he led the team in scoring with a 33.1 points per game average throughout his junior and senior seasons. His game started to attract national attention. In 1965, Lebanon played Crawfordsville High School at Hinkle Fieldhouse with 10,000 people in attendance. He scored 57 points in the game. On February 14, 1966, Mount became the first high school athlete to appear on the cover of *Sports Illustrated*, which featured him standing in front of a barn located in his Boone County

The nemesis of IU players, Rick Mount became Purdue's all-time leading scorer before graduating.

After considering committing to Miami University (Ohio), he decided to attend Purdue, just 35 miles from home, to play basketball under head coach George King. As a freshman, Mount was unable to play on the varsity team due to NCAA regulations then in effect

In his first varsity game of the 1967–68 season, Mount scored a game-high 28 points in a last-second, two-point loss to a top-ranked UCLA team and Lew Alcindor. It was also the first game played in Mackey Arena. Averaging 28.4 points per game and leading Purdue to a 15–9 record, he was named a second-team All-American and first-team All–Big Ten his sophomore season.

In his junior season at Purdue, along with seniors Billy Keller and Herm Gilliam, he led the Boilermakers to a Big Ten Conference title and the school's first NCAA Tournament appearance, leading to the NCAA Finals game, where they lost again to a Lew Alcindor-led UCLA. Purdue led the nation with 94.8 points per game during the 1968–69 season, fronted by Mount's 33.3 average points per game. They beat IU 120–76 in the closing game of the regular season, becoming a school record for most points in a game.

In his senior year, Mount had two 53-point games plus a 61-point game. Leading Purdue to an 18–6 season, he averaged 35.4 points per game and took his second-straight first-team All-American and Big Ten Player of the Year honors. Mount left as the school's all-time leading scorer with 2,323 points throughout only three varsity seasons. At the time, it was also the Big-Ten scoring record, surpassing the total of Indiana's Don Schlundt. It is currently held by Indiana's Calbert Cheaney's 2,613.

On February 10, 1970, the last time Mount faced IU, he hit 16 of 28 field-goal attempts and nine of ten free throws. Purdue won that night 98–80. Mount's team beat IU five times without a loss. After that last game, IU coach Jerry Oliver said, "I'm happy to see that number ten [Mount] graduating, and I'll enjoy watching him as a professional."

Mike Phipps: A Rhodes Scholar?

Phipps was recruited to Purdue from Columbus High School. He began his college career when he replaced All-American Boilermaker quarterback Bob Griese. His first major victory was a 28–21 upset of defending–national champion Notre Dame Fighting Irish in 1967. Combining strong passing skills with excellent mobility helped Phipps establish a new school single-season record for total offense and earn the Boilermakers a share of the Big Ten Conference title. That year, IU beat Phipps and the Boilermakers to also win a share of the Big Ten title and a trip to the Rose Bowl.

The following year, Phipps suffered an ankle injury that kept him out of two games. His Boilermakers were the top-ranked team in the country until the Ohio State Buckeyes upset them. That year, Purdue won back the Old Oaken Bucket, 38–35, some say because Phipps made the referees remeasure an IU first down, stopping a great Hoosier comeback.

In 1969, Phipps became the focal point of Purdue's offense, throwing for five touchdowns in a 36–35 thriller over Stanford, including throwing for a two-point conversion with three minutes left. He also defeated Notre Dame for the third consecutive year. After

falling behind by three touchdowns in the Bucket game, he brought the Boilermakers back for a 44–21 win in front of 56,223 fans at IU Memorial Stadium.

Phipps finished second in the voting for the Heisman Trophy to the Oklahoma Sooners' running back Steve Owens. Although he was awarded the 1969 Sammy Baugh Trophy, he declined a Rhodes Scholarship to concentrate on a professional football career.

Phipps was picked third in the 1970 NFL Draft by the Miami Dolphins, who traded him to the Cleveland Browns. He played in Cleveland from 1970 to 1976 and finished his career with the Chicago Bears, playing from 1977 to 1981.

Otis Armstrong: Monster Game against IU

Otis Armstrong came to Purdue from Farragut High School in Chicago. He played for Bob DeMoss, who succeeded the great Jack Mollenkoph as head football coach. As freshmen were not eligible, Armstrong waited until his sophomore year to suit-up for the Boilermakers. That year his impact was felt as he rushed for 1009 yards. Only Leroy Keys had accomplished this before 1070.

. In 1970, Purdue beat the Hoosiers, 40–0, in the Bucket game. In his junior year, IU prevailed in the Old Oaken Bucket battle, 38–31, in a game marred by a fight at the IU bench. Purdue quarterback Danielson was chased out of bounds on the Indiana sidelines in the final half-minute, and in a matter of seconds, fists began to fly. It started when Purdue's Gary Danielson fired the football into a pack of IU players, an act that might be described as brave but foolhardy. Danielson claimed he was punched in the mouth. Ted McNulty later said he grabbed Danielson to keep him from falling. Both benches emptied, fans poured out of the stands, and a full-scale donnybrook erupted. Before the end of that game, Armstrong broke a 44-yard run for a touchdown.

As a senior, in his final Bucket battle, he had a monster game, rushing for 276 yards, the highest rushing mark in school history.

During that senior season Armstrong was a consensus All-American and rushed for 1,361 yards.

Armstrong finished his three college seasons with 4,601 all-purpose yards (3,315 rushing yards, 897 yards from kickoff returns, and 389 passing yards). He also scored 24 touchdowns (17 rushing and seven on returns). He was selected the Big Ten MVP in 1972, leading the league in rushing and total offense, while being selected first-team All-Conference. He participated in four All-Star games; the Hula Bowl, the East–West Shrine Game, the Coaches' All-American Game, and the Chicago College All-Star game.

After college Armstrong played in the NFL for the Denver Broncos and led the league in rushing his second season with 1,407 yards. He played with Denver from 1973 through 1980 and made the Pro-Bowl twice.

He was inducted into the Purdue Intercollegiate Athletics Hall of Fame in 1997, the College Football Hall of Fame in 2012, and the Chicagoland Sports Hall of Fame.

Joe Barry Carroll: Shot Blocker

An All-American at Denver East High School in Colorado, seven-foot Joe Barry Carroll opted to go to Purdue and play for Fred Schaus. In his senior year, he averaged 20.3 points and 12.2 rebounds per game while scoring 41 points in one contest.

In the 1976–1977 season, Carroll helped lead the Boilermakers to a 20–8 record. In his first national televised appearance, which was against Indiana, he scored 12 points, had six rebounds, and three blocks in 20 minutes off the bench in an 86–76 win. That was the second win for Carroll and his Boilermakers over the Hoosiers during the season. He recorded 206 rebounds and averaged 7.4 per game in his first season, the most for a Purdue freshman. Carroll also holds the freshman record for most blocks in a season with 82.

In the 1977–78 series, Carroll set school records with 105 blocks for the season and averaged 3.9 blocks per game as a sophomore. That

year Carroll helped the boilermakers to a 77–67 win over IU. In that game, he not only blocked shots, but he grabbed 10 rebounds, was given a technical foul, and scored 15 points. He made 5 of 8 shots from the field and 5 of 6 from the free-throw line.

Head coach Fred Schaus stepped down in 1978 and was replaced by Lee Rose. Playing with a slower, more-controlled system compared to Schaus' fast-paced style, Carroll led Purdue to a first-place Big Ten tie with a Magic Johnson–led Michigan State. He averaged 22.8 points per game for the season and was named first-team All–Big Ten and a third-team All-American, while leading the Boilers to a 27–8 record. He grabbed a school-record 352 rebounds for the season.

During his senior year, he led the Boilermakers to two victories over IU and an NCAA Final Four appearance, losing to UCLA in the semi-finals. Leading Purdue to a 23–10 record for the season, he was named a first-team All-American and a second-straight first-team All–Big Ten selection. He played 1,235 minutes for the season, the most by any player in school history. Carroll holds the all-time school records for career rebounds (1,148) and blocks (349).

Carroll's teams had a 6–4 record against the Hoosiers.

Mark Herrmann: He Sold Out the Stadiums

Herrmann was recruited as a quarterback from Carmel High School.

He also played on Carmel's state championship basketball team in 1977.

Herrmann played for Coach Jim Young's Boilermaker football team from 1977 to 1980. The crowd at Ross–Ade Stadium would always begin to roar as he'd drop back into a shotgun formation.

In 1977, Herrmann passed for 2,453 yards with 18 touchdown versus 27 interceptions in 11 games. In that season, he lost to IU in Bloomington 21–10 in front of a sold-out house.

In 1978, Herrmann passed for 1,904 yards with 14 touchdown versus 12 interceptions in 11 games. That year, he beat IU 20–7 at a sold-out Ross–Ade Stadium.

In 1979, he connected for 2,377 yards with 16 touchdown versus 19 interceptions in 11 games. The sold-out Bucket game was in Bloomington, and the Boilermakers won 37–21.

In Herrmann's senior season, he had his best passing year, throwing for 3,212 yards with 23 touchdown versus 17 interceptions in 11 games and a sold-out 24–23 Bucket battle victory in West Lafayette. That year, he also won the Sammy Baugh Trophy.

In 1980, he was recognized as a consensus first-team All-American, he was selected as the Big Ten Conference's Most Valuable Player, and he finished fourth in voting for the Heisman Trophy. His 9,946 career-passing yards set an NCAA record. He is one of only three Purdue quarterbacks to start in three consecutive bowl games. Herrmann won all three of his bowl games and was selected Most Valuable Player in each of them, the 1978 Peach Bowl, 1979 Bluebonnet Bowl, and 1980 Liberty Bowl).

He was elected to the College Football Hall of Fame in May 2010.

Rod Woodson: He Played All 80 Plays In '86

Woodson decided to play football at Purdue because of a desire to pursue a degree in electrical engineering, but switched his major to criminal justice as a sophomore. He played primarily as a cornerback and kick returner, but also saw time on offense as a running back and wide receiver. He beat IU almost single-handedly in 1978 by playing all 80 plays in the game on both defense as a corner and offense as a tailback. He led the team in rushing with 93 yards and receiving with 67. His coach, knowing that the Hoosiers were a heavy favorite, asked Woodson to go both ways to inspire and elevate the Boilermakers.

He was named an All-American defensive back in 1985 and 1986 and an All-American returner in 1986. He was a three time All–Big Ten first-team selection. In his final collegiate game, Woodson gained

over-150 combined rushing and receiving yards in addition to making 10 tackles and forcing a fumble, leading Purdue to a victory over arch-rival Indiana.

Woodson left Purdue with 13 individual records, tying the school record with eleven career interceptions. He currently is ranked in the top ten in career interceptions, solo tackles, total tackles, passes deflected, and kickoff return yardage as a Boilermaker.

In addition to playing football, Woodson was also an accomplished track-and-field athlete, where he was twice awarded All-America honors. He finished second at the 1985 NCAA championships in the 55-meter hurdles and third at the 1987 NCAA championships in the 55-meter hurdles. He earned five Big Ten championships while at Purdue. In 1984, he qualified for the Olympic Trials in the 110-meter hurdles but elected to continue his football career in the NFL after graduating from Purdue with a degree in criminal justice.

He was drafted by the Pittsburgh Steelers. He also played for Baltimore and Oakland. He is among the NFL's all-time leaders in games played as a defensive back in his 17 NFL seasons

Woodson was inducted into the Purdue Intercollegiate Athletics Hall of Fame in 2003. In 2009, he was inducted into the NFL Pro Football Hall of Fame, and in 2016, Woodson was selected for induction in the College Football Hall of Fame.

Glenn Robinson: "I won."

Glen Robinson was recruited by Frank Kendrick out of Gary Roosevelt High School. During his senior season (1990–91), he led his team to an Indiana state basketball championship. Robinson won the 1991 Indiana Mr. Basketball award, edging out Alan Henderson, IU's future All-American.

Robinson struggled with NCAA eligibility because of Proposition 48, which requires minimum academic standards. Thus, he had to redshirt for his freshman season.

In his sophomore season, Robinson led the Boilermakers with an average of 24.1 points and 9.4 rebounds per game in his first season as a Boilermaker. He led them to an 18–10 record in the regular season and an NCAA tournament appearance. He received first-team All–Big Ten and second-team All-American honors.

In his junior season, Robinson built upon his previous season's averages with averages of 30.3 points and 11.2 rebounds per game, while becoming the first player since 1978 to lead the Big Ten Conference in both categories. He became known as the "Big Dog", in reference to his hustling style of basketball play. Along with teammates Cuonzo Martin and Matt Waddell, he led the Boilermakers to a Big Ten Conference Title and an Elite Eight appearance, finishing the season with a 29–5 record and a third overall ranking. Leading the nation in scoring and becoming the conference's all-time single-season points leader with 1,030 points, Robinson was unanimously selected as the Big Ten Conference Player of the Year. He also unanimously received the John R. Wooden Award and Naismith Award, the first Boilermaker honored as National Player of the Year since John Wooden himself did it in 1932.

On January 18, 1994, the eighth-ranked Hoosiers traveled to Purdue to play the twelfth-ranked Boilermakers. It was to be a match between the "Big Dog" and IU's beloved big man, Alan Henderson. ESPN covered the game, which turned into an epic battle of come-from-behind efforts by both teams. Purdue trailed by 10 in the first half, and IU trailed by six in the second. The game ended in a tie and went into overtime. The battle between Alan Henderson and Glen Robinson raged as Glen had two facials (blocked shots) by Alan. The Big Dog ended with 33 points and 12 rebounds. Henderson had 24 points and 12 rebounds.

Purdue won 83–76. After the game, a member of the press asked Robinson how he matched against Henderson. He said, "You guys have the stats. But we won the game. So, if you ask me, I won."

Drew Brees: Basketball on Grass

Drew Brees did not even play tackle football until high school and was on the flag football team at St. Andrew's Episcopal Junior High School. In high school, he was a varsity letterman in baseball, basketball, and football and considered playing college baseball rather than football. College recruiters quickly ran after Brees. He overcame an ACL tear during his junior year and was selected as Texas High School 5A Most Valuable Offensive Player in 1996. He led the Westlake High School football team to 16–0 record and state championship. Brees had hoped to follow his father and uncle's footsteps and play for the Texas Longhorns or Texas A&M Aggies, but was not heavily recruited despite his stellar record. He received offers from only two colleges, Purdue and Kentucky, and chose Purdue for its highly rated academics.

After a relatively uneventful freshman season at Purdue, Brees was given his first start during his sophomore year. He immediately became an integral part of coach Tiller's high speed "basketball on grass" spread offense. He served as offensive captain during his junior and senior years. He had the option to make himself available for the 2000 NFL Draft but chose to return for his senior year to complete his studies. In 2000, he led the Boilermakers to memorable last-minute upsets against top-ranked Ohio State and Michigan, passing to the Boilermakers' first Big Ten championship in over three decades.

Brees was a finalist for the Davey O'Brien Award as the nation's best quarterback in 1999. He won the Maxwell Award as the nation's outstanding player of 2000 and the NCAA's Today's Top VIII Award as a member of the Class of 2001. Brees was also fourth in Heisman Trophy voting in 1999 and third in 2000. As a senior, Brees became the first Boilermaker since 1989 to earn Academic All-American honors. Additionally, he won Academic All–Big Ten honors a record three times and was awarded the Big Ten Medal of Honor and the NFF National Scholar-Athlete Award. Brees also was awarded Purdue's Leonard Wilson Award for unselfishness and dedication.

In his college career, Brees set two NCAA records, 13 Big-Ten-Conference records, and 19 Purdue-University records. He left Purdue with Big-Ten-Conference records in passing yards (11,792), touchdown passes (90), total offensive yards (12,693), completions (1,026), and attempts (1,678). He tied an NCAA record with the longest pass ever (99 yards), to receiver Vinny Sutherland against Northwestern on

September 25, 1999 and held the NCAA record for pass attempts in a game (83) for fifteen years.

As the Purdue quarterback, Brees was 3–0 against the Hoosiers. He graduated in 2001 with a degree in industrial management.

JaJuan Johnson: 3–1 against IU

JaJuan Johnson played for Franklin Central High School in Marion County, Indiana. He finished his senior year with averages of 20.6 points and 9.1 rebounds per game. He was named to the Indiana All-Star Team with five future NBA players including IU's Eric Gordon. Considered a four-star recruit by Rivals.com, Johnson was listed as the number-nine power forward and the number-42 player in the nation in 2007.

Johnson, a six-foot, ten-inch forward/center, committed to the Purdue University Boilermakers to play under head coach Matt Painter as part of a top-five recruiting class. He averaged 5.4 points and 3.1 rebounds per game, while starting in 17 of the 34 games he played in during his freshman season. He helped the Boilermakers to a second straight NCAA Tournament appearance, including a game against Baylor in the first round, where he scored 10 points, grabbed eight rebounds, and blocked two shots in 20 minutes.

Johnson averaged 13.4 points (second-highest on the team) and led the conference with an average of 2.2 blocks per game, for which he was named a first-team All–Big Ten selection as well as to the Big Ten All-Defensive Team. He also led the conference shooting 54 percent from the field. He recorded five double-doubles for the

season, all coming in conference play. Johnson led Purdue to the program's first Big Ten Tournament Championship, was named to the all-tournament team, and helped lead them to a Sweet Sixteen appearance. In the last seconds of the second-round game in the NCAA Tournament against Washington, he blocked back-to-back shots to seal the win while adding 22 points and a total of four blocks. Finishing with a 27–10 record, he is one of four Boilermakers to share

the school record for most games played in a season. He also moved amongst Joe Barry Carroll in the Purdue records with the third-most blocks in a season: 78.

He began his junior season as a preseason first-team All–Big Ten selection by CBS Sports. In the season, he recorded nine double-doubles, while leading Purdue to its best start in 16 years (14–0). On February 4th, Johnson led the Boilermakers to their first win in nine tries at Assembly Hall. In that rollercoaster, down-to-the-wire game, IU used an 8–0 run to take a 69–66 lead on a three-point basket in transition by Jordan Hulls with 5:43 to play. Purdue answered with a 9–0 run of its own and took a 75–69 lead at the 1:15 mark. Johnson led scoring with 21 points.

In three seasons at Purdue, Johnson's teams went 3–1.

Caleb Swanigan: Biggie

Caleb Swanigan inherited two key features from his biological father—height and a tendency to obesity. His large size was the reason his aunt nicknamed him "Biggie." Caleb was adopted by Roosevelt Barnes, a former three-sport star at Purdue who played on the school's 1980 Final Four team and a successful sports agent.

As a senior, he was named Indiana Mr. Basketball and led Homestead to a first-ever state title. He was ranked as a top-20 national prospect in his class. He was named a McDonald's All-American. Swanigan averaged 22.6 points and 13.7 rebounds his final year. Academically, Swanigan maintained a 3.1 GPA and graduated in three years instead of the usual four.

Swanigan had several teams recruit him and offer scholarships: Arizona, Kentucky, Cal, and Duke were among the schools that gave Swanigan an offer. Caleb Swanigan verbally committed to Michigan State on April 10, 2015, but rescinded that commitment on May 7. He decided to stay in-state and chose Purdue on May 19. Swanigan announced his decision by tweeting "#BoilerUp." Swanigan was Purdue's first Indiana's Mr. Basketball recruit since Glenn Robinson.

Purdue's junior class came to West Lafayette to change the program's culture and lead it back to relevance in the Big Ten Conference.

On March 1, 2017, the most raucous night in years in Mackey Arena, number-16 Purdue locked up the program's first Big Ten title since 2010 with an 86–75 victory, which gave the Boilermakers a sweep of the Hoosiers. Caleb Swanigan returned to double-double form with 21 points and 10 rebounds. The Boilermakers ultimately pulled away by making the post a priority again. No one on IU's team figured out a way to defend Swanigan without fouling the Big Ten Player of the Year, who seemed to score every time he got the ball.

The 14,804 people in attendance witnessed something no Purdue fans had before a Big Ten championship-clinching victory at home over Indiana.

Rondale Moore: He Outran Our Defenders

Rondale Moore went to New Albany High School, where he was part of the 2016 4-A Indiana State basketball championship team with Romeo Langford. Then he transferred across the Ohio River to Trinity High School, where he was a four-star football recruit. At first, he committed to play for Texas. He led Trinity High School to its 25th (and second consecutive) state championship to cap off back-to-back perfect 15–0 seasons. Rondale was named MVP of the game. Then he rescinded his commitment to Texas, citing that he didn't have all the time he needed to evaluate schools during the season. In January,

Moore committed to Purdue. He was the first four-star recruit to commit to Purdue in years.

In his first-ever game with the Boilermakers, and his first game overall, Moore's 313 all-purpose yards was the record for most in program history and the highest since Otis Armstrong, who had 312 in 1972. In that same game, Moore had a 76-yard rush to score a touchdown. During the 2018 season, Moore was named Big Ten Freshman of the Week four times. The fourth time came after the Old Oaken Bucket game in Bloomington, where Moore beat IU almost singlehandedly with 12 receptions, two touchdowns, and 141 all-purpose yards.

At the conclusion of the 2018 regular season, Moore had recorded 1,164 receiving yards and 203 rushing yards to go along with thirteen combined touchdowns. Moore's 2,048 all-purpose yards were the most since Dorien Bryant recorded 2,121 in 2007, and the second-most in school history.

At the end of the 2018 season, Moore was the recipient of the Paul Hornung Award, given to the most versatile player in all of college football. Moore was also named a first-team All-American by the Associated Press as an all-purpose back. He was also named a first-team All-American by the Football Writers' Association of America. Moore was also named the CBS Sports Freshman of the Year.

Coaches We Hate

Noble Kizer: Purdue's First Real Winner in the Big Ten

From Plymouth, Indiana, just south of South Bend, Noble Kizer played for Notre Dame at right guard under Irish coach Knute Rockne from 1922 to 1924. In 1925, he became an assistant coach at Purdue under James Phelan. He inherited the head coaching position upon Phelan's departure for the University of Washington.

Kizer was the head football coach at Purdue from 1930 to 1936. During his tenure as head coach, he won two Big Ten Conference titles and compiled a record of 42–13–3, with 26–9–3 in the Big Ten. Kizer was also the athletic director from 1933 until his death in 1940. He had a 3–3–1 record against IU during his tenure at Purdue. From 1931 to '33, his Boilermakers won three-straight Bucket games with a score of 63–10.

In February of 1934, it seemed to Purdue alumni that Ohio State was attempting to hire Kizer to rebuild their football program. Ohio State gave very vague answers to a telegram sent by the Purdue Alumni Association in regard to accusations that Ohio was proselytizing Purdue employees. Maybe that's why there seems to be bad blood between the two schools.

Ward "Piggy" Lambert: Purdue's First Great Coach

In 1917, Ward "Piggy" Lambert was named head basketball coach of the Boilermakers. Until he retired in 1946, he amassed a 27–16 record against the Hoosiers. He was in the forefront of developing a faster-paced game where the scores began to climb into the 40s and 50s. Lambert got his nickname from the pigtails he wore as a child.

While coaching at Purdue, Lambert developed 16 All-Americans and 31 first-team All–Big Ten selections. The 1932 National Player of the Year was none other than John Wooden, later of even more honors as the coach of the UCLA dynasty, and a three-time consensus All-American. Wooden was the first college player to be named a consensus All-American three times. Lambert compiled a career record of 371–152, a 70.9 winning percentage. His 228 wins in Big Ten play have been bested by only Indiana's Bob Knight and former Purdue head coach Gene Keady. Lambert won an unprecedented 11 Big Ten Championships, which Bobby Knight later tied for most in conference history.

Low-key off the court but frenetic during games, Lambert's coaching method stressed self-confidence, aggressiveness, speed, and positive attitude. He is one of the coaches that pioneered the fast break, an offensive drive down the court at all-out speed. Lambert retired from coaching in 1946 and served until 1949 as commissioner of the professional National Basketball League, a forerunner of the NBA.

Until Branch McCracken became coach at IU, Lambert's teams held sway, 24–8, over the Hoosiers. But after coach Mac's teams competed against Purdue, Lambert won only three and lost eight.

Jack Mollenkopf: Purdue's Best Ever

Kenneth "Jack" Mollenkopf was an assistant coach at Purdue from 1947 to 1955 under Stu Holcomb and became the head football coach at Purdue in 1956. He directed the Boilermakers until 1969.

Mollenkopf is widely acknowledged as the greatest football coach in Purdue's history because he leads all Purdue coaches in Big Ten Conference wins (58) and conference winning percentage (63.7). Mollenkopf's Boilermakers were nationally ranked for 80 weeks, the most under any Purdue head coach, and were ranked number one for the first half of the 1968 season.

On January 2, 1967, Mollenkopf coached the school's first appearance in the Rose Bowl that Purdue won 14–13 victory over USC. His teams dominated both in-state rivals, Notre Dame and IU. Against Notre Dame, he went 10–4 and was 11–2–1 versus IU.

He was known for recruiting and developing top-notch players. From 1966 to 1969, a Purdue player finished in the top three in Heisman Trophy balloting every year. Quarterback Bob Griese was second in 1966, halfback Leroy Keyes placed third in 1967 and second in 1968, and quarterback Mike Phipps finished as runner-up in 1969. Mollenkopf's inaugural season in 1956 was the only losing campaign of his tenure as head coach at Purdue, but his team still won the Bucket game, 39–20.

Extremely well respected nationally, Mollenkopf served as head coach of the 1958, 1959, and 1960 Blue–Gray Football Classics; the 1962 and 1963 East–West Shrine Games; the 1964, 1967, and 1970 Hula Bowls; the 1968 All-American Bowl; and the 1969 North–South Shrine Game. He was inducted into the College Football Hall of Fame in 1988, the Bowling Green State University Hall of Fame in 1965, and the Indiana Football Hall of Fame in 1975. In 1994, Coach Mollenkopf was inducted as a member of the inaugural class of the Purdue Intercollegiate Athletic Hall of Fame.

George King: Took Purdue to the Final Game

George King took over the reins for Purdue basketball in 1966 and stayed until 1979. Prior to coming to Purdue, he coached as an assistant to Fred Schaus (future Purdue coach) for the West Virginia Mountaineers. Schaus left WVU to coach the Lakers in the NBA. King took over the WVU program and managed an overall record of 102–43 and led them to three Southern Conference tournament championships and three NCAA Tournaments.

George King's best team at Purdue was in 1969 when they won their first conference title in 29 years and advanced to the 1969 NCAA Finals game, led by All-American Rick Mount, where they would fall to former Purdue great, John Wooden, and his UCLA Bruins squad.

During his tenure at Purdue, King's teams compiled a 109–64 record. King's record against IU was 12-10.

For the next 21 years, after his retirement from coaching basketball, King stayed on as Purdue's seventh athletics director. King directed the Boilermaker program through a period of tremendous growth and change. He oversaw the emergence of women's athletics at the varsity level at Purdue in the 1976–77 season. Extremely revered by his peers in the profession, King served as President of the National Association of Collegiate Directors of Athletics.

He was one of the youngest collegiate athletic directors in the nation and was the only AD who also coached in the 1971–72 season. King is a member of both the Purdue and the University of Charleston Athletic Halls of Fame.

Jim Young: Brought Back Winning Football

In December 1976, Purdue University hired the 41-year-old Jim Young away from Arizona, where he had a record of 31–13 in four seasons. Prior to Arizona, he had been the defensive coordinator for Bo Schembechler at Michigan. He had great success at Arizona, posting records of 9–2 in 1974 and 1975, the latter ending with a

number 13 and number 18 ranking in the Coaches' and AP Polls, respectively. Boilermaker fans met Young with high expectations.

When he arrived at Purdue, knowing pure talent when he saw it, he named freshman Mark Herrmann as the team's starting quarterback. Herrmann was a high-school standout at Carmel in both football and basketball. Herrmann proved Young right by throwing for 2,041 yards through the team's first eight games. Herrmann broke the NCAA record for passing yards (2,453) and passing touchdowns (18) for a freshman. In 1978, Young lead Purdue to a 9–2–1 record and a victory over Georgia Tech in the 1978 Peach Bowl. He was named the Big Ten's Coach of the Year, the first Boilermaker head coach to ever win the award.

During his five seasons, Young had three wins against Indiana. At a game in Bloomington, Herrmann was tackled on the southwest sideline after hot pursuit from the IU defense. As he lay to be tended to by medics, the IU fans booed assuming Purdue was stalling. This incensed Young was visibly upset and verbally attacked the nearby crowd. The final that day was 37–21.

After a disappointing 1981 season, Young resigned from his position as head coach at Purdue, citing his desire to concentrate on athletic administration. Young left Purdue to coach for the Army and compiled an excellent record there during eight seasons. His Army teams were often ranked, beat the Navy five times, and went to three bowl games.

Young was inducted into the College Football Hall of Fame as a coach in 1999.

Lee Rose: Took Purdue to the Final Four

Lee Rose came to Purdue in 1978 from the UNC Charlotte where he had taken the team to the Final Four of the NCAA Tournament. He took Purdue to the Final Four in 1980 and is one of only ten coaches in NCAA history to take two different schools to the semifinals of the

NCAA Tournament. Rose had two seasons at Purdue and compiled a 50–18 record. Against IU, he was 3–1.

Even though Rose only coached the Boilermakers for two years, they were two very memorable seasons. His first season, 1978–79, Purdue was in a three-way tie for the Big Ten championship. Back then, only one team from each conference could go to the NCAA tournament. Michigan State got the Big Ten's bid. Magic Johnson led them to a national championship in a classic game against Larry Byrd and Indiana State. That year Rose's team started conference play 0–2, losing at Ohio State and Indiana, partly because of travel problems trying to fly out of Hawaii after playing in a holiday tournament. Because of snow storms on the mainland, the team couldn't get back to West Lafayette with time to prepare for the games.

The Boilermakers reached the Final Four in Indianapolis Rose's second season, losing to UCLA in the semifinals. That team was led by seven-foot Joe Barry Carroll, who became the first pick in the NBA draft. Rose was a brilliant tactician and communicator with his players.

Rose left Purdue after his second season to start the program at South Florida. Many people are confused as to why Rose would leave a winning program. He says it just wasn't a good fit, but clearly, his relationship with athletic director George King was strained. He also was frustrated by home-state recruiting against Bob Knight at IU and Digger Phelps at Notre Dame.

Gene Keady: Had a Winning Record Versus IU

If there's something IU fans do not like about Mackey Arena, it may be the name of the court. It's the Keady Court, named after a coach who was a real thorn in the side of Hoosier basketball for most of the 25-years he coached the Boilermakers. His head-on record against the Hoosiers was 21–20 at a time when Indiana was winning NCAA championships, Big Ten titles, and all the glory in the Hoosier state press. Gene Keady seemed to be able to win with players that were not in the spotlight like the IU players of the time.

*Purdue's 25-year coach Gene Keady led them
to victories over Big-Ten champion IU.*

In 1980, Gene Keady, was named the new head coach of the Boilermakers. Over the next 25 years, Keady led the Boilermakers to six Big Ten Championships and 17 NCAA Tournament appearances with two Elite Eights. Keady's teams began to be recognized nationally, and, in the 1987–88 season, they were ranked as high as second in the nation. In 1991, Keady got his first big-name Indiana recruit, Glenn Robinson, from IHSAA-state-champion Roosevelt High School in Gary. Robinson was Mr. Basketball in that year. Under Keady, he ultimately became an All-American and Purdue's second player named National Player of the Year. A few years later, Purdue managed to recruit the program's first of many foreign players when they picked up Matt ten Dam from the Netherlands. In December 1997, Keady became Purdue's all-time winningest head coach, surpassing Piggy Lambert with his 372nd win. He also became the second-winningest coach in Big Ten history behind Bobby Knight.

In October 2010, newly-hired St. John's coach Steve Lavin hired Keady to be his assistant coach. His main roles as an assistant to

Lavin were breaking down game film and serving as a bench coach on game days.

Many of Keady's former assistant coaches and players throughout the years have gone on to enjoy success as head coaches. Included in the Gene Keady–coaching tree is Purdue's current head coach Matt Painter, former St. John's head coach Steve Lavin, Pittsburgh head coach Kevin Stallings, Kansas State head coach Bruce Weber, Wisconsin-Green Bay head coach Linc Darner, UNC Charlotte head coach Alan Major, Missouri head coach Cuonzo Martin, Missouri State head coach Paul Lusk, and Illinois State head coach Dan Muller.

Internationally, Keady coached on the 2000 Dream Team and won a gold medal in the Olympic Games in Sydney. As the head coach of various USA Basketball teams, Keady racked up a record of 22–2, (91.7 percent) in four different tournaments from 1979 to 1991. He led Team USA to two gold medals: one in 1979 at the National Sports Festival, and another in 1989 at the World University Games.

In 2007, The Big Ten Network hired Keady to be a basketball analyst, along with former Big Ten basketball players Tim Doyle and Jim Jackson. Keady is also an occasional commentator for the network. He now attends Purdue home games on a regular basis.

Joe Tiller: Fast Break Basketball on Grass

After an exceptional final season at Wyoming, where his Cowboys went 10–2 and ended the season ranked 22nd in the nation, Joe Tiller was hired by Purdue in 1997. Tiller inherited a program that had only had two winning seasons in the previous 18 years.

In his first season, Tiller's Boilermakers made headlines by upsetting Notre Dame on national TV. Purdue proceeded to go to 10 bowl games in Tiller's 12 seasons as head coach. In his third season, he took the Boilermakers to the 2001 Rose Bowl. The 2000 season also saw the Boilers' first Big Ten title in 35 years. Prior to Tiller's tenure as head coach, Purdue had played in only five bowl games.

In 2008, against Central Michigan, Tiller won his 85th game at Purdue to become the winningest coach in school history, topping the previous mark set by Jack Mollenkopf (1956–1969). Tiller's "basketball on grass" offense was well-renowned for its ability to score and score effectively, befuddling opposing defenses. This was especially the case when quarterback Drew Brees led the team from 1997 to 2000. His Purdue squads were shut-out only once by Penn State in a 12–0 defeat at Ross–Ade Stadium on October 28, 2006.

Tiller retired following the 2008 season, ending with a 62–10 Old Oaken Bucket win at Ross–Ade Stadium. Hoosier fans always felt that Tiller would run up the score by playing his starters late into games with a huge lead. He had games against IU with winning scores like 62–10, 63–24, 52–7, and 56–7. His teams went 11–1 against the Hoosiers, with an average margin of victory of 26 points.

Matt Painter: Won Multiple Big Ten Titles (2005–present)

As Gene Keady was preparing to retire from his head coaching position at Purdue, the Boilermakers hired Matt Painter to be his replacement, but they made him an associate head coach for one year to ease the transition (2004–05). Painter, who had played for Keady during the early nineties, was head coach for only one year at Southern Illinois, but he led the Salukis to a 25–5 record and an NCAA appearance.

Painter's first season at Purdue, without Keady, was disappointing at 9–19. However, he re-invigorated Purdue basketball in the summer of 2006 by signing a top recruiting class, allowing the Boilermakers to make one of their biggest turnarounds ever. In 2006, Painter's Boilermakers went 22–12 and made it to the NCAA tourney. He repeated this feat for six years.

During the 2010 season, Painter's Boilermakers had a start that tied the school record, winning their first 14 games. They also had the most wins ever (29), and they won the Big Ten. In 2011 season,

the team went 26–8 and finished second in the Big Ten. That year, they went on to a Sweet Sixteen appearance in the NCAA tourney. In the 2012 season, Painter's team started with a 12–3 record and held a 27 home-game winning streak. That year, they led the nation with the fewest turnovers per game average (8.7) and completed their sixth consecutive season of 22 or more wins (a Purdue record).

The following two seasons were below-par for Painter, and after a moderate 8–5 preseason campaign during the 2015 season, Purdue got back on track, finishing third in the conference. The 2015 season ended after losing in the NCAA tourney to Cincinnati in overtime. It was the first time that the program lost its opener in the NCAA Tournament in 22 years, breaking a 14-game win streak. After making it back to the NCAA tourney, the program landed its biggest recruit since Glenn Robinson when Fort Wayne–native Caleb "Biggie" Swanigan, a five-star recruit, rescinded his commitment to Michigan State. With Biggie, they opened the 2016 season with an 11–0 record, while setting a program record with consecutive double-digit victories and were ranked as high as ninth in the nation. In May 2016, it was announced that the 2017–18 Purdue team would represent the US at the 2017 World University Games in Taipei. The team would go on to win the Silver Medal at the Games, winning every game until losing to Lithuania in the Gold Medal game.

Painter's Boilermakers won the 2017 Big Ten Conference title outright, along with Caleb Swanigan being named unanimous Big Ten Player of the Year. In the 2017 NCAA Tournament, Purdue reached the Sweet Sixteen, losing to number-one seed Kansas. In the 2017-2018 season, Purdue spent several weeks at number three while being on a program-record and nation-leading 19-game winning streak. During that time, the Boilers led the nation in scoring margin, points per game, three-point shooting, and was one of only two teams with a top-three ranking in both offensive and defensive efficiency. Purdue finished second in the conference at 15–3 and got a four-seed in the Big Ten Tournament. They made it to the championship game,

where they lost to Michigan, whom they had beaten twice during the Big Ten season.

Painter's Boilermakers were seeded second in the East Region of the 2018 NCAA Tournament, their highest seed in recent history. They easily won their first-round game, then the hearts of the Purdue fans were broken in the second half of the game as seven-foot dominating senior center Isaac Haas fell and broke his elbow as he hit the ground fighting for a rebound, ending his Purdue Basketball career. Painter's team still won the game and advanced to the Sweet Sixteen but lost, ending their season with 30 wins, the most wins in program history.

Painter's Boilermakers made it to the elite eight in the 2019 NCAA tourney before losing to Virginia in overtime. His team beat IU twice during the season climaxing with a last second heart breaker 48-46 win in Bloomington. This gives Painter a 12-9 winning record against the Hoosiers.

Jeff Brohm: Brought the Fans Back

In 2016, Jeff Brohm took the head coaching position at Purdue University, where he took the Boilermakers to a 7–6 record in his first season. Purdue was on a losing streak against IU, who had added four consecutive "I" links to the Old Oaken Bucket chain.

Brohm began by recruiting primarily the offensive and defensive lines, as well as wide receivers, bringing in five graduate transfers to help get instant depth.

Many Purdue fans thought that this could be the turnaround they had been waiting for since the retirement of Joe Tiller. They had their first sell-out crowd since 2008. Purdue would reach the high point of the season upon taking the Old Oaken Bucket in a win, 31–24. Both teams were 5–6 for the season, meaning the winner would become bowl-eligible. Purdue's win was the first for the program against the Hoosiers since 2012. The six wins that season was enough to get Purdue into the 2017 Foster Farms Bowl, where they would face the University of Arizona. The bowl game made Brohm only the second

head coach in Purdue history—along with Joe Tiller—to take Purdue to a bowl game in their first season as head coach.

Purdue would head into the Foster Farms Bowl game as slight underdogs, but would go on to beating the Arizona Wildcats, 38–35, thanks in part to an Elijah Sindelar touchdown pass in the closing minutes of the game.

The next season, Purdue came to Bloomington and beat IU, 28–21. The outcome didn't sit well with Hoosier fans as the huge Purdue contingent taunted the IU crowd. Hoosier fans were consoled by Purdue's 63–14 loss to Auburn in the 2018 Music City Bowl. The story is told that Auburn won the coin toss and elected to kick the heck out of Purdue.

Traditions We Hate

World's Largest Drum—Not

The "World's Largest Drum" is actually a full nine feet smaller than the true world's largest drum in Korea.

Purdue students and alumni think that their big bass drum, the "World's Largest Drum," is the biggest drum in the world. After all, it stands 10 feet tall on its field carriage and must be handled by a crew

of four band members. It takes two guys to beat the drum. The drum draws attention wherever it goes from ethnocentric Boilermaker fans that want their picture taken with the instrument. They really believe that it is the biggest drum in the world. Others, however, dispute the Purdue assertion.

It's often said, "Everything is bigger in Texas!" The university of Texas claims their Big Bertha to be the world's largest drum; it measures 8 feet in diameter, 44 inches in depth, and stands 10 feet tall when on its four-wheeled cart. The drum weighs more than 500 pounds. Big Bertha is wheeled onto the field during varsity football games and is used in other occasions such as parades and spirit rallies. The drum is managed by the Bertha Crew, sometimes called "drum wranglers." The crew moves the drum and play it after touchdowns. Big Bertha is nicknamed the "Sweetheart of the Longhorn Band."

Big Bertha was built for the University of Chicago and first used in the 1922 football game versus rival Princeton. When the University of Chicago ended its varsity football program, the drum was stored under the school's bleachers. It later became radioactively contaminated as a result of research for the Manhattan Project conducted at Stagg Field during the 1940s. Colonel D. Harold Byrd, a former Longhorn Band member, brought the drum to the university in 1955 after purchasing it from the University of Chicago for $1 and paying to have it decontaminated and restored.

But alas, neither school has the world's largest drum. The *Guinness Book of World Records* lists a Korean drum as the largest. The world's largest drum measures 18 feet, 2 inches in diameter is 19 feet, 6 inches tall, and weighs 15,432 pounds. The drum was created in South Korea on 6 July 2011.

Boilermakers—Hired A Team?

The moniker for the University's athletics teams has become a popular reference for all things Purdue. A reporter first used the name in 1891 to describe the year's winning football team and quickly gained approval from students.

In the 1880s, Purdue students experienced hands-on education at the university, including the maintenance of a fully-operational steam locomotive. So, in 1889, when Purdue beat Wabash College, 18–4, students from the college and citizens of Crawfordsville began calling the Purdue players "a great, big, burly gang of corn-huskers," "grangers," "pumpkin-shuckers," "rail-splitters," "blacksmiths," "cornfield sailors," and "foundry hands."

It was suggested that Purdue was adding bulk to their team by hiring workers from the nearby Monon railroad yards to play football. The Monon Railroad had its main locomotive shops in Lafayette, not far from campus.

Purdue defeated Wabash College again in 1891, 44–0. An account of the game in the *Crawfordsville Daily Argus News* of October 26, 1891 was headlined, "Slaughter of Innocents: Wabash Snowed Completely Under by the Burly Boiler Makers from Purdue." Purdue became known as the boilermakers the next year.

Grand Prix—A Knock-Off

The Purdue Grand Prix is a 50-mile, 160-lap go-kart race. Its backers call it "The Greatest Spectacle in College Racing," taken from the description "The Greatest Spectacle in Racing" used by the Indianapolis 500. There are 33 participating karts, all made from scratch by student teams. The event has been raising money for student scholarships since it began in 1958. The primary purpose of the race is to raise around $10,000 in annual funds for student scholarships.

Student organizations—including residence halls, co-op houses, and Greek organizations—build and race go-karts on a purpose-built race course located on the Purdue University campus. The event is open to all members of the student body, including students at regional campuses. Students at the Indianapolis campus (IUPUI) have won the race on several occasions, possibly due in part to the motorsports technology major offered on that branch campus. Teams qualify for starting positions much like Indycar road course races.

Though the race is held on a Saturday, associated festivities begin the weekend before, resulting in an entire week of parties and other events, both sanctioned and unsanctioned. A newer tradition which precedes the race itself is the Breakfast Club. Early on the morning of the race, local bars re-open to hordes of costume-clad students and alumni. Screwdrivers and other alcoholic drinks are served to patrons dressed in a variety of costumes—the more outrageous or inventive, the better.

Indiana students and alumni consider the Purdue Grand Prix to be a knock-off or little sister of IU's Little 500, which began seven years before than the Grand Prix. Purdue's track has limited public seating on the bleachers and a section for sponsors. By contrast, the Little 500 draws about 25,000 fans annually. When the race was held at the old IU Memorial Stadium on 10th Street, the crowd attendance actually reached as many as 30,000 people.

IU Sucks—From the Jealous Little Brother

At every Purdue home football and basketball game, no matter who the Boilermakers are playing, the student section yells in unison "IU Sucks." They yell it at basketball games after the band plays "Hail Fire." Football games are similar.

Most Indiana fans and alumni don't know about the IU Sucks cheer because they only pay attention to Purdue when IU plays them. And if, by chance, they are watching a Purdue game on TV, the IU-Sucks cheer is seldom allowed on the network audio. But IU students in today's era of ultra-communications are well aware of this tradition. A general thought expressed by an IU student on Reddit is, "They chant 'IU Sucks' at every game, whether or not they're playing IU. Proof that they're the jealous little brother."

Purdue basketball coach, Matt Painter, a class-act in himself, has asked the students to stop the cheer. This was after the IU student section in Bloomington chanted "F—— Harms" at Purdue center

Matt Harms during a basketball game with Purdue. The IU students were way out of line, and Athletic Director Fred Glass sent an apology to Purdue. He promised it wouldn't happen again. But Purdue students, however, don't feel the same way.

The *Purdue Exponent*'s (student newspaper) sportswriter Konner Klotz said, "Here at Purdue, we've got two sports [football and men's basketball] in which fans partake in the Boilermaker ritual of degrading our number one in-state rival. Personally, I don't believe we should chant 'IU sucks' unless we're actually playing the Hoosiers, but it seems I'm in the minority with that belief. Last week, we ran a poll via The *Exponent* Sports Desk Twitter page, in which we asked, "If Purdue is NOT playing Indiana, should the fans still chant 'IU sucks' during games?" Overwhelmingly, sixty-three percent of our respondents said yes."

Old Gold and Black

Purdue's colors, old gold and black, were proposed by the captain of the football team and adopted in 1887, the first year of Purdue football. It was decided that colors were needed to achieve distinction. Whether those colors exude distinction or not in today's wardrobe is a matter of opinion. Most IU fans find black depressing and appropriate for funerals or a desire to be unnoticed after nightfall.

So, whether you believe Purdue colors exude elegance or depression, wealth or stress, think about wearing clothes to a football game. When looking at the fans at a game, black and old gold are rather dull and unexciting.

POTFH

From urbandictionary.com, the definition of POTFH is "P— on the F—— Hoosiers." Commonly used on the Purdue University, West Lafayette campus in reference to the Indiana University Hoosier athletic teams.

Here's Urban Dictionary's example of using the phrase properly:

Joe: "Dude, IU is kind of good this year, if they get one more win, they could go to a bowl game."

Dave: "I don't care. POTFH. The Boilers are gonna murder them."

IU fans could care less when Purdue students use this phrase on their campus. After all, Purdue students are starved for a bar scene, and have a permanent inferiority complex. The only problem Hoosiers have with POTFH is when "artistic" Purdue students come to Bloomington and paint the letters on sidewalks, walls, streets, cars, or—heaven forbid—, on the limestone front of Ernie Pyle Hall, as they have done in the past.

Purdue Pete—Scared the Kids

What started as an advertising logo for the Purdue University Bookstore in 1940 has become one of the most recognized symbols for the school. The owners of the bookstores gave him the name "Pete;" no one today knows why this was chosen to be his name.

Over the years, the appearance of Purdue Pete has gone under several drastic changes as well as several minor changes. His original head was made of paper-mâché pasted onto a chicken wire frame. This was very inconvenient for the person inside the costume because it would limit his movements, yet he was still expected to move around and do stunts. Later, the head was changed to fiberglass and the person inside used a harness to support it. This was also impractical due to the sheer size of it. In the 1980s, Purdue Pete acquired the current look.

Purdue attempted to redesign Purdue Pete's costume due to concerns that the over-sized head was perceived as scary by younger fans, however, the redesign was met with outrage and criticism. The redesign plans for Purdue Pete involved no jersey, a full-body suit rather than just a head, and no hammer. At the spring 2011 Black & Gold game, the loudest fan reaction was to boo the redesigned costume.

IU fans dislike the Purdue Pete for several reasons. Mainly, they think Pete looked stupid with a huge top-heavy head. His puffed-up fake muscles and pads were meant to resemble a person working on railroad steam boilers of the old days that has suited-up in a football jersey for the game. He is also unpopular because he stirs-up fans at Bucket games in Bloomington. He stands in the south end zone and waves his fake hammer at the crowd.

One game, long ago, Pete took off his heavy costume head to rest his shoulders during the half-time. A high-spirited IU undergrad climbed the short south–end zone fence, scooped up Pete's vacant pantomime head, and darted toward the IU west stands. The headless Pete took up a chase, and the crowd roared. Pete caught the culprit, and security took him away to the disapproval of the IU students.

Boilermaker Special

The Boilermaker Special is a truck with a Victorian-era locomotive replica built on its frame. The locomotive design of Purdue's official mascot celebrates the University's renowned railroad programs. In the 1890s, Purdue had become a leader in the research of railway technology.

The Boilermaker Special is the official mascot of Purdue. Contrary to popular belief, the burly boilermaker Purdue Pete is not the official mascot of the university.

The Boilermaker Special is frequently seen around the main campus, at athletic contests, and at local community events, where it is used to promote the university. The members of the Purdue Reamer Club travel with the train to nearly every football game, including bowl games. During the football season, caps bearing the logos of defeated opponents are attached to the Boilermaker Special's cow-catcher.

IU fans are generally annoyed by the Boilermaker Special because of its presence on the IU campus every other year hours before the Old Oaken bucket games, honking and bell-ringing. The Purdue fans that are on the campus are all hypnotized by the sight and sounds

and are induced to hoot and holler. These are the people that drive to Bloomington, put up signs that say "Ross–Ade South," and try to take over the parking lot. It's funny that, after a Purdue loss, these fans are nowhere to be found.

IU students more into cross-communications with Purdue undergrad friends, also dislike the truck/train, leading Claire Hitchins to say, "That train of theirs travels around their campus like one of the kiddie trains at the mall."

We Hate Purdue's Campus

West Lafayette

Unlike Indiana University in Bloomington, Purdue's campus doesn't appear in national rankings like Conde Nast, Best College Reviews, *Travel and Leisure,* or the *USA Today* reader's poll of Best Beautiful College Campuses. To add to this snub, the city of West Lafayette was voted last in the Big Ten for a college town in an Athlon Sports poll conducted among Gerry DiNardo, Dave Revsine, Tom Dienhart, and Brent Yarina of Big Ten Network; Teddy Greenstein of the *Chicago Tribune;* Adam Rittenberg of ESPN; Kevin McGuire of College Football Talk; Sean Callahan of HuskerOnline.com; Kevin Noon of BuckeyeGrove.com; and Braden Gall of Athlon Sports and SiriusXM. From this group of ten, West Lafayette received seven last-place votes.

Ambiance

When you think about it, the Purdue campus sits on a vast agricultural plane that's almost as flat as a tabletop, save for the Wabash River's occasional steep banks. The campus looks like something from a brown brick colored Lego project. W. Burchell, after receiving his master's degree in Fine Art from Purdue, jokingly said, "They took one little brick and added a million more just like it and made Purdue."

"The Boilermaker"

The first use of the term "boilermaker" in connection with the Purdue football team was in 1891 and was used in a derogatory manner towards Purdue football opponents by newspaper.

Just outside of Ross–Ade Stadium, between the Intercollegiate Athletic Facility and the Mollenkopf Athletic Center, sits "The Boilermaker." An 18-foot bronze statue depicting a nineteenth-century boiler-room worker, "The Boilermaker" dons the jersey of a different player on the football team each football weekend. "The Boilermaker" was commissioned on behalf of an anonymous donor.

"The Boilermaker" statue probably more closely resembles one of the many statues and drawings to honor the worker developed in The USSR after the overthrow the Tsar than it does a nineteenth-century man working on a boiler.

Ross–Ade Stadium

Ross–Ade Stadium's seating capacity presently is 57,282. It once had a capacity of 68,000, but the number of seats has since been cut down due to comfort and safety concerns. The larger capacity came from an attempt to have Purdue seat more people than their former rival Notre Dame. With all the wisdom of an engineer, someone at Purdue decided to reduce the number of square inches each spectator would be allotted for his or her seat. They accomplished this by repainting the lines on the stadium bleachers to allow for more seats without adding more bleachers. This gave each spectator less butt room. Of course, this act didn't sit well with spectators, no pun intended. A spectator with a seat on the end of a row tended to lose his or her place to sit when the crowd rose to cheer and sat back down.

The Ross–Ade playing field features the PAT, or Prescription Athletic Turf system. Developed by Purdue staffers in the 1970s, the PAT system features a network of pipes connected to pumps capable of keeping the field playable, even during a storm dumping one inch of rain per hour.

When the turf system was initially installed, the field tended to incur an excessive number of divots where big sections of the grass would flip over. It seemed that, many times, as a player would dig his cleats into the field, a chunk of turf would peel back. Jokingly, the Executive Secretary of the Purdue Ag Alumni Association Mauri Williamson said at a Press Club Roast that he was dreaming about a fresh-plowed field, only to wake up and realize that it was the playing surface of Ross–Ade Stadium.

After a game with the Demon Deacons of Wake Forest, the post-game press-conference leader asked John Mackovic, the Deacon head coach, what he thought of the PAT turf. Mackovic said, "That was the worst playing surface I've ever seen in college football."

Despite the addition of many new parts to improve the stadium, when one looks at the concourse below the seating areas, Ross–Ade Stadium still gives the impression of a somewhat-temporary facility, with exposed steel girders that give the appearance of hasty construction.

The exposed girders and functional architecture of Ross–Ade Stadium make many visitors feel as though the huge stadium is permanently unfinished.

Ross Ade stadium looks functional and fits perfectly into the Purdue campus. The joy and happiness of beauty in design and architecture are sacrificed at Purdue for functionalism.

I Love IU

Why Hoosier Fans Love the Cream and Crimson

I Love IU

Why Hoosier Fans Love the Cream and Crimson

Joe Drozda

BLUE RIVER PRESS

Indianapolis, Indiana

Contents

Foreword

I came to IU in 1973 and learned quickly that, no matter where you traveled in Indiana, there was a spirited rivalry between fans from IU and fans from Purdue. Joe Drozda was the first IU fan I met living in the most hostile territory in the whole state, West Lafayette. In 1971 he formed the Lafayette Chapter of the IU Varsity Club and gave Tippecanoe County's huge local contingent of Hoosier fans an outlet for their pent-up Indiana University pride.

In 1976 Joe began to do a radio talk show that I appeared on during a trip to cover the IU–Purdue game at Mackey Arena. During that show I received a phone call from the voice of Purdue, Johnny De Camp, and then another from one of his staff. This good-natured banter was fun on the air and showed how neat the IU–Purdue rivalry was. All that season Joe attended the Indiana home games and then stopped at WTTS (radio) in Bloomington to pick up a tape of the game and take it with him back to Lafayette. The game was replayed, tape delayed, on a local station for Hoosier fans that couldn't pick up the Indiana games on their radios.

In this book Joe covers many of the great games, players, and coaches I've covered as the voice of the Hoosiers. Joe also writes about some great Purdue athletes and coaches while poking some fun at the campus and traditions of Purdue. This book really covers the rivalry between IU and Purdue.

—Don Fischer

Introduction

The rivalry between the Indiana University (Hoosiers) and Purdue University (Boilermakers) encompasses the two largest schools in the state of Indiana. And their collegiate rivalry is regarded as one of the most intense in the United States. Among all of college sports rivalries, *Huffington Post* listed it as the fifth-best rivalry over all, ahead of Army–Navy, and *Newsweek* listed it among the top 12.

IU has more than 33,000 undergraduates and is located in the forests, hills, and limestone cliffs of southern Indiana. It is known for music, business, medicine, law, and the arts. Obviously, Indiana University is named after the state of Indiana.

Purdue has just over 31,000 undergraduates and is in the northwest portion of the state on the banks of the Wabash River surrounded by flat farmland. Purdue is known for engineering and agriculture. Purdue is named for businessman and benefactor John Purdue.

Some die-hard IU fans really hate Purdue—the school and anything about it—with an animosity that lasts 365 days a year, even on Christmas. And the feeling is mutual. But whereas most of the Hoosier Nation dislike Purdue, very few really hate the Boilermaker players or the students that attend Purdue. After all, many of them

are neighbors or even family. It's just that IU fans find it unacceptable that Purdue and her faithful can believe that their teams or schools are as good as Indiana's. The more the Boilermakers fanaticize about being as good and try to prove it, the more Indiana fans don't like it. This feeling lasts all year even when the two school's teams are facing other opponents. Schadenfreude aptly describes the fans of these two schools' teams. It means the experience of pleasure, joy, or self-satisfaction that comes from learning of or witnessing the troubles, failures, or humiliations of another. This is evidenced in a statement common to IU fans, "My two favorite teams are IU and whoever is playing Purdue."

What fans of both schools really hate is losing to each other. It's been like this since 1891, the year of their first football game, won by the "Bad Guys," 60 – 0. Some things never change, and all the predictions indicate that this rivalry will continue for as long as collegiate sports exist.

The rivalry's season is kind of like a mini-fiscal year, beginning in the fall with the first game of football season and ending in early summer. The summer season is a time of hoping: hoping to continue the past season's victories, or hoping to regain some past glory.

One would conjecture that, since IU and Purdue most often have had great, highly-ranked basketball teams, football wouldn't be important. In reality, that's not the case at all. From the onset of football season, IU fans observe oddsmaker predictions and final scores for Purdue games as a yard stick against which to measure their Hoosier teams. An early loss for Purdue is universally enjoyed by IU fans.

As the football season progresses, the schools begin to add up wins to get a sense of possibilities for a bowl game. Many times, the final game of football season, The Old Oaken Bucket game, determines which school's team plays in a bowl and which team stays home.

Introduction

When IU and Purdue play the Old Oaken Bucket game, all IU nation and Boilermaker fans pay attention. IU and Purdue fans and alumni are conditioned to look forward to this game because of all the national attention to rivalries. It seems like everyone in America takes a side in the Army–Navy game. Traditionally everyone has watched or followed the score of "The Game" between Harvard and Yale. There's also "The Game" between Michigan and Ohio State, the "Red River Shootout" between Texas and Oklahoma, and "The Iron Bowl" between Alabama and Auburn. These are just a few of the great rivalries when the home-team fans and alumni can come back to college for one more "Saturday in the sun;" to sing the fight song and to tear up for the alma mater. The Old Oaken Bucket Game is the season-ending clash that means so much to Indiana and Purdue alums. And those alums must live with the outcome for 365 days.

The intensity of this rivalry is augmented by the deep passion within the state of Indiana for basketball. That's not just college basketball, but high school where, over the years, most high schools, no matter how small, competed with their rivals head-to-head and in county and state tournaments. Some of the stars of those teams made a name for themselves by playing collegiate basketball, and most of the best played at IU and Purdue.

Basketball at IU is regularly the most important event on the school sports calendar. When school is in session, men's basketball at Assembly Hall is always sold out. Tickets to the 17,000-plus seat Assembly Hall games are sold to students, alumni, faculty, staff, and the general public. Students, faculty, and staff get tickets to several of the home games on a lottery basis. Alumni and general public tickets are sold on a point system, meaning that donations determine the availability and placement of seats. Alumni, students and fans of IU feel that Bloomington is the basketball capital of the world.

Crew in IU helmets and conductors manned the "victory train" carrying fans to Purdue on November 22, 1930.

We Love Beating Purdue

1930: Indiana 7, Purdue 6—First Bucket Win

November 22, 1930 was a day to remember in the annals of Hoosier football. On a glorious autumn afternoon, 20,000 Purdue spectators watched in disbelief as their heavily favored (10–1 odds) Boilermakers lost their first-ever Old Oaken Bucket game to the Indiana Hoosiers. Purdue, which had a 30–3–1 record for three seasons before and after this game, was such a heavy favorite that their officials didn't even think it was necessary to bring the bucket to the stadium!

Early, in the game Purdue scored a touchdown on a pass from Lew Pope to Jim Purvis, but when the extra point kick by George Van Bibber failed, the Black and Gold were held at a 6–0 lead. The Purdue team didn't seem concerned because they felt they would have plenty more points against the IU team that hadn't scored all season in the Big Ten.

The rest of the game was a defensive struggle until the fourth quarter, at which time the Hoosiers mounted a drive to the 15-yard line. After being held to virtually no gain by the stout Purdue defensive line on the next three plays, Gene Opasik threw a pass like a laser to Ray Dauer to score the game-tying touchdown. The

score was 6–6 as the IU kicker Ed Hughes, who had been kept out of the game due to an injury, peeled off his warm-up clothes and came onto the Ross Aide Stadium turf to attempt the go-ahead point after. Hughes's toe met the leather, and the ball sailed straight through the upright. IU had a 7–6 lead.

Purdue was not going to go away quietly. They made a first down on successful 15-yard pass from their own end zone, but then IU intercepted another pass to seal the victory. Indiana's line was bolstered by the play of Joe Zeller, a freshman from East Chicago, who would be the subject of Knute Rockne's remarks a year later when he said, "I wish to goodness that I had one lineman like that fellow Zeller."

Stats for the day showed Purdue dominated with 84 passing yards to IU's 36, but they were sunk by being intercepted six times to IU's one.

After the game, a Purdue representative took the Old Oaken Bucket to the train station, where he came across a group of IU students. The students claimed they were given the responsibility of taking the bucket to the IU campus, but it was revealed that the Old Oaken Bucket never made it to IU. The students were actually Purdue students dressed in IU clothing. The trophy was later recovered in Lafayette.

That afternoon, in Bloomington, as news of the victory over Purdue spread, students from the campus came to town and began to celebrate by lighting bonfires, ransacking basements for wooden boxes and barrels to feed the flames. One huge fire at the southeast corner of the court house square was so big that the fire department tried to put it out while rowdy students kept feeding the flames. Eventually the fire brigade just circled the square with their bells ringing to try to protect the businesses.

During the celebration on the square, some students tried to rush the movie theaters and were only held back by managers promising free movies on Tuesday and pictures of the game. Still

looking to celebrate, more students headed for the Monon train station to await the victorious Hoosier football players and what they thought would be the arrival of the Old Oaken Bucket.

1940: Indiana 51, Purdue 45—Huge Crowd

March 2, 1940—Purdue Field House had opened three years earlier (1937) with seating for 7,500 fans. For the big 1940 home game with Indiana, 9,150 fans jammed into the arena. The IU 7th Street Fieldhouse was opened in 1928 and held only 8,000 spectators. Looking for revenge, Boilermaker fans were upset because Indiana had already beaten Piggy Lambert's Boilermakers, 46–30, in Bloomington, giving Purdue their only conference loss.

The Boilermaker players came out with payback on their minds as they built an early seven-point lead starting with free throws of Beretta and Fisher, but IU had a spurt of their own led by Paul Armstrong to gain the lead, 30–25, at the half.

In the second half, Purdue shooters brought the score to only a one point difference but Bob Dro made three field goals in rapid succession and the Hoosiers kept the lead. IU defeated Purdue, 51–45, and marked the Hoosier's second win of the season over the Boilermakers. For the season, Purdue had only lost twice in 11 games, and both were to the Hoosiers.

The Hoosiers were led by Bob Dro with 13 points. Paul Armstrong and Jay McCreary each scored in double figures with 11. Indiana made 21 baskets in 78 attempts (26.7 percent), compared to 16 out of 70 (22.8 percent) for the losers. Indiana made 9 of 15 free throws (60 percent), while Purdue made 13 of 22 (59 percent).

Purdue scoring was led by their top three scorers for the season. Sprowl, a forward, had 14; their center Fisher scored 13; and forward Blanken netted 9.

1940: Indiana 3, Purdue 0—White Wins It

Saturday, November 24, 1940 was soaked by an all-day rain in West Lafayette. The game-long downpour took its toll on the 28,000 spectators as well as the play of the game. Both teams had frequent fumbles on the muddy field. There were only 11 first downs all day, and six were by the Hoosiers. Purdue tried only three passes all afternoon. Indiana passed eight times with three completions. In the first half, Purdue only moved the ball into Indiana territory once and that play was brought back by a 15-yard penalty.

In the waning seconds of the contest, as many of the throng of rain-soaked Purdue spectators were headed out of Ross–Ade Stadium expecting the game to end in at least a 0–0 tie, their misery was compounded as IU won the battle with a field goal. With just 13 seconds on the clock, Gene White kicked a 33-yard field goal from the right side.

Late in the game IU's Cobb Lewis intercepted a pass at his own 35 and returned it to the Purdue 40. After two runs failed, Harold Red Zimmer circled the left end taking it to the Boilermaker 19, where White booted his winning field goal. It was said the kick bracketed the target "as if a slide rule and dividers had been called into play."

1945: Indiana 26, Purdue 0—Undefeated Season

After a snowfall earlier in the week, the weather moderated and the sun came out making November 24 a beautiful fall Saturday. It was Thanksgiving week, and yet 27,000 spectators crowded into overflowing Memorial Stadium to watch their beloved Hoosiers play Purdue for the Old Oaken Bucket. Extra seating had been placed on the field in front of the white concrete wall, a huge set of bleachers was erected in the open west end zone, and additional bleachers were set, where terrain permitted, on the knoll above the east end zone's regular seats. IU fans were excited in anticipation

of an undefeated season. And most importantly, another "I" on the Bucket and another year of bragging rights at home in Indiana.

The 1945 football team celebrates an undefeated season, a 26–0 drubbing of Purdue, and an "I" on the Old Oaken Bucked. Bo McMillin, being hugged by his players, is still wearing his suit and tie.

As the final gun sounded, many of the spectators swarmed the field and, along with the team, swept IU coach McMillin up onto their shoulders and carried him off the field. The crowd was jubilant because this game allowed the Hoosiers to finish with an undefeated season and the Championship of the Western Conference (Big Ten). The game seemed to be a grand achievement with the conference title, continued annual dominance of Purdue, and the culmination of Bo McMillin's major rebuilding project. A decade earlier, Bo had inherited a Hoosier team that had averaged an eighth place finish in the conference for the ten years preceding his arrival in 1934. Now Indiana finished the season ranked first in the conference, first in the state, and fourth in the nation.

The final score, 26–0, was misleading because, for most of the game, the battle raged as a defensive struggle. At halftime, the score was 0–0. There were two rapid-fire touchdowns within a two-minute span in the third quarter. Then the Crimson scored two more in the fourth.

Hoosiers future Hall of Famers George Taliaferro, Pete Pihos, and Ted Kluszewski (Klu) dominated and became very well-known to Boilermaker coaches, players, and fans. Taliaferro caught a 30-yard pass from Ben Raimondi to the Purdue one-yard line, then Pihos ran it for a 6–0 lead. The Charles Armstrong kick made it Indiana, 7–0. After the kickoff, a fumble was recovered by Kluszewski on the Purdue one-yard line. Pihos ran the ball in for the game's second touchdown, and the rout was on as the score was 13–0.

The fourth quarter featured great catches by both Kluszewski and Taliaferro, as well as Pihos and Taliferro runs that broke the back of the Boilermakers, who were beginning to fade down the stretch. Klu scored on a 10-yard reception making it 19–0. Next Raimondo intercepted a Purdue pass and ran it back to the Boilermakers' 34. Soon a pass to Bob Ravensberg had the ball first-and-goal for the Hoosiers. Then a pass to Lou Mihajlovich got the touchdown. Armstrong kicked the extra point, 26–0.

In the locker room, after the game, there was a huge celebration, and silver-haired Bo McMillin was seen with tears of joy streaming down his face. His lifelong friend Robert (Chief) Myers, who played football with Bo back in Fort Worth, Texas, had watched him play as an all American at Centre College when McMillin scored the only touchdown to defeat number one–ranked Harvard and end their 26 game winning streak. He asked Bo, through the din of the locker room, which game had given him the greatest thrill, that day or the win over Harvard? McMillin didn't hesitate and answered quickly. "Today"!

1953: Indiana 113, Purdue 78— Record-Breaking Performance

By rule, in the 1950s, no student at IU could have a car on campus until they were 21 years old. Consequently, almost every student going to a basketball game at the fieldhouse would be walking. The dorms were at least five blocks away, as were most of the fraternities and sororities. So students, bundled against the cold February air, headed north in small groups from Third Street, shortcutting on paths around the Union Building and crossing the Jordan River to get to the game against Purdue, the rival that IU soundly whipped earlier in West Lafayette.

It was a cold Monday night outside, but inside the IU fieldhouse all was warm, or, as the newspapers of the day said, "White hot!" That night, the Hoosiers ran all over Purdue with a 113–78 victory. Indiana's 113 points was the highest ever in the Big Ten, breaking a 1944 record set by Iowa when they scored 103 against Chicago. The Hoosiers also broke the IU Fieldhouse record of 105 set earlier in the season against Tony Hinkle's Butler Bulldogs.

The Hoosiers scored early and often with a 10–4 run in the first three minutes. The first period ended with IU holding a commanding lead, 37–14.

The second period started as hot as the first as the Hoosiers connected on five of their first six shots to run the score to 47–18. Mercifully, coach McCracken pulled super-star big-man Don Schlundt out of the game midway through the second period. The halftime score was Indiana 61, Purdue 35. Schlundt was again pulled in the third quarter, but early in the fourth quarter, Dick White fouled out, and the Indiana students immediately began a chant "We want Schlundt." Finally, coach McCracken motioned to Schlundt to report in, and the whole crowd came to their collective feet and cheered with a deafening roar. Schlundt was again pulled with the score 98–66 and 5:33 left on the clock. Don Schlundt led all scorers with 31 points, while Bobby ("Slick") Leonard had 16.

Schlundt reached 367 points for the season, giving him a two-year total of 882. That broke the Big Ten record for two seasons previously held by Iowa's Chuck Darling. Schlundt also broke Bill Garrett's IU record of 792 points. The Boilermakers were led by Blind with 19 points.

Coach Branch McCracken refused to run-up the score more. He had 13 players that scored in the game.

After the win, Indiana led the Big Ten with a 14–0 record. The next closest team was Illinois at 11–3. Purdue's record was a lowly 3–12 in the conference.

1954: Indiana 86, Purdue 50—Twelve in a Row

Any season where IU beats Purdue twice is always fun for Hoosier fans. And a season where IU can dominate is even better. On Monday, January 16, 1954, the Hoosiers beat the Boilermakers in Bloomington in a surprisingly close 73–67 game. Boilermaker fans were encouraged by their team's good showing and packed their fieldhouse on Monday, February 15, planning to finally beat Indiana after 11 straight losses. The Hoosiers, however, traveled to West Lafayette and proved their complete dominance by dismantling the Purdue squad in front of their own fans, 86–50. In taking this victory, IU moved into first place, undisputed, in the Big Ten.

The Boilermakers never saw a lead, and the only tie was in the opening seconds as Joe Sexson tipped a Ted Dunn shot in for a 2–2 score. After that, Purdue just watched as Don Schlundt—the six-foot, ten-inch Hoosier center—outscored all the Boilermakers in the first period with 11 points. At the end of the first period, the score was 25–7, 43–17 at the half. Schlundt wound up with 23 points on five baskets and 13 free throws. Schlundt's total, added to Bobby Leonard's 19 points and Burke Scott's 15, would have beaten the Boilermakers without further help. But coach McCracken let others join the fun.

Purdue tried everything, but to no avail. They tried a slow-down, deliberate style of play that went on the rocks with bad passing, missed connections on cripple shots, and just plain poor shooting. Coach Ray Eddy even ran the six-foot, nine-inch Don German, who rarely played, in with six-foot, seven-inch Dave Rodenkirk in the losing battle to contain Schlundt and Kraak, but that didn't work either. Kraak grabbed 20 rebounds, more than anyone else, and zipped passes down court for basket after basket. And when Kraak and Schlundt (who grabbed 12 rebounds) were not controlling the boards, Leonard was standing outside hitting long shots, and Burke Scott was jumping and hitting from the free-throw line. In the third and fourth periods, Indiana just seemed to coast out in front by a comfortable 25 or 30 points.

The Hoosiers shot 42.4 percent from the field, connecting on 31 of 73 shots, and Purdue helped by shooting only 19 percent on 16 of 86 shots from the field. Sexson led all Purdue scorers with 15 points. Denny Blind had nine. The victory marked the Hoosiers' 12th straight decision over Purdue.

1962: Indiana 12, Purdue 7—
Marvelous Marv Woodson

Fourteen years—fourteen long years—that's how long it had been since IU had beaten Purdue for the Old Oaken Bucket. But November 24, 1962 was different. That day Indiana finally broke the streak and upset Purdue 12–7, in front of 50,243 stunned fans at Ross–Ade Stadium. Since the schools were on break, most students were at home listening to the game on the radio. Only a contingent of Hoosier students and alumni remained in the stadium for more than an hour and a half after the game, laughing and crying tears of joy, as the Crimson had finally broken the hex. As an onlooker said about the absence of Boilermaker fans that day, they, "sorta died."

Purdue started the day as normal with quarterback Ron DiGravio steering the Boilermakers down the field to where FB

Roy Walker scored on a ten-yard run. After the kick, Purdue led, 7–0. Then Indiana struck back with two field goals to make it 7–6. Late in the first half, Purdue seemed to be on the verge of another touchdown with a first down at the IU fourteen-yard line, but DiGravio's pass deflected off a receiver and was picked off by IU's Marvin Woodson at the eight-yard line. Woodson, one of the Big Ten's top running backs, showed his form as he returned the ball up the east sideline. DiGravio had the angle to get to Woodson at the 25, but Woodson made a series of fakes, cuts, stops, and cut backs which had DiGravio hesitate and hope for help. The help came, but it was for Woodson as Guard Don Croftcheck leveled DiGravio and allowed Indiana to score the 92-yard return with little more than a minute left in the half. The score was 12–7, and the Purdue fans became quiet.

The second half was scoreless, with IU fighting off numerous Purdue scoring threats. Woodson played great pass defense and Rushers Rudy vvKuechenberg and Bob DeStefano harried Purdue's DiGravio unmercifully. Time ran out when Purdue's Ray Schultz was tackled at the IU 7.

Meanwhile, down in Bloomington, fans took to the streets shouting, waving flags, and tooting horns in celebration. There was no caravan of cars back to Bloomington because many team members headed to their homes to celebrate what was left of the Thanksgiving break.

On Sunday evening, as students returned to campus from break, a pep rally was held in the auditorium to celebrate the Old Oaken Bucket victory. The rumor was that classes would be cancelled Monday. There were cheerleaders and a pep band. Unfortunately, Dean of Students Robert Shaffer announced that there was a faculty council rule prohibiting holidays for celebrating sports victories.

After the game at Ross–Ade Stadium, IU coach Phil Dickens was hoisted onto the shoulders of his players, but watched horrified as his wedding ring came off and fell to the turf under the cleats of

his team. Later, scores of IU fans were visible combing the turf for coach's ring as the sun faded behind the press box. After the season, Purdue excavated the surface of Ross–Ade Stadium to be able to lower the field to allow the addition of more seats. The joke at IU was that Purdue dug up their field looking for Phil Dickens ring.

1967: Indiana 19, Purdue 14— California Here I Come

IU wins the 1967 Bucket game, 19–14, and a trip to the Rose Bowl. The game was in doubt as Purdue was driving toward the IU end zone. The defense stepped up as Ken Kaczmarek (52) hit PU's Perry Williams causing a fumble recovered by Mike Bughman (33) at the one-yard line.

Indiana drew 52,770 fans to see IU pull-off an unbelievable upset of the highly-favored Boilermakers, 19–14. Indiana hadn't beaten the Boilermakers in Bloomington since 1947. This win capped off an unbelievable season for these "Cardiac Kids." "Kids" because some of the notable players were just sophomores (freshmen were not eligible in '67). "Cardiac" because almost every game during the season was a nail-biter, with only a few points between the win and a loss. They beat Kentucky by two, Kansas

15

by three, Iowa by four, Michigan by seven, Wisconsin by five, and Michigan State by one.

Purdue entered the contest ranked number three in the nation, and one game ahead of IU and Minnesota for the Big Ten championship. Their conference record was 6–0, while Indiana's and Minnesota's were both 5–1. The oddsmakers had Purdue the heavy favorite, with future NFL first-round picks Mike Phipps at quarterback and Leroy Keyes at running back. Phipps was a record-setting quarterback from Columbus, Indiana that was recruited by almost every big school in America. Keyes was a four-star recruit from Virginia and played both offense and defense for Purdue. IU's quarterback was Harry Gonzo, a future lawyer and trustee on the IU Board of Trustees. Terry Cole, IU's running back came from tiny Mitchell, Indiana about a half-hour south of Bloomington. The idea that Indiana could beat Purdue was a longshot at best.

The Hoosiers flat out outplayed the Boilermakers. Terry Cole outshone Leroy Keyes with a career-long, 63-yard touchdown run and a 42-yard run to set up another score. Cole ended the day with 155 yards. Quarterback Harry Gonzo had his usual exciting afternoon. He dazzled the fans and Purdue with unexpected calls at the right time. But the IU defense made the difference. Late in the game when Purdue, behind, 19–14, was driving for the winning score, Ken Kaczmarek took a chance with 6:39 left in the fourth quarter, shot the gap and hit Perry Williams so hard the Purdue fullback fumbled on Indiana's goal line. Safety Mike Baughman recovered for Indiana at the one-yard line. And the countdown to defeat began for Purdue.

The Hoosiers took three tries for a first down, and on fourth down, sophomore John Isenbarger boomed a 63-yard punt out of the end zone to put PU at their own 40-yard line. IU held them and won, 19–14, and clinched their first Rose Bowl trip.

Indiana, Minnesota, and Purdue finished in a three-way tie for first, but Indiana got the Rose Bowl bid because Purdue had gone the season before, and Minnesota had been to the Rose Bowl after

the 1961 season. Because of the IU success, John Pont was selected as national coach of the year.

All that night and into the wee hours, from every bar with a band or piano on Kirkwood and College Avenues, Walnut Street and even in the infamous "Levy," raucous music could be heard. The prevailing tune, sung over and over until all voices were hoarse was Al Jolson's, "California Here I Come."

1971: Indiana 38, Purdue 31— Root Beer Celebration

On a cold and cloudy late-November Saturday in Bloomington, nearly 51,000 fans celebrated as IU beat Purdue 38–31. Just like pro athletes do with champagne during victory celebrations, the IU football team sprayed each other and coach Pont with wild enthusiasm. The only difference was that the Indiana team did it with root beer! That's right, their beverage of choice was sprayed and poured over the jubilant players and even dripped off the balding head of smiling coach John Pont. Believe it or not, root beer sprays better than champagne. It actually tastes pretty good, and more importantly, it's legal on campus.

The Boilermaker football team came into the game a ten-point favorite because their lineup featured future pro stars like quarterback Gary Danielson and three first-round draft picks in running back Otis Armstrong, wide receiver Daryl Stingley, and defensive tackle Dave Butz. Key players for IU were quarterback Ted McNulty, running backs Ken St. Pierre and Ken Starling, and an unheralded offensive line.

The underdog Hoosiers ripped into Purdue from the opening kickoff with their offensive unit and were never in worse shape than early ties at seven and ten. Indiana poured it on, building a lead, 31–10, after that. Ken St Pierre had 144 yards rushing, which was more than the whole Purdue team. Ken Starling added 89 more yards as the IU line pushed the huge Purdue defense out of the way.

Purdue's last scores came after the game had been decided, as Stingley caught a pass and ran for 70 yards, which made it 38–23. Unfortunately, some decided it was time to literally fight over the Bucket. Purdue quarterback Danielson was chased out of bounds on the Indiana sidelines in the final half-minute, and, in a matter of seconds, fists began to fly. Both benches emptied, fans poured out of the stands and a full-scale donnybrook erupted. It started when Purdue's Gary Daniel fired the football into a pack of IU players, an act that might be described as brave but foolhardy. Danielson claimed he was punched in the mouth. Ted McNulty later said that he grabbed Danielson to keep him from falling.

After the field was cleared, Purdue's Armstrong broke a 44-yard run to make the final score 38–31. Then things digressed as if TV wrestling promoters wrote the script. The Purdue band took the field as IU students rushed to meet them. A few fans charged into the band and got what they deserved, including one who got a horn in the mouth and had to go to the hospital.

1975: Indiana 104, Purdue 71—
We're Number One

IU fans had become reluctant to commit any act that would anger coach Bob Knight after he called a technical foul on the Assembly Hall crowd during a Notre Dame game two years earlier. The week of this game with twentieth-ranked Purdue, the Hoosiers had risen to the number one spot in the polls, and it seemed that every basketball fan in the country knew it.

On this Saturday afternoon, the biggest crowd (17,823) in IU basketball's history packed Assembly Hall. The fans were emotional and very loud, but no chants or other actions that may upset Knight were done. In the second half, as the rout was on, a fan-chant started in the area under the south basket by the pep band whom, by the way, all wore red and white bumper stickers on their white straw hats reading "Indiana No. 1." A cheer began, rather muted at first, by a handful of students chanting, "We're number one. . . . We're number

one. . . . We're number one". It got louder and louder, and eventually, what seemed like 17,000 voices were picking up the chant. Knight, the consummate teacher, seemed to not care about the rankings and thus didn't react and seemed to be preoccupied trying to make the players, mostly reserves by then, play as well as the starters who had built a big lead. It wasn't till a year or more later that it was revealed that Knight was happy about the ranking and had called a friend at a newspaper more than once asking about the wire service reports on (IU's) college basketball rankings in the polls.

With this huge victory (104–71), IU extended its Big Ten lead and pushed the two-season winning streak to 21 games. This was the second-largest spread an Indiana team ever registered over the Boilermakers. Only in the 86–50 clash of 1954 was the difference so pronounced. In reflecting on the slaughter, Purdue Coach Fred Schaus admitted, "I thought the clock would never run out. I've never spent a longer forty minutes in my life!" For all practical purposes, the game was decided early in the second half when the undefeated Hoosiers sprinted from an intermission lead to a 73–48 cushion with 11:29 to play. That's when the fan-chant began in Assembly Hall.

Purdue battled sportingly for the first seven minutes of the contest and led by four points on three occasions. But they trailed at the half, 54–42, and never were in it thereafter. The Hoosiers posted their eighteenth consecutive triumph of the season and ran their Assembly Hall record to 40–2.

Six-foot, seven-inch starter Steve Green sat out the entire game due to the flu. This didn't seem to bother the Hoosiers, though, as "super sub" John Laskowski plugged the gap. Laskowski scored 13 points in 34 minutes of play. Scott May had the game high of 23 when Coach Bob Knight began wholesale subbing at the 6:00 mark. Green sat colorless, but not necessarily quietly, on the bench the entire game. Alongside Green and May, in a marvelous display of balance, came the other three starters in double figures: Quinn Buckner, 18; Kent Benson, 14; and Bobby Wilkerson, 13.

Purdue retaliated with a two-man punch as seven-foot John Garrett scored 18 points, and guard Bruce Parkinson had 15. From there, the drop-off was to nine by Tom Scheffler, and seven of his were long after the game had been decided.

Garrett sat out a lot of the first half with three personals, and for the rest of the day with 10:32 remaining, as his fifth foul helped Tom Abernathy complete a three-point play on a rebound bucket to boost the lead to 78–52. Purdue, meanwhile, made 26 of 59 shots (44 percent). The Boilers killed their own chance of staying in the hunt time and again with damaging errors. They finished with 31 errors. Nineteen were charged in the first half, and almost every time they made a mistake, the Hoosiers scored. Sixteen of Indiana's 54 points before the half came directly off a Purdue miscue or steals by the tenacious IU defense. Some of the difference might be explained by these figures: Indiana notched 25 assists (including nine by Buckner and seven by Wilkerson) while committing 17 errors. Purdue came up woefully short with 9 and 31 in that order.

1976: Indiana 20, Purdue 14—Thanks Jack

November 20, 1976, was an unusually sunny day for November in West Lafayette. Ross Aide Stadium was filled with 63,220 fans, mostly wearing the Old Gold and Black of the Boilermakers, expecting to put another P on the Old Oaken Bucket. After all, Purdue hadn't lost to the Hoosiers there since 1962 and had a four-game winning streak against IU. They also had All-American running back Scott Dierking, who was nearing a 1000-yard rushing season. He had run roughshod for wins over big-time opponents like Michigan during his four-year career at Purdue. The Boilermakers also had five other players selected in the next NFL draft and just needed this "W" to have a winning season.

What the fans didn't realize was that Indiana had their own top-notch running back in Mike Harkrader, and his dynamic

replacement, Darrick Burnett, was finally healthy and ready. The IU pass defense was also ready.

To open the game, the Hoosiers scored via Purdue quarterback Mark Vitali's passing arm on the third play, as Walter Booth picked-off the quarterback's first pass of the day. This led to an IU touchdown when fullback Tony D'Orazio caught Scott Arnett's pass in the end zone. On Purdue's ninth play of the quarter, Steve Sanders made an interception, leading to a Dan Freud's 21-yard field goal. These two defense-initiated scores gave Indiana ten points in the first quarter.

Indiana coach Lee Corso later credited the day's pass rush to the late Jack Mollenkopf. "I got the best advice on pass defense from a man you all know, Jack Mollenkopf," Corso said, referring to the late Purdue coach. "The day before we played Minnesota my first year, I called him up, and he told me to go after the passer. . . . Go after the passer, or at least talk about it and don't do it. It's sort of ironic, we beat Purdue with Mollenkopf's advice." Vitali only completed one of seven passes all day, and Harold Waterhouse got the third IU interception during the game.

Not trusting their air attack, the Boilermakers then ground out 67 yards to pay dirt with 17 runs. Vitali ran the touchdown in from the one. It was

10–7 until Kevin Kellogg added three points on a 47-yard field goal to give the Hoosiers a 13–7 at the half.

In the second half, Purdue wanted to get the ball and score quickly to change the momentum. They did just that as Kim Cripe caused an Arnett fumble, recovered by tackle Ken Louis at the IU 21. Soon, Purdue jumped to their first lead at 14–13.

Unlike the previous year's 9–7 loss, it was Indiana that struck last with an epic march as star freshman tailback, Mike Harkrader suffered a broken ankle on a late hit out-of-bounds into the Purdue Band by Boilermaker defender Rock Supan. No flag was thrown, and now the Hoosiers had a huge hole to fill. Harkrader rushed

that day for 79 yards, giving him 1,003 for the year. The Hoosiers needed to fill the hole with a good back, and that's what they got from Darrick Burnett, who was seeing his first action after missing seven games due to a knee injury. Burnett came off the bench to rush for 70 yards in 16 carries which included the game-winning run, off guard, to the south end zone. Burnett and Harkrader each averaged 4.4 yards per carry on the day.

Scott Dierking hobbled by an Achilles injury only rushed for 40 yards, which got him to exactly 1000 yards for the season.

1979: NIT Indiana 53, Purdue 52—
IU Takes the Rubber Match

After winning the NCAA tourney and four of the last six Big Ten championships, a 21–12 record and fifth place in the conference was somewhat of a letdown. To make things worse, Purdue had won one of the two games against the Hoosiers during the season (55–48 in West Lafayette). So, getting to play them again for the NIT championship provided a chance for redemption.

The NIT championship was on March 31, 1979, for a national TV audience and 14,000 people in Madison Square Garden. This game was to provide these spectators a chance to see what the Indiana–Purdue rivalry was all about.

IU and Purdue had played each other 133 times in this legendary rivalry. This night was to be no exception in the thrilling history of IU–Purdue as Butch Carter sank the winning shot for the Hoosiers with just six seconds to play. Not giving up, Purdue inbounded to guard Jerry Sichting, who took a shot with two seconds remaining that rimmed out. The final score was Indiana 53, Purdue 52. This game climaxed a real comeback season in which the Hoosiers had lost five of their first six Big Ten Games.

Carter's 18-foot shot from the top of the key accounted for the only points scored in the final 6:31 as both teams engaged in a monumental struggle of ball control and hard-nosed defense. Purdue did not score after 8:49 to play when Boilermaker seven-foot center Joe Barry Carroll connected on the first of two free throws. The charity toss gave the Boilermakers a 52–47 lead. Then center Ray Tolbert (MVP of the tournament with Butch Carter) made a sky-hook shot at 8:05 for a 52–49 score. At 6:31, Woodson dropped a 15-foot jump-shot to bring IU to within one point at 52–51. Sichting missed a shot at 4:35, and for the next three and a half minutes, Indiana went into a delay game while the Boilermakers sat back in their 2–3 zone.

Then the Hoosiers finally went on the attack. Carter tried a pass to Woodson that was intercepted by Boilermaker Mike Scearce at 1:10. After the first of seven time-outs in the final 70 seconds, Carroll was fouled by Carter but missed the free throw (he missed six of eight tries), and Landon Turner rebounded for IU at 0:16. Between them, the two coaches called six time-outs in those last 16 seconds. Indiana's play was designed for Woodson, but he was covered, so Carter moved to the top of the key, faked once, then went up with the shot over Sichting. It swished. By the time Purdue called time, there were four seconds to play. Purdue's last play got Sichting loose in the corner. But his shot rimmed away, and the game was over.

Bob Knight had always liked to play in the NIT when he coached Army (West Point) and made that known when he said, "I've never had a bigger ambition than to win the NIT. This is as satisfying as the NCAA title [which Indiana won in 1976]." Knight claimed that, before this game, he had never ordered his team into a delay game. But tonight, he wanted the ball held until the clock was under 90 seconds so that Purdue couldn't get a three-point lead with another basket.

The pre-game expectation was that there was going to be a scoring duel between IU's Mike Woodson and Joe Barry Carroll of Purdue. Woodson scored just ten points and was 5 of 16 from the floor. Carroll had only 14.

For Purdue Hallman finished with 12 points, and Morris, nine. Sichting could account for only six points as he hit only three of nine shots.

Ray Tolbert, whistled for two early fouls, had to sit out a lot of the first half, but his replacement, freshman forward Landon Turner did a good job guarding Carroll. Turner wound up leading the Hoosiers with 13 points. Tolbert had 12 points and 10 rebounds. Carter had 12 with six assists. Guard Randy Wittman had 7 assists with four points.

In the first half, Indiana shot 11 of 29 (37.9 percent) from the field and improved to 13 of 23 (56.5 percent) after the break. The Boilermakers were 13 of 28 (46.4 percent) in the first half and led by five at the break. In the second half, they made 10 of 25 shots (40.0 percent).

The Boilermakers finished their season at 27–8, the most wins they ever had. Indiana won 10 of its last 11 games to finish with another national title (the NIT) to go with NCAA championships in 1940, 1953, and 1976.

1982: Indiana 13, Purdue 7—Defense Steals It

It was five days before Thanksgiving, and there was a lot for which to be thankful for Indiana. On a soggy 67-degree fall Saturday, 69,745 Ross–Ade Stadium spectators watched the Hoosier defense commit a series of larcenies. They intercepted three passes, swiped a fumble, stole a Purdue football, and came away with a 13–7 victory. This Indiana team became the first Hoosier eleven since 1946 to defend its ownership of the Old Oaken Bucket.

The game started in lackluster fashion, with the Hoosiers scoring both touchdowns in the first half following Purdue turnovers. The first came as Chris Sigler intercepted a Scott Campbell pass to Bruce King at the Purdue 18. The ensuing 18-yard, five-play drive culminated in Bobby Howard's four-yard dart to the end zone for the score. A freshman tailback, Howard suffered a broken hand in the first quarter but still played the entire game. Purdue punter Matt Kinzer bobbled a high snap and was tackled for a 20-yard loss at the Boiler 31. Again, Howard charged two yards to the end zone for his second touchdown. Mark Rogers, subbing for Doug Smith, who was sidelined with a pulled leg muscle, kicked the conversion after the first touchdown, then missed his second try.

Purdue's offense was almost nonexistent in the opening half. It began to assert itself in the third period running 30 plays to only six for Indiana. Despite all this grinding, the Boilermakers failed to cross the IU goal line. Their first second-half drive came to a screeching halt at the Indiana 30 when Campbell was sacked twice by Steve Moorman, and tailback Mel Gray juggled a pass as he fell out of the end zone. Their second drive, which started at Purdue's one-yard line, following Dan Anderson's interception of a Babe Laufenberg pass, reached Indiana's 17 before Tim Wilbur pilfered another Campbell pass. The Boilers finally scored with 9:45 remaining as Campbell hit Benson who was running down the left sideline. Wilbur went for the football but missed the interception at midfield. The receiver had no one between him and the goal line. Purdue so dominated the final half that it had 62 plays to Indiana's 17, and it outgained the Hoosiers 306 yards to 60. The only problem was the Boilers couldn't finish when they were in the red zone. Indiana, which finished the season 5–6 overall and 4–5 in the Big Ten, stopped Purdue's passing game in the first half with a pair of new looks. They turned their defensive linemen loose more than any other time in the year, which allowed them to put extreme pressure on Campbell as he hunted receivers. While the big men were pursuing the quarterback, Indiana's secondary used what they term a "pick" defense to cover Purdue's pass catchers.

The game-saver for the Hoosiers came late in the fourth quarter as Indiana free safety Mark Sutor turned in the defensive gem of the afternoon with a play that will be etched forever in the minds of Crimson faithful along with the 13–7 victory. Sutor, on the final play of his college career, slammed Boilermaker quarterback Scott Campbell to the turf at the Hoosier 17-yard line as the clock ticked down to 0:00. The sack ended Purdue's hopes of a dramatic fourth-quarter rally and permitted Indiana to claim possession of the Bucket for the fourth time in seven years.

With time for one more play, Purdue was at the Indiana six and poised to score the tying touchdown and winning extra point. Sutor blitzed and drew a bead on Campbell, who had drifted left, searching for an open receiver in the end zone before Sutor leveled him. Only moments before, Campbell had dashed into the end zone with what seemed to be the game tying touchdown only to have it nullified because of an illegal procedure penalty.

After the game, defensive back Tim Wilbur stood in the corner of the stout brick building in the southwest corner of the end zone, the outdated visitor's locker room. Wilber stood with a football tucked under one arm. "Congratulations on earning a game ball," a bystander told Wilbur.

"This isn't one of our game balls." Wilbur replied. "This is a Purdue ball. I stole it." Wilbur's theft was the last of a series of Hoosier larcenies that day.

1987: Indiana 35, Purdue 14— Peach Bowl Bound

The Saturday before Thanksgiving was sunny and warm for November 21 with the temperature reaching 50 degrees, a perfect day for football. That day, a partisan Crimson crowd of 51,951 fans entered Indiana's Memorial Stadium hoping that IU could win back the Old Oaken Bucket after four years of losing it to Purdue.

In the end, everything turned up peaches as Indiana's defense converted four turnovers into 28 points, thus bailing out a struggling Hoosier offense and providing the Cream and Crimson with a 35–14 Big Ten football victory. The win was the Hoosiers' eighth of the season and assured them a second-place finish in the Big Ten with a 6–2 record, the best IU finish since the '67 Rose Bowl team. It also sent them to the January 2 Peach Bowl to face Tennessee in Atlanta.

More importantly to IU alumni, the Hoosiers also regained possession of the prized Old Oaken Bucket. This meant that, finally, IU grads could rub it in with neighbors and co-workers who attended Purdue after receiving years of good-natured ribbing. This was the first victory for IU over Purdue since Lee Corso's team in 1982, and the first of what was to be many Bucket wins for Coach Bill Mallory.

After digging a huge hole, 21–0, the determined Boilermakers made a comeback in the second quarter. Employing back-up quarterback Doug Downing and a defense that held the Hoosiers to minus yardage through most of the second and third quarters, Purdue closed to 21–14 with 11:35 remaining. Then they regained both the football and the momentum when IU fullback Andre Powell fumbled at the Boilermaker one-yard line.

But Indiana's vaunted defenders, who had intercepted two passes, blocked two field goals, and recovered two fumbles, weren't through. Three plays after covering Powell's fumble, the Boilermakers coughed up the ball as quarterback Shawn McCarthy, subbing for an injured Downing, miscued on a handoff. Willie Bates covered the fumble for IU at the Purdue four-yard line, and, two plays later, Hoosier tailback Anthony cheanson scored his third touchdown. This tied a school single-game record and gave his team a lead, 28–14, and some breathing room with less than seven minutes left.

Outside linebacker Van Waiters was credited with only one tackle, but that tackle put a stamp on the IU victory. Called "The

Moving Van" by *Indianapolis Star* reporter Bob Collins, Waiters got to Purdue quarterback McCarthy nine yards behind the line of scrimmage. He jerked the ball out of the quarterback's grasp and took it 47 yards for a touchdown. That made it 35–14 with 4:59 left. The celebrating among the Crimson crowd began in earnest, culminating at game's end when fans stormed the field and tore down both goal posts just as they had done after the victory over Michigan four weeks earlier.

1988: Indiana 52, Purdue 7—Liberty Bowl

On a cold, gray, late-November Saturday, 67,861 spectators packed Ross–Ade Stadium to watch the continuation of the Old Oaken Bucket series. Of the 67,861, it's probably safe to say not a single one was expecting a 52–7 IU rout, but the game turned into the most lopsided Hoosier win in the history of the Old Oaken Bucket series. It was the win that allowed the Hoosiers (5–3 in the Big Ten) to retain possession of the Old Oaken Bucket and move on to face 8–3 South Carolina in the Liberty Bowl in Memphis.

Indiana's defense was dominating and limited the Boilermakers to just ten first downs, 230 total yards, and a mere 17 yards rushing in 25 attempts. Purdue's freshman quarterback Brian Fox completed 15 of 29 passes for 166 yards but was under constant pressure. He was sacked four times and threw three interceptions. The defense was in his face all day.

Safety Brian Dewitz intercepted two passes, returning the first 34 yards for a touchdown to begin the track meet. His second interception also set up a score as the Hoosiers broke a deadlock, 7–7, after the first quarter with 24 points in the second quarter. Indiana turned the three interceptions and three fumbles into 31 points in storming to a 31–7 halftime command.

The Hoosier offense was led by tailback Anthony Thompson, who rushed for 167 yards and three touchdowns to reach 24 touchdowns for the season. IU established the run in a big way

by collectively rolling up 392 yards on the ground, 30 first downs, and 537 yards of total offense. Trying to not run up the score, coach Mallory used ten different runners and three quarterbacks. Mercifully, Thompson was taken out of the game half way through the third quarter. Barry Way, subbing for Thompson, made the game's last two touchdowns on runs of one and five yards.

Purdue's only success of the day came on a trick play as Shawn McCarthy lined up to punt on fourth-and-two in the first quarter but instead flipped a pass to Ernie Schramayr, who then completed a 47-yard scoring play and put the Boilermakers into a tie, 7–7. Purdue then moved into position to take the lead on its next possession, but the IU defense struck again as Mike Dumas tipped Fox's end zone pass into teammate Marc Ferry's hands for an interception. The Hoosiers then began to take control.

Rob Turner's leaping catch of a 48-yard pass from Bolyard put IU on the Purdue seven-yard line, and Thompson scored on the next play a short time later. Next Dewitz intercepted Fox's pass on the fly and sprinted into the end zone for 21 points. Dewitz's second interception led to Bolyard's scoring pass to Turner for a lead, 28–7, with 20 seconds left in the half.

On a day when almost everything went wrong, Purdue's Curtis McManus fumbled the ensuing kickoff, allowing IU's Pele Stoyanovich to add a 34-yard field goal and make the score 31–7 at the intermission. The Hoosiers added to the rout in the second half with three long-scoring drives, two of more than 60 yards each, and one of 45. The Hoosiers reached 58 points on a late touchdown, but a penalty resulted in calling the play back. The Hoosiers settled for 52 points, which was still the most Indiana had ever scored on Purdue football.

Anthony Thompson ended the game as Indiana's all-time leading rusher with 3,366 yards. He also set his single-season school record at 1,546 yards. Pete Stoyanovich kicked a school single-season record 15th field goal and extended his Big Ten conversion record

to 103 straight. IU also set a single-season team scoring record. The Hoosiers' 362 points broke the old mark of 314 set by the 1979 team. IU's Turner had just four catches, but the team were good for 108 yards and a touchdown.

1990: Indiana 28, Purdue 14— Georgia on My Mind

It was cool but sunny as 51,393 spectators spent the Saturday after Thanksgiving in Purdue's Ross–Ade Stadium watching Indiana win a Peach Bowl bid because of an opportunistic defense and Boilermaker turnovers.

The Hoosiers jumped out to a 7–0 lead on Mark Hagan's 21-yard pick-six interception and a Scott Bonnell extra point. Then in the second quarter Damon Watts intercepted a pass and returned it to the Purdue 14, which led to a four-play drive and a Vaughn Dunbar touchdown from the one-yard line. To end the half, IU mounted a 98-yard, 16-play drive that was aided by penalties. Twice, Purdue stopped the Hoosiers on third down only to be called for holding. The touchdown was made by Vaughn Dunbar on a nine-yard run, and IU led, 21–0.

In the second half, Purdue bounced with a 67-yard, eight-play, seven-minute drive featuring a 41-yard pass from Eric Hunter to Jeremy Ross. The extra point made it 21–7.

The fourth quarter started with another Purdue drive to the IU 24-yard line. Closing in on a score, Hunter lofted a pass to the left corner of the end zone, only to see free safety Mike Dumas intercept it and return it 99 yards to the Purdue one-yard line. That one-yard drive took three plays for Dunbar to score, but the game was no longer in doubt. The scoring finished with a 14-play, 80-yard drive ending with a one-yard Hunter run and a Wambold kick. With only four minutes left, the score was 28–14.

On Purdue's last possession, Scott Hoffman, who replaced Hunter because of a bruised knee, was sacked by Chris McCoy, and frustrated fists started flying. Skirmishes broke out on the field, and two players were kicked out from each side.

Purdue frustrations were understandable. The Boilermakers outgained the Hoosiers, 393–187, and had 26 first downs to IU's 12, but the Boilermakers also had seven turnovers on four interceptions and three fumbles. IU converted three of the miscues into touchdowns.

Purdue, suffering through an eight-loss season, was averaging only 36,421 fans at most their home games. The crowd for this bucket game, bolstered by a huge, Hoosier, red-clad contingent, was more than 15,000 above their norm. Crimson fans vastly outnumbered the Purdue faithful in the South end zone and in the north end of the horseshoe. As Mike Dumas ran his crucial interception 99 yards toward the huge red section in the North end zone, the fans rose like a Crimson wave.

The IU Marching Hundred pep band sat in the South end zone. As the game's final minutes ticked off, the band started playing "Georgia on My Mind," a tune written by IU Alumnus Hoagy Carmichael. The happy Hoosier fans seemed to all join in with the band singing the chorus. After all, the Hoosiers were bound for the Peach Bowl in Georgia!

1991: Indiana 24, Purdue 22—Goal Post Goes

On the last Saturday before Thanksgiving, Memorial Stadium was cold, and gusty breezes turned the playing surface into a huge wind tunnel. 51,596 fans rose to their feet as one to watch Purdue's Joe O'Leary attempt the 35-yard field goal that would win the game for the Boilermakers with 28 seconds to play. As O'Leary's kick drifted a few feet right of the south goal post, Indiana students stormed the field to tear down the other goal post. A gallant Purdue comeback effort had become a great IU victory.

Purdue scored first as Boilermaker Ernest Calloway picked up an IU fumble and rumbled 77 yards for a touchdown. When the wind-blown kick failed, the score remained 6–0. Then the roof seemed to cave in for the Boilermakers. Indiana got on the board with 54-yard drive as quarterback Trent Green hit Thomas Lewis with a 40-yard pass, but the drive stalled. They had to settle for a Scott-Bonnell, 27-yard field goal. Indiana scored again on a 12-play drive as Green found Scott McGowen for nine yards to the Purdue 12-yard line. From there, All-American Vaughn Dunbar ran it in for a touchdown. Bonnell kicked the extra point, and IU had a 10–6 lead. On the next series, the IU defense smothered Purdue, forcing a punt that gave the Hoosiers the ball at the Boilermakers' 45-yard line. Trent Green completed a 34-yard pass to Lewis for the touchdown, and Bonnell added the extra point. Now IU held a 17–6 lead

On the next series, the Purdue punter Eric Brunn dropped the snap and tried to kick the ball while it lay on the ground. The play went for a yard loss and a penalty of half the distance to the goal line. Green hit Eddie Thomas for a 13-yard touchdown, and Bonnell added the extra point.

A shoulder injury to ineffective freshman Matt Pike prompted Purdue coach Jim Colletto to go with Eric Hunter at quarterback in the second half, and Hunter provided the spark that nearly burned the Hoosiers. He got the Boilermakers back in the game by completing nine of 12 passes for 133 yards and two touchdowns. Indiana helped Purdue by committing four turnovers and managed just 119 yards in the second half after rolling up 296 during the first two quarters.

Purdue got on the board quickly with a Joe-O'Leary, 22-yard field goal ending an eight-play drive which made it 24–9. The comeback by Hunter continued as tight end Ryan Grigson caught a three-yard touchdown pass from Hunter, but a two point conversion failed, and the score remained 24–15. Hunter continued

the relentless attack by hitting wide receiver Tedman Brown with a 15-yard pass for a touchdown. With the kick, Purdue trailed only 24–22 but the wind-blown kick, with 28 seconds left, made that the final score.

The Old Oaken Bucket was awarded after the final gun. While Indiana's players celebrated, Scott Bonnell sought out his Boilermaker counterpart Joe O'Leary. Bonnell first offered his hand, then he opened his heart. O'Leary had just missed a 35-yard field goal attempt that would have given Purdue a stunning comeback triumph. It was his fourth miss in five tries, but O'Leary was not entirely to blame, since the timing from the long snapper was off. But on the final attempt, O'Leary smoothly whipped his right leg into the ball and watched as it drove through the gusts.

Officials at the game announced that IU would get their bid to play 8–3 Baylor in the Tucson, Arizona Copper Bowl on New Year's Eve.

IU tailback Vaughn Dunbar rushed 29 times for 153 yards to push his season total to 1,699 yards. Quarterback Trent Green completed 18 of 33 passes for 258 yards and two touchdowns with three interceptions.

1992: Indiana 106, Purdue 65— Largest Victory Margin Ever

Purdue fielded a very young Boilermaker team at Assembly Hall, with only one senior and two juniors on their 13-deep roster. The Hoosiers squad started five players that would all eventually end up on the list of the top 12 scorers in IU history, including Calbert Cheney who was National Player of the Year. Indiana had three Mr. Basketballs on the team. Purdue's inexperience against high-scoring talent produced a 41-point Indiana win, the largest margin of victory in the series. The previous record had been set by the 1954 team at 86–50 at Purdue's fieldhouse.

Indiana shot 38 of 57 from the field for 67 percent. Their defense held Purdue to 40 percent shooting with 20 shots for 50. IU dominance lasted most of all the game. Indiana's defensive pressure and offensive execution yielded a halftime lead, 51–24. Calbert Cheaney scored Indiana's first eight points, and when the rest of the Hoosiers got going, Purdue had no answers. Indiana had runs of 10–0, 9–0, and 10–1 during the opening 20 minutes.

IU's largest lead of the night was 46 points at 106–62, but with a second to go, Woody Austin hit a three-pointer for Purdue. Austin, Purdue's leading scorer for the season, ended the night with only 15 points, forced by the defense to be mostly from outside. Link Darner came off the Boilermakers bench to make four baskets on five shots. He topped Purdue with 19 points, including 17 in the second half.

The Boilermakers couldn't begin to cope with Calbert Cheaney's quickness and slashing cuts, although Cuonzo Martin, Matt Painter, Ian Stanback, and Matt Waddell all tried. All were a step behind as Cheaney scored 23 points on 10 of 14 shots. Purdue just couldn't get started. The old adage that you can't score without the ball proved true. Indiana stole the ball 13 times, part of Purdue's 25 turnovers. Indiana turned the ball over only nine times.

In the middle of the second half, Knight took Cheaney, Eric Anderson, and Damon Bailey out of the game, but the other Hoosiers continued to shine as Greg Graham had 13 points and three steals. Chris Reynolds had seven assists and three steals. Jamal Meeks had six assists, and Alan Henderson and Todd Leary scored 11 points each. Because of strep throat, Henderson missed the two previous weeks' games. He had four steals and played only 19 minutes.

1996: Indiana 33, Purdue 16— Mallory Goes out a Winner

It was cool, overcast, and misty for a November 23, just five days from Thanksgiving. The paid attendance in Ross–Ade Stadium was announced at 50,750, but many of them came disguised as empty seats. By the time the final seconds ticked away, most of the Boilermaker fans had joined Elvis and left the building.

The Hoosiers opened the scoring on a Bill-Manolopoulos, 27-yard field goal after a seven-play, 49-yard drive. Purdue tied the score on a 36-yard field goal by Shane Ryan after a 12-play, five-yard drive.

In the second quarter, Purdue scored on a 90-yard pass from Rick Trefzger to Brian Alford to take a lead, 10–3. Then Indiana's defense got a score as Kywyn Supernaw intercepted Trefzger for a 13-yard pick-six that tied the score. Purdue went back into the lead on an Alford 22-yard pass reception from Trefzger, but the extra point failed, and the lead was 16–10.

Indiana's defense, ravaged by teams in the Big Ten for the previous two seasons, stepped-up in the second half. It started when defensive end Nathan Davis blocked punt and was followed four minutes later by the Purdue quarterback being sacked in the end zone for a safety. The Hoosier defense intercepted Trefzger four times in the second half and sacked him on four other occasions. IU's two defensive ends accounted for eight tackles (four behind the line), two and a half sacks, a pass deflection, and a forced fumble.

In the second half, it was all Indiana. Smith's two-yard, third-quarter run capped an eight-play drive of 61 yards that had two big third-down conversions. Receiver Ajamu Stoner earned the first on a six-yard pass, and Steve Lee then took Chris Dittoe's 31-yard floater to the Purdue 18-yard line. On third-and-eight from the 16-yard line, Dittoe threw to Dorian Wilkerson in the end zone, where a pass interference flag gave IU the ball at the two-yard line. Two plays later, Smith scored for a 17–16 lead. On the next possession, Purdue had fourth-and-five with the Purdue fans yelling for the

Boilermakers to go for it. Instead, Coach Colletto decided to punt. The Hoosier's Nathan Davis blocked the punt and returned it 51-yards for a touchdown. Bill Manolopoulos made the kick, and IU led 24–16. Coach Mallory had told Davis that he could go for the block, and Colletto later said that Davis ran right over the blocker.

To add to the defense's fun, they next had a safety on a team tackle of Trefzger in end zone. Now the score was Indiana 26, Purdue 16. After the safety, Purdue kicked off from their 20-yard line. The Hoosiers received the kick and then mounted a quick drive of 59 yards, ending in Smith's seven-yard run. Manolopoulos made the kick, and Indiana led 33–16.

This Old Oaken Bucket effort gave Coach Bill Mallory a win that allowed him to end his 13-year career at Indiana with a winning record (7–6) against Purdue.

IU linebacker Jamie Baisley walked off the field with the cherished Old Oaken Bucket balanced on his head. He was taking the Bucket to coach Mallory, who was being carried off the field IU team. An inebriated Purdue fan tried to punch Baisley after the game. He later said, "That was the hardest hit I took all day, but it wasn't enough to lose the bucket."

2001: Indiana 13, Purdue 7— Randle El Celebrates

The 2001 football season was interrupted on September 11 by Muslim terrorists hijacking planes and crashing them into New York's World Trade Center and the Pentagon in Washington, D.C. Suddenly, football didn't seem as important in the minds of students, alumni, and fans across America. All football games for that weekend were postponed, and most were made up at season's end. The IU–Kentucky game was moved all the way back to December 1.

On November 24, there was a cold, driving rain coming down in Bloomington as heavily-favored Purdue, which had already won six games to IU's three, came to town. Cocky Purdue fans drove

into the lots with signs calling the IU stadium "Ross–Ade South," and some even taunted IU die-hards who, trying to tailgate, huddled under shelters and tarps outside of Memorial Stadium. But that day, it would be the Hoosiers that celebrated.

IU's star quarterback, Antwaan Randle El, was to finish his illustrious career at IU without playing in a bowl game. He hadn't had much chance to celebrate with his teammates during his Indiana career, so when the Hoosiers won, 13–7, he wasn't about to wait to get his hands on the Old Oaken Bucket. After a perfunctory hand shake, most of the players went right over to the Purdue sideline and got the bucket. The Hoosiers passed it among themselves as they ran excitedly around the field. Soon, some younger IU fans in the crowd of 36,685 ran onto the field and tore down the goal posts at the south end.

Randle El and tailback Levron Williams were brilliant early in the game as the Hoosiers jumped to a 13–0 lead. IU scored on its first possession when Williams, who rushed for 94 yards on 21 carries, ran for a 52-yard touchdown. Then after another drive, Randle El added a 10-yard scoring run early in the second quarter, but the Hoosiers missed the extra point.

IU's much maligned defense shut down the Boilermakers' offense just enough to get the victory, and could point with pride to one great play. With the score at 13–7 early in the fourth quarter, Purdue had the ball fourth-and-goal from inside the IU one-yard line. Montrell Lowe took a handoff and seemed to be ready to score when IU linebacker Martin Lapostolle stopped him before he could cross the goal line.

The Boilers rushed for minus-15 yards during a miserable first half. But when the heavy rain stopped at halftime, Purdue coach Tiller decided to drop the run and almost exclusively to the pass in the second half. Quarterback Kyle Orton completed 31 of 62 passes for 263 yards, and Purdue cut the lead to 13–7 when he hit John Standeford with a 14-yard touchdown pass with 10:52 remaining

in the third quarter. Purdue, however, never took advantage of the momentum. The Boilers got the ball inside the IU 30-yard line five times in the second half but scored only once.

After the game, few Purdue former-zealots were present in the tailgate lots. The signs and cars mysteriously schlepped away. Since the rain had stopped, IU tailgaters were having a last snack before driving home. One departing Purdue fan, walking through the lot was heard to say, "If it weren't for the rain, Purdue would have scored two more touchdowns". Which was answered by an IU Alumnus, enjoying a hot Irish coffee, "If it weren't for the rain, IU would have had five more touchdowns. Have a nice ride home."

2002: Indiana 66, Purdue 63— Duel in the Dome

This game, dubbed "The Duel in the Dome", didn't count in the Big Ten standings, but you couldn't tell from the reaction of the players who went down to the wire in a 66–63 Hoosier victory. Michael Pointer, a beat writer covering Purdue for the *Indianapolis Star*, estimated that the raucous crowd of 32,055 at the RCA Dome consisted of mostly IU fans.

The nonconference duel had all the excitement of any February battle in Mackey Arena or Assembly Hall. IU senior forward Jeff Newton scored all of his team-high 16 points in the final 14 minutes to lead number-seven Indiana to the victory. Newton, who had just two rebounds in the first half, recorded his fifth consecutive double-double with 16 points and 10 more rebounds in the second half. He was also money at the foul line. This was a tremendous improvement from a player who was a 53 percent foul shooter his first two seasons at IU.

This game had been scheduled because the Big Ten decided that IU and Purdue would only meet once in conference play that season. Indiana (8–0) continued with its best start for a season since the 1989–90 campaign. The favored Hoosiers discovered that

this game was anything but easy. Purdue led by six in the first half and for most of the game. At 11:22, IU finally took the lead on two Bracey Wright free throws, 39–37. The second half featured nine lead changes, with IU taking the lead for good on a 17-foot jumper by Wright with 5:37 to play. Wright, who hadn't practiced all week after injuring his right shooting wrist in a shoot-around before practice, hit the second of two free throws with 1.2 seconds to play, giving the Hoosiers a 66–63 lead. Kenneth Lowe's long baseball pass on the game's final play was intercepted by Newton to end the game.

IU's biggest lead was five at 65–60 with less than 25 seconds remaining, following a pair of free throws by Wright. After a turnover seconds later, IU got the ball back and should have been able at the very least get back to the foul line and attempt to increase the lead. But freshman Marshall Strickland made a freshman mistake. Driving the ball into the lane, he tossed an alley-oop pass in the direction of Wright, but the ball flew out of bounds, giving Purdue the ball with 10.9 seconds remaining. At the other end, Purdue freshman guard David Teague knocked down a three-pointer from the left wing with 4.1 seconds to play to cut the lead to two at 65–63.

On the subsequent inbounds, however, Wright took a pass from Tom Coverdale and dribbled to mid-court where he was fouled by Willie Deane with 1.2 seconds to play. Deane led all scorers with 21 points. George Leach had 11 points and 14 rebounds. He also had four blocked shots. Chris Booker and Lowe each scored 12 points for the Boilermakers. Booker had a double-double, also recording 11 rebounds. Neither team shot the ball well, Purdue at 32 percent (19 of 59) and the Hoosiers at 37.5 percent (21 of 56). Indiana, which had made at least seven three-pointers in each of its first seven games, was 3–14 from beyond the arc.

The lack of rebounding hurt the Boilermakers this day as it had done to them all season. They were averaging less rebounds per game with each of their previous opponents. Today the Hoosiers capitalized on this weakness by winning the battle of the boards

49-35 and by 16 to 10 on the offensive end. IU"'s inside tandem of George Leach (14) and Jeff Newton (12) grabbed more than half of the rebounds.

2007: Indiana 27, Purdue 24—Play Thirteen

The 2007 Bucket game kicked off at 3:30 on a beautiful, sunny, 57-degree late-November afternoon. By the time it ended under the Memorial Stadium lights with Austin Star's 49-yard field goal, the Hoosiers had the Old Oaken Bucket, a winning season, a bowl bid, and tears of joy as the team fulfilled the battle cry of their late coach Terry Hoeppner to "play thirteen." Hoeppner had become the Indiana head coach for the 2005 season and died of brain cancer the summer before the 2007 campaign. His goal for the 2007 season was to play 13 games, the 12 regularly scheduled contests plus an additional post-season bowl game.

Many of the 50,741 Hoosier spectators, including Hoeppner's wife Jane and daughters Amy and Allison, were on the field to congratulate the team after time expired. This was a game and a season where the Indiana players felt inspired by coach Hoeppner. Their motivating attitude was that they were playing this season for Coach.

IU led 17–3 at halftime. The scoring began as IU quarterback Kellen Lewis made a nine-yard scamper with only 37 seconds left in the first quarter. Austin Starr kicked the extra point, and the score was 7–0. Purdue put three-points on the board late in the second quarter with a 37-yard field goal by Chris Summers. Then IU added an Austin-Starr 42-yarder to take a 10–3 lead with 2:43 left in the half. After a Purdue fumble, IU scored again when Lewis hit James Hardy with a pass as he flashed from east to west in the south end zone just 34 seconds before the end of the half.

In the second half, IU scored again on a Lewis eight-yard run and Starr kick to lead 24–3. But the Boilermakers weren't done and rallied for 21 unanswered points to tie the score at 24. First, they

got a touchdown as Kory Sheets sneaked it in from a yard out, then another Sheets plunge and Summers kick made it 24–17. To tie the game, Purdue scored on a five-yard pass from Curtis Painter to Jake Standeford with 3:39 to play.

Purdue kicked off to IU's 24-yard line. Indiana moved 45 yards in 12 plays to set up Starr for the game-winning field goal try. On the drive, the Hoosiers converted a pair of third downs, including a 12-yard pass from Kellen Lewis to James Hardy on third-and-five at the Purdue 45-yard line. One of the passes accounted for 41 yards. Earlier in the game, Starr had made a 42-yard field goal to set an IU record for field goals in a season with 18. Marcus Thigpen ran for a career-high 140 yards on 19 carries, and Kellen Lewis ran for two scores and threw for a third to lead Indiana to the victory.

After IU made the field goal to go on top 27–24, Coach Billy Lynch told Starr to do a squib-kick and keep the ball away from dangerous Purdue kick returner Dorien Bryant. Hoosier radio voice Don Fischer expected the same thing and reacted with amazement when Starr, seeing Purdue's deep men move up, tried to kick it over their heads. The ball was returned by Bryant to the Purdue 30, but a late hit moved it all the way back to the 15. Painter then threw three passes—one was incomplete—the third of which was an unsuccessful hook and ladder to end the game.

2013: Indiana 97, Purdue 60—Sheehey's Flex

The number-three Hoosiers put together one of their most complete efforts of the season as they buried the Boilers 97–60 in front of a Mackey Arena crowd of 14,845 in 2013. They also made series history as they won by the largest margin of victory by an Indiana team in 97 trips to West Lafayette. The previous high had been 36 points in 1954.

Prior to the contest, the IU team warmed up in the end zone right in front of the infamous student section called the "Paint Crew," named after Purdue coach Matt Painter. These rowdies

always take pleasure in harassing the opponents as they warm-up. This game they were exceptionally vocal with chants of "IU Sucks" and yells of a few obscenities as well.

For the most part, Indiana (19–2, 7–1 Big Ten) let its game do the talking. Purdue largest lead of the contest, two points, came just over a minute into the game. From that point, Indiana dismantled Purdue's locomotive bolt by bolt and quieted the fans by going on a 9–0 run. Jeremy Hollowell, Remy Abell, Will Sheehey, and Victor Oladipo scored in the run. Later in the half, the Hoosiers used a 13–0 run to go ahead 47–25.

Will Sheehey came off the bench for seven points and seven assists in 18 minutes. He also hardly endeared himself to the Purdue Paint Crew by snagging a long rebound and scoring down the lane with a thunder dunk with 9:07 remaining. Sheehey was fouled on the play, looked right at the student section, pounded his chest, flexed his arms like a Mr. America body builder, and gave a roar. The bib overall, hard hat-wearing fanatics went so berserk that game officials feared for Will's safety. To calm the students, they took Will over to the Indiana bench and asked IU coach Tom Crean to calm him down. Of course, Coach Crean grabbed Sheehey and talked with him for a moment, but it wasn't Sheehey who needed calming, it was the Paint Crew.

Here are some facts from the day which show IU's total domination. Cody Zeller had his fourth double-double in Big Ten play and sixth of the season with 19 points and 11 rebounds. Christian Watford and Victor Oladipo had 17 points each. Yogi Ferrell had 11 points, including a trio of three-pointers. Jordan Hulls had 10 points, rounding out the players in double figures. The Hoosiers shot 57 percent from the field in the second half as they built on a 20-point halftime lead. Overall, IU hit 49 percent, just missing the 12th time it would have made more than 50 percent of the shots in a game that season.

Indiana made a season-high 12 three-pointers, including seven of 10 in the second half. Watford hit four of five, and Ferrell made three of four. It was the second time in three games that Ferrell had made a season-high three three-point shots. After making 59.6 percent of its free throws the previous two games, Indiana showed why it was the top free throw-shooting team in the Big Ten, making 19 of 20 against Purdue. Indiana also dominated the backboards, especially on the offensive end. IU had 18 offensive rebounds in its total of 39. That led to 24 second-chance points and 36 points overall in the paint.

IU got so far ahead that it basically took the crowd out of the game. At one time in the second half, the IU faithful started chants. These chants would normally not be heard over the Boilermaker fans, but as the Purdue crowd started leaving the building in the final ten minutes, with the Hoosiers on top by 30 points, the crowd balance was more apparent. Even the Paint Crew had no eloquent reply.

The one bright spot for Purdue (11–10, 4–4) was the play of freshman center A. J. Hammons. The seven-foot player from Carmel scored a career-high 30 points, hitting 10 of 14 shots from the field and 10 of 12 from the line. His previous best had been 20 points. That means he scored half of Purdue's 60 points.

IU moved into a first-place tie with number one Michigan atop the Big Ten at 7–1.

We Love Winning March Madness

1940: Indiana 60, Kansas 42

In Kansas City, Missouri on March 30, Jay McCreary—a gum-chewing, blond guard in a forest of physical giants—scored 12 points, as did teammate Marv Huffman, as Indiana defeated the University of Kansas, 60–42, for the NCAA Championship in front of 10,116 fans in the Kansas City municipal auditorium. Coach McCracken regularly started five different players for each game, choosing from among his six top players. This night, McCreary was not in the starting line-up for the Hoosiers, but once he got onto the floor, Coach Branch McCracken realized Jay should play. He had only 2 of his 12 points in the first half and scored five times from the field in second half.

It took Indiana eight minutes to get its first basket, but after that there was no stopping them. Kansas stymied the Hoosiers the first eight minutes by relentlessly pushing them back to mid-court. Then the Hoosiers got underway by picking and cutting down the center of the floor. At the half, IU walked to their dressing rooms ahead, 32–19.

Although he went out early on fouls, Indiana's big captain Marvin Huffman was spectacular, making baskets each time Kansas

started to gain momentum. Once the victory was no longer in doubt, the Hoosiers turned loose spectacular passing attacks which seemed to hypnotize the fans and almost put the Kansas athletes to sleep.

1953: Indiana 69, Kansas 68

In Kansas City, Missouri, Indiana University, best in the Big Ten, once again was the NCAA's best basketball team. The Hoosier fought, and fought, and fought before they could down a courageous Kansas team, 69–68 in front of 10,000 screaming fans, including some 500 Indiana students and followers. Indiana downed the defending NCAA champs, the same team it beat in 1940 for its initial NCAA cage crown, when Bob Leonard sank the second of two free throws with 30 seconds left. Kansas called time. When play resumed, Kansas got the ball down court in good fashion, working it around and looking for the basket that would give the Jayhawks their second straight title.

Center Jerry Alberts got the ball in the right corner and fired with three seconds left. The ball hit the far side of the rim and bounced away. The horn sounded before possession of the ball was gained by either team. The Hoosiers fought for their basketball lives in a game jam-packed with pressure. Indiana was in front or tied for the lead all of the last quarter. Three times the Jayhawks knotted the count in those last hectic 10 minutes. Dean Kelly deadlocked the score at 68-all with 38 seconds remaining. But it was this same Kelley who committed the costly foul against Leonard when the Hoosier guard drove for the basket with 30 seconds left.

Kansas, it must be said, put up a tremendous battle with Allen Kelley and B. H. Born leading the way. For Indiana, Don Schlundt (30 points) and Charlie Kraak, who played his best game of the year, were outstanding. Leonard got 12 points, far below his average, because of some fine defensive play by Dean Kelley. It was Schlundt and Kraak who kept the Hoosiers going in the first half, with Leonard coming on in the second as Kraak loaded up with fouls.

Bench strength was a major factor in the Hoosiers' victory. Kraak, Schlundt, Dick Farley and Burke Scott were all forced to the bench at various times because of personals. Jim DeaKyne, Dick White, Phil Byers, and Paul Toff filled the gaps in fine style.

Indiana got off to a 2–0 lead on Schlundt's hook shot. Born and Allen Kelley put Kansas ahead, 4–2, and the Jayhawks never trailed again until the waning minutes of the first quarter. Scott put IU on top, 15–14, on a jump shot. Born's two buckets, and one by Allen Kelley, pushed Kansas to a 19–15 lead before Schlundt and Scott got the Hoosiers ahead, 21–19, at the quarter's end. Shortly after the second period started, Kansas ran up leads of 28–24 and 39–35 the latter with 3:45 remaining in the quarter. Then Kraak, Schlundt, and White tied the score and the half ended in a 41-all tie.

Indiana came out in the third quarter and grabbed a quick 47–44 lead. Back came the Jayhawks, paced by Born, Harold Patterson, and Dean Kelley. They ran up a 53–49 advantage before Leonard and Schlundt cut it to 53–51. The last five minutes of this period, the lead changed hands four times with Indiana finally managing only a 59–58 three-quarter advantage. Into the home stretch they went.

Allen Kelley made it 60–59 on a pair of free throws. Schlundt scored on a sleeper, but Born tied it at 61 on DeaKyne's personal foul. Schlundt made one free throw on Gil Reich's foul. Schlundt added another charity toss on Horn's fifth foul, making it 63–61 with 5:36 to go. When Born was finally charged with his fifth personal, it settled a three-minute rhubarb in the third quarter. The official scorer somehow had Born with five when he had only four. The loss of Born did not help the Kansas cause in the least, but the Jayhawks hung on as Allen Kelley hit a jump shot from the side for a 63-all tie. Schlundt once again put IU ahead, 65–63, with a hook shot. Kansas called time with 3:57 left, hoping to have the ball when it headed into the last three minutes and the mandatory two-shot foul rule.

"They were a courageous team," was all Coach Branch McCracken, with his second NCAA title in his back pocket, could say as he was pummeled by his team.

Bob Houbregs poured in 42 points and broke the four-game field-goal record. He totaled 57 points, breaking Clyde Lovellette's record of 53 set the previous year. Schlundt and Leonard were named to the all-tourney first five. Born was named the most valuable player.

The team was met outside Bloomington for a parade and were honored at a banquet in the Union Building. The final result marked the first time in the playoffs that a winner had been held to a one-point margin. Indiana broke the team record for total points in four tourney games with 310. Washington had set the old record of 307 when the Huskies beat Louisiana State. The Hoosiers also broke the four-game free-throw record with 108, and Schlundt set a new series mark with 49 free throws.

1976: Indiana 86, Michigan 68

In Philadelphia, in front of a capacity crowd of 17,540 persons in the Spectrum, Indiana experienced an emotion-shattering 86–68

IU wins, 86–68, over Michigan to win the NCAA. Buckner and May hoist that 1976 NCAA trophy as coach Knight, in a plaid sport coat, helps celebrate IU's championship and third win of the year over Michigan. This was Knight's first of three NCAA championships at IU.

victory over Big Ten–rival Michigan, which came as hard as any triumph all season long.

Besides having a bull's-eye on their backs as the number one–ranked team in the nation, Indiana was again facing a Michigan team that was looking for revenge. The Hoosiers had narrowly beaten them twice, once in overtime, 72–67. Steve Grote, the fiery leader of the Wolverines, predicted that this game was to be World War III since Indiana won the first two games and tonight was the third one. Adding to this, the Hoosiers lost Bobby Wilkerson, a key member of the team. He was completely and instantly knocked out when he caught an elbow from the Wolverines' Wayman Britt with 17:17 left in the opening period. The senior was treated on the floor for almost 15 minutes, then taken to Temple University Hospital for a concussion.

Officials ruled the collision and knockout an accident and called no foul. Few teams ever have been more stunned in the opening moments of such an important game and still come back to triumph. Most teams would have quietly wilted and called the accident one of those saddening strictures of fate, but not this team. Knight himself termed the team, "one that won't let itself be beaten."

Instead of showing any signs of panic, the Hoosiers rallied and refused to roll over and curse the fates. It wasn't easy, nor was it a quick road to victory. Knight used three different guards to replace Wilkerson, and the Hoosiers were having trouble getting either the offense or defense functioning properly. The Wolverines found themselves out in front by hitting nine of their first 12 shots. By this time, the fans wondered if they were watching an unattainable dream.

But the team hadn't factored in the determination of Buckner and Benson, who combined for such a show of strength on both ends of the floor that Indiana kept climbing. The team finally took a 27–26 lead with six minutes left in the half when May, college player

of the year, tossed in a long shot from the corner. The Hoosiers lost the lead and went into the dressing room behind, 35–29.

In the first half, Michigan shot a phenomenal .615 from the field (16 of 26). This wasn't the first time Indiana had been faced with a staggering road to comeback, and the confidence it picked up in traveling the road to the NCAA championship over the previous four years was evident during the second half as Knight's basketball team went into high gear. Benson, May, and Buckner led the charge that brought ties at 41 and 43 followed by a three-point lead with 12:13 still to play. The Wolverines, with Steve Grote running the offense, weren't going to concede either, and struck back three times to tie the score before May's basket put IU in front permanently. Five straight points were scored in the surge before Michigan could answer, and when Buckner stepped to the free-throw line on Phil Hubbard's fifth and final foul with 7:27 left, his free throw was the beginning of the end.

May and Benson added four points. Buckner calmly put in a pair of free throws at the 5:28 mark for a nine-point advantage. When Britt fouled-out 30 seconds later, the Wolverines were starting to falter. Not even a stern press could have thrown off the charge to victory. The lead was sliced to eight points before Jimmy Wisman, May, and Buckner added the final and clinching points that sealed the victory and started a victory celebration with 44 seconds left and Indiana in front. With tears flowing, Knight talked about this win being the objective of the previous two years' teams. He spoke of how hard the players worked both years.

Kent Benson, a unanimous choice for most outstanding player, had 25 points and nine rebounds. Quinn Buckner, still the heart and soul of this club, scored 16 points. May gave Knight a tearful and happy hug, then huskily told his coach, "We worked so hard, so hard for this, and we finally beat 'em, baby." Knight said that, without Wilkerson, the team wasn't able to pressure as much. He commended the team's great job, particularly in the second half.

He also commended Quinn Buckner for playing a great game and bringing the team down to the end. Abernethy, who played 35 minutes despite a taped-up knee that had been badly bruised in Saturday's semifinal, also did an outstanding job, scoring 11 points and grabbing four boards. And giving an outstanding performance was Wisman, who contributed six assists and ran the IU offense quite well the entire second period. Steve Grote credited Wisman with the reason the Indiana offense ran well in the second half. Michigan, finishing at 25–7 for the season, had 18 points from Green, 12 from Grote, 11 from Britt, and 10 from Hubbard but faded in the second half when Indiana outshot them, .600 to .355, to show once again how strong their defense was.

After doctors attended Wilkerson on the floor, he was taken by stretcher to the Indiana dressing room. Upon deciding that he needed to be hospitalized, the ambulance that was supposed to be stationed at the Spectrum was nowhere to be found. After a fruitless search, Dr. Joseph Torg of Temple University, the physician in charge, asked if the Police Paddy Wagon was there. So, instead of an ambulance, Wilkerson rode 9.9 miles to Temple Hospital in an unlit police wagon. Later, one Spectrum official was overheard saying to a man from Temple, "I hope there's never a real emergency here."

1981: Indiana 63, UNC 50

American college's most prized possession, the NCAA championship, came back home to Indiana University. A team of Hoosier basketball players overwhelmed North Carolina, 63–50, in front of 18,276 spectators in Philadelphia. This marks the fourth time the Hoosiers reached the pinnacle of college basketball. The first two NCAA championships were in 1940 and 1953, both in Kansas City at the Municipal Arena as both victories were over Kansas. The last two NCAA championships came in the Spectrum in Philadelphia against Michigan in 1976 and 1981 against North Carolina. In addition to being the Hoosiers' fourth title, the 1981

championship marks the sixth-consecutive year the crown remained in the Mideast region. IU began the streak in 1976 and was followed by Marquette, Kentucky, Michigan State, and Louisville before it made the full circle back to Bloomington.

This game was just like the Indiana victory over LSU two days earlier. In that contest, the Hoosiers trailed, 30–27, at the half and came back to win convincingly, 67–49. Against North Carolina, the Hoosiers also took control of the game in the second half. The star of the game was Isiah Thomas the six-foot, one-inch sophomore guard with the boyish smile. Named the most outstanding player in the finals for his brilliant effort, Thomas climaxed the season with 19 second-half points to propel IU past the Tar Heels. When the clock read 13:17, Isiah had pumped home 10 points and his club was sailing toward the championship, 43–34. Thomas's effort was symbolic of the entire squad, which hit 12 of 19 field goal attempts in the last half after a dismal 11-of-29 effort in the opening 20 minutes. Along with shooting five assists, he got four steals which contributed mightily to the Indiana cause. Three times in the half's opening minutes, Thomas was there to swipe the ball, drive the length of the floor, and deposit layups at the other end. And before anyone, particularly the Tar Heels, could comprehend what had transpired, Indiana was sitting on a nine-point lead.

Also playing a big role was the other Thomas, a sophomore guard named Jim from Fort Lauderdale, Florida. For the fourth-straight game, Jim Thomas proved to be the super-sub. Monday night, he came into the game with IU trailing, 16–8, at 9:25 of the first half. For the next 29 minutes, he dished out eight assists, grabbed four rebounds, and shut off North Carolina forward Al Wood in the crucial early minutes of the second half.

The Game against North Carolina was Knight's third NCAA championship. He had one as a player at Ohio State and two coaching Indiana. The team ended the season 26–9, winning five

games in the NCAA tournament by a grand total of 113 points. North Carolina's 50 points was the lowest scored by a losing team in a title game since Kentucky beat Oklahoma State, 46–36, in 1949.

Indiana had its problems early as Ted Kitchel picked up three fouls in four minutes. He was replaced by Steve Risley, who eventually gave way to Jim Thomas. IU, scoreless for more than four minutes when it fell behind at 16–4, missed six of its first seven shots. Indiana led for the first time as the clock hit 0:00 in the first half. Randy Wittman did the bombing, drilling a shot from deep in the right corner for two of his 16 points and a 27–26 lead. Seconds earlier, Wittman had shouted "come on, come on," to Isiah Thomas. Wittman moved to the front line when Jim Thomas moved into the picture. He responded well, just as he had during the season. Against Carolina, Wittman was 7-of-13 from the field and, when IU went into its delay game midway through the final half, he was one of the men called upon to protect the basketball. Carolina used a zone for the first 30 minutes, then was forced to a trapping man defense because Indiana had opened up a lead ranging between 11 and 13 points.

Indiana's title was achieved in a game that was almost not played Monday evening because of the assassination attempt earlier in the day on President Ronald Reagan. That fact weighed heavy in the mind of Ray Tolbert, the Hoosiers' valuable senior center.

"We didn't know for a long time if we would play, but that wasn't important," said Tolbert. "We are happy that we won, but we are even happier that the President is alive and doing well." Tolbert termed Indiana's effort "the best forty minutes of basketball we've played." He grabbed 11 rebounds, dominating play under the boards in a struggle against the Carolina frontline—considered the best in the nation by many associated with the game. Indiana's final 12 points came at the free-throw line.

1987: Indiana 74, Syracuse 73

On Monday night, 64,959 fans, mostly wearing the red of the IU Nation, filled the New Orleans Super Dome to see the NCAA men's basketball championship. The game was tight, right down to the last four seconds when Keith Smart hit The Shot—a 17-foot jumper from the right corner—to give Indiana the win and their fifth NCAA title. The title was IU's fifth, pulling it abreast of Kentucky. Only UCLA had more with 10 titles. It was the Hoosiers' third national championship under Coach Bob Knight, who also won in 1976 and '81. That put him behind just two men, legends both: UCLA's John Wooden (10), and Kentucky's Adolph Rupp (5).

The Hoosiers weren't favored to win the national championship in 1987 as UNLV was top ranked coming to Louisiana. North Carolina, another team ranked ahead of IU, didn't make it to the final four. Pre-season, Indiana wasn't even favored to win the Big Ten. A key for the Hoosiers' march to the championship was winning a number-one seed in the tourney so they could play close to home. To do that, they would have to win the Big Ten. On the last day of the conference season, Michigan knocked over Purdue, and Indiana beat Ohio State to allow the Hoosiers and Boilermakers to tie for the conference championship at 15–3. Number three–ranked Indiana thus was given a one-seed. The driving distances to the games before the Final Four would be very short, Indianapolis and Cincinnati.

That Monday night, the Hoosiers weren't quite up to the standard from two days earlier when they knocked off number one–ranked UNLV at their own game. On Saturday, the Hoosiers ran right along with the Runnin' Rebels, knocking them off, 97–93, in a game in which IU was ahead most of the way. Late in the game, as time was running out, Indiana had a 10-point lead.

The Hoosiers, however, were up to the standard of beating Syracuse. Indiana just let Keith Smart lead the way to the win. Smart, the Final Four Most Valuable Player, was playing at Garden City Community College in Kansas the year before. The six-foot,

one-inch junior scored 21 points for IU, gave out six assists, took down five rebounds, and made a career's worth of big plays to keep Indiana in the game through the second half. Smart scored 12 of Indiana's final 15 points.

Indiana led, 34–33, on a three-point shot a second before the halftime buzzer and pushed the margin to 41–37 before the Orangemen started to fight back. A 15–3 run, including three-point plays by Seikaly and Derek Bower and a three-point shot by Monroe, gave Syracuse a lead, 52–44, with 13 minutes to play. Smart brought the Hoosiers back with three points and a pair of assists as IU scored 10 straight points to go back into a lead at 54–52. It was a footrace the rest of the way. Syracuse held Indiana to 48 percent shooting, committed just 16 personal fouls, and won the battle on the boards, 38–35. The Orangemen fell largely because their free throws didn't. Syracuse went only 11 for 20 at the foul line.

"I just took what was given to me," Smart said. "Syracuse was sagging inside and covering Steve [Alford] tight, so he was looking for me and that worked. Having a player like Steve opens things up so much for the others on the team." Alford had to be guarded closely because he was deadly all night from outside, hitting seven of 10 three-point attempts and scoring 23 points. Alford wound up with 2,438 career points, just one short of the Big Ten record held by Michigan's Mike McGee. Alford's 749 season-points were four short of the Indiana record held by Scott May.

Thomas repeatedly stepped into the lane to break open and gave the Hoosiers 20 points and seven rebounds. Center Dean Garrett had 10 points and 10 rebounds and made a pair of crucial blocks down the stretch. Point guard Sherman Douglas topped the Syracuse lineup with 20 points. Center Rony Seikaly and guard Greg Monroe both added 18 points each.

It could have been Syracuse doing the celebrating. With only 28 seconds to play, Orangemen forward Derrick Coleman missed a free throw with a chance to put the game away. Syracuse Coach

Jim Boeheim pulled all his players away from the free-throw lane to prevent a foul. With no one on the lane looking to rebound, Daryl Thomas secured the rebound for the Hoosiers. Indiana took a timeout with 28 seconds to play. Knight had IU run 10 seconds off the clock and look for Alford. Syracuse defender Howard Triche, had Alford covered. Smart penetrated and dumped the ball to Thomas on the baseline, who faked a shot and passed up a jumper over the six-foot, nine-inch Coleman. Less than 10 seconds remained.

"Daryl was smart," said Knight. "He didn't take a panic shot or make a move and get in trouble with the basketball." Smart cut behind Thomas, took the ball from the Hoosiers forward and, with Triche in his face, buried the Orangemen and the basket.

You'd think that Syracuse would immediately call a time-out to get a good shot, but the team seemed to be in shock. In looking at the replay, it's obvious to the viewer and game commentators that they did not call a TO. It seems that the referees gave them a sympathetic TO at one second left. After a minute huddle to figure out a play, the Orangemen threw in a lob pass to none other than Keith Smart at mid-court. It was over.

Captain Dean

Players We Love

Everett Dean: Outscored the Opposition

Everett Dean was born in Livonia, Indiana, and was a three-sport athlete at Salem High School. He came to IU in 1918 and played both football and basketball. He didn't letter in football, although he caught a touchdown pass against Kentucky.

As a player, Dean outscored IU's opponent in seven different basketball games, one of which was Notre Dame. This is an

IU record. Between 1905 and 1928, an IU player outscored the opponent 40 times. Dean's seven is the record for the most times.

Dean played basketball for three years at Indiana University and was named to the 1921 Helms Athletic Foundation All-America team. He has the distinction of being the first basketball All-American from IU. He became head baseball and basketball coach at IU from 1924 to 1938. In 1938, Dean became the only coach named to both the Naismith Basketball Hall of Fame and the College Baseball Hall of Fame. He was inducted into the Indiana Basketball Hall of Fame in 1965.

Branch McCracken: The Dominating "Big Guy" from Monrovia

Emmett Branch McCracken was born and raised in Monrovia, Indiana, just 32 miles north of IU. At Monrovia High School, he became the basketball team's star, leading the tiny school of only 32 male students to consecutive Tri-State Tournament championships (1925–1926). The Tri-State Tournament was an annual basketball tournament played in Cincinnati between more than 50 high school teams from Indiana, Ohio, and Kentucky. In 1925, big school powers from Indiana included Anderson, Columbus, and Logansport. It took six wins for Monrovia to become Tri-State Tournament champion. Tournament officials selected McCracken to the mythical All Tri-State Team, a testament to the skills he exhibited during the tournament.

Monrovia again won the tournament the following year. McCracken, captain of Monrovia's team, won the highest individual honor for a player, receiving the medal for Most Valuable Player both years.

McCracken was recruited to IU by Everett Dean for the basketball team. However, upon arriving in Bloomington as a freshman, McCracken pledged the Kappa Sigma fraternity. The chapterhouse was way east on 3rd street. So far out, in fact, that the rest of the Greeks called the chapterhouse "the Granary." At

night, when Branch would be sound asleep, he would occasionally be awakened by the shout, "Where's the Big Guy?" coming from one of the older members of the chapter who had been playing the piano and drinking with his cronies at a local bar. This older member was none other than IU's legend of movies and songs, Hoagy Carmichael. Hoagy would then give Branch an unappreciated swat from his fraternity paddle.

McCracken's first varsity sport at IU was football, where he went on to win three letters. Strange as it may seem, Branch, the basketball All-American to be, scored a touchdown before he ever scored a basket at IU. On the 1927 football team, he recovered a fumble and ran it 20 yards for a touchdown and a 14–14 tie against a previously-unbeaten Minnesota Gopher team.

During McCracken's first basketball season, he was a strong presence on the court throughout the season. Despite his youth, he was the high-scorer for the Hoosiers and led the Big Ten Conference in scoring for most of the year, only losing the lead to Bennie Oosterbaan of Michigan in the last few weeks of the season. McCracken finished the season tied for second place in conference scoring with 171 points and a 10.1 average per game.

The next year McCracken returned as center and continued to put up big points, again finishing second in Big Ten scoring with 146 points. McCracken's last season in 1929-1930 would prove to be his best as McCracken plowed his way through conference foes to score a total of 206 points to top all other players and to break the all-time record set the previous year by Charles "Stretch" Murphy of Purdue. McCracken was named on nearly every all-conference team.

McCracken graduated from IU in 1930, and accepted a position as head basketball coach at Ball State in Muncie, Indiana soon after. After Ball State, McCracken became the first IU head basketball coach that would lead the Hoosiers to an NCAA Championship.

Billy Hillenbrand: Mr. Everything

Billy Hillenbrand was born in Armstrong, Indiana. In high school (Evansville Reitz Memorial), he was a winner and a leader. He was All-State in football three times (1937, 1938, 1939) and was his class president for three years. He was a four-year varsity letterman in football, basketball, and baseball; was All-State in Basketball, and won the Catholic Sportsmanship Award at the ISHAA state basketball tournament. He also set Evansville single-year basketball scoring record with a four-year total of 485 points. His teams won four City Championships, posting record 36–2–2 and won the Mythical National Championship 1937 and Mythical State Championship 1938. There were no tournaments to prove the rankings, so the media dubbed them mythical champions.

Billy Hillenbrand graduated from Reitz Memorial in 1940 and stunned recruiters for Notre Dame and Purdue by deciding to attend IU and play football for Bo McMillin's up-and-coming Hoosiers. Billy played IU football 1941–42 and was MVP in 1941, All–Big Ten in 1941 and 1942, and All-American in 1942 and led the Hoosiers in rushing, passing, and scoring. He still owns all IU punt-return records with 65 for 1,042 yards and a 16.0 average. After Billy's junior season in 1942, he was a consensus All-American, having been selected as a first-team All-American halfback by *The Sporting News*, United Press, Central Press Association, NEA wire service, *Collier's Weekly*, *New York Sun*, and Walter Camp Football Foundation. He also finished fifth in the Heisman Trophy voting, the first IU player to make the final voting.

After that 7–3 IU season, World War II was on Billy's mind, as it was for numerous college stars. Hillenbrand was drafted by the New York Giants in the first round (sixth pick overall) in the 1944 NFL Draft, but went to the Army instead. While serving in India, he completed his IU degree by correspondence in 1946.

After his discharge, he went to the NFL's competitor the AAFC where he played three seasons from 1946–1948 for the Chicago

Rockets and Baltimore Colts. He played in a total of 41 professional games. He was a versatile player who scored 186 points gained over 4,000 all-purpose yards in three years. He was an All-AFL second-team All-Star Selection in 1947 and 1948, held several individual Colt records, and was the team scoring leader 1946, 1947, and 1948. His total of 970 receiving yards and an average of 11.2 yards per touch were AAFC League's best in 1948.

Upon retiring from football, Hillenbrand ran a food brokerage firm for 21 years back home in Evansville.

Hillenbrand has been selected into the Indiana University Athletics Hall of Fame and the Indiana Football Hall of Fame.

John Tavener: More than Football

John Tavener came to IU from Granville, Ohio, where he was one of Ohio's top high-school football players.

An extremely versatile player at IU, Tavener called the offensive signals at center, excelled on defense, and kicked extra points. John won football letters in 1941, 1942, 1943, and 1944 as a center, and was honorary captain in 1943. He was captain in 1944 and Indiana's Most Valuable Player in both 1943 and 1944. John was first-team All-American in 1944. He played in the 1943 East–West game, in the 1944 Blue–Gray All-Star game, and played professionally for Miami Seahawks and Green Bay Packers. He was named to six different All-America teams following his senior season in 1944.

When putting together a list of IU's greatest football players of all time, John Tavener is not a name that will come to many people's minds right away. He played in the mid-1940s and was a center— certainly not a glamorous position. But when you review Tavener's credentials, there is no doubt he belongs on any list of IU's "best of all time". Tavener was a star for the Hoosiers on the field, and he was a major reason why the 1940s were a particularly bright era for IU on the gridiron. While he may have grown up and died in Ohio, he will always be remembered as a great Hoosier.

After football, John retired and pursued a banking career in Ohio. After retiring from the business in 1986, he became a volunteer assistant coach at Denison University in Granville, Ohio. Dennison used a single wing, and he coached the centers and implemented a direct long-snap to the team's tailback. It was the same technique he had been taught while playing for the Hoosiers.

He continued to reside in Johnstown, Ohio, where he was an outstanding public speaker, a leader in Baptist Church activities, a 32nd-degree Mason, a Shriner, and a past treasurer of Ohio Young Republicans.

Tavener was enshrined into both the College Football Halls of Fame and the IU Athletics Hall of Fame in 1990.

Ted Kluszewski: Major League MVP

Growing up as the son of Polish immigrants in the western Chicago suburb of Argo, Ted Kluszewski (Klu) surely didn't expect to be a college football star and a major-league MVP. He graduated from high school in 1942 and went to work full-time at the local starch plant. Tragically, his mother Josephine passed away in August 1943, and his father John died in March 1944. The six Klu children were left to fend for themselves, but Ted spent the summer of 1944 working hard to save money, hoping to earn enough to marry his high-school sweetheart, Eleanor Guckel.

Work was Klu's focus, and baseball wasn't on his radar. He did play some sandlot football, however, and his life would take a dramatic turn thanks to one of those amateur games. During one of those games, he was noticed by someone who happened to be a close friend of Indiana University head football coach Bo McMillin. When coach McMillin heard about Ted, an IU official was sent to Argo to offer him a scholarship to play football.

The war had stripped Indiana of most of its talent, and McMillin scrambled to find enough experienced players to fill out a roster.

Only 48 players came out for the first practice in 1944. Of the 48, 20 were classified as 4-F by the draft board. Klu had a childhood pelvic operation that made him unfit (4-F) for the military.

Klu quickly made his fitness felt, earning a spot with the first team at end and backup-kicker. His first game was a 72–0 rout of Ft. Knox, a nearby military base whose team was full of college players still in the Army. Following a loss to Illinois the next week, Klu made an impact as the Hoosiers stunned the college football world by beating Michigan 20–0 in Ann Arbor. In the fourth quarter with IU up, 13–0, Klu caught a pass and rambled 38 yards to the Michigan 27-yard line, setting up Indiana's final score of the day and sealing the win. It was Michigan's first conference loss since 1942 and served notice that McMillin was putting together something special in Bloomington. The Hoosiers would go on to a 4–3 record in conference and a 7–3 mark overall. Klu was fit enough to play 441 out of a possible 600 minutes for the Hoosiers in IU's single-platoon system, showing his toughness.

In 1945, the Hoosiers went undefeated and ended the season ranked fourth in the country. Klu again played end on offense and outside linebacker on defense and was an integral part of the Hoosier success. The team had other stars like All-Americans: George Taliaferro, Pete Pihos, Russ Deal, Bob Ravensberg, and Howard Brown.

Being a great football player wasn't all that Klu is remembered for. He was also one of the greatest baseball players for the Hoosiers as well.

Legends of his mammoth home run shots are almost unbelievable. At the time, the Hoosier baseball team played at Jordan Field, which was located where today's main parking lot for the Indiana Memorial Union is located. The southeast corner of that lot was home plate, and the outer perimeter ("outfield wall") was a berm or terrace that encircled much of the field and still exists to this day. It is the northern border of the parking lot.

In his first college game, Klu came up to bat with the game tied 5–5 in the bottom of the ninth inning against the Michigan State Spartans. *The Indiana Daily Student* reported that "The big outfielder belted the first ball pitched to him far over right field and the adjacent roadway onto the green grass of the B and E Building lawn for a home run and a seven-to-five verdict."

Another of Klu's great blasts is reported by several witnesses and football All-American Russ Deal. It is said to have hit the roof of the fieldhouse, 600 feet from home. "The biggest story my dad told is that he saw Ted Kluszewski, in the spring of 1945, hit a ball out of right field off the top of the Old Fieldhouse there," says Mark Deal, IU's current director of football operations and the son of Russ Deal, an IU Hall-of-Famer and a member of the Hoosiers' undefeated 1945 team. "When you stand down there and look, and you think that he hit a ball off the top of the roof there, you say, 'Wow. That's quite a poke.' I know it's true, because my dad saw it. He said he saw him do it."

Oddly, these aren't the only stories about Klu's tape-measure homers. But then again, the man they called the "Big Klu" enjoyed an unbelievable time at Indiana. He was a stellar football player during the 1944 and 1945 seasons. But it was his short baseball career, and a brush with fate, that really sets him apart in IU history.

The outbreak of World War II caused the need to ration and sacrifice in many ways. Such sacrifices included travel restrictions, and in late 1942, the Director of War Defense Transportation Joseph Eastman asked Major League Baseball to curtail the travel of teams during spring training as much as possible. In response, the Cincinnati Reds and the minor-league Indianapolis Indians agreed to relocate their spring training camps to Bloomington. The Reds' first order of business was to dispatch their groundskeeper from their home park in Cincinnati to Bloomington to take a look at the facilities.

Klu was in the market to earn some money, and his physical strength would be an asset for the Red's groundskeeper. He also hoped to play a little baseball to stay in shape for football season. Little did he know that fate was about to touch him on the shoulder yet again.

Each day, the Reds would go through their paces on Jordan Field first, then the IU Baseball Hoosiers would take to the diamond to conduct their workout. The Red's grounds crew would stick around while IU went through its practice, then they would take over the field when the Hoosiers were finished to get the field ready for the next day.

Exactly what drew Marty Schwab's (head groundskeeper) eye to Klu, outside of Ted's massive physique, has been lost to the ages, although there naturally are a few legends. The book *The Big Klu* says that, while Schwab watched, Klu hit a few balls over the centerfield embankment at Jordan Field, a feat none of the Reds' hitters could match. Consequently, the feat was communicated to the Red's manager and he wanted Klu.

To the benefit of IU, Klu stayed for the undefeated 1945 football season, ending in a 26–0 win over Purdue that was nationally broadcast on both the NBC and Mutual radio networks in front of a huge live crowd of more than 27,000 fans in the 10th Street Memorial Stadium. In baseball, IU's season ended with a 12–8–2 record. Klu finished his only year of IU baseball with a .443 batting average, the highest in IU history at the time. The record stood for decades. In 11 conference games, he hit .409 with 18 hits and 11 runs.

After two years at Indiana, Klu was paid a bonus to sign with the Cincinnati Reds and begin in the minors, where he would be taught how to play first base. After that, he was called-up to be the Red's first baseman and didn't disappoint. He hit .274 with 12 homers and 57 RBIs during his first season, and he hit .309 with eight homers and 68 RBIs in 1949. His breakout year came in 1950 when he hit

.307 with 25 homers and 111 RBIs, and three years later, he landed on the NL All-Star team during a season that saw him hit .316 with 40 home runs and 108 RBIs. In 1954, he was an All-Star again, and he finished second in the MVP voting after hitting .326 with 49 homers and 141 RBIs.

He enjoyed a 15-year career for the Reds, Pittsburgh Pirates, Chicago White Sox, and Los Angeles Angels before a back injury in 1956 took its toll and he retired in 1961 at the age of 36. He finished his career as a four-time All-Star who was a career .298 hitter with 279 homers and 1,028 RBIs.

Klu ran a restaurant (Jack and Klu's Charcoal Steakhouse) after retiring. Then in 1968 the Red's lured him back to baseball as their minor-league hitting instructor. For the next 18 years, he would spend time working at both the minor- and major-league levels with the Reds' hitters.

The Reds have erected a statue outside Great American Ballpark in Klu's honor, and his number (18) has been retired by the Reds. In 1962, he was inducted into the Cincinnati Reds Hall of Fame. In 1974, he was inducted into the National Polish American Sports Hall of Fame. He was elected to the IU Athletics Hall of Fame as part of the inaugural Class of 1982.

Klu spent just 18 months on the campus of Indiana University, but the stories that surround his short stint at IU have stood the test of time. Nearly 70 years after his only baseball season in a Hoosier uniform, he is still regarded by most as Indiana's best baseball player of all time, and his legend will live in Bloomington forever.

Pete Pihos: Greatest All-Around Football Player

Peter Louis Pihos was born to Greek immigrants Louis and Mary Pihos in Orlando, Florida. Pete's father ran an all-night restaurant. Pete attended Orlando High School, where he played football as a tackle and basketball as a guard. After Pete's father was

killed by a robber at his restaurant, his mother moved the family to Chicago, where he attended Austin High School as a junior. Indiana coach Bo McMillin recruited Pihos as one of the building blocks to his Hoosier football dynasty.

Mark Deal, Indiana's Assistant Athletic director in charge of Alumni Relations, had only the highest praise for Pihos, saying, "Pete Pihos . . . —in my opinion, in my father's opinion [who was a team captain and his teammate], and in George Taliaferro's opinion [who was his teammate]—is the greatest football player to ever play at Indiana University." As for professional football accolades, former Eagles coach Greasy Neale felt Pihos was virtually unstoppable, once saying, "When he gets his hands on a ball, there isn't much the defense can do. He just runs over people."

Pete Pihos was a man who defined what it meant to be a warrior both on and off the football field. So, in addition to earning honors as an All-American football player, Pihos earned honors for his bravery; he was one of the men who stormed the beaches at Normandy. He served in the 35th Infantry Division under George S. Patton, who awarded him a battlefield commission to second lieutenant. He was awarded the Bronze Star and Silver Star medals for bravery. He was granted a furlough to return to Indiana University in September 1945 while awaiting his final discharge.

When Pihos returned to Indiana after his military service, he played fullback for the 1945 Hoosier team that compiled the only undefeated record (9–0–1) in IU football history, won IU's first Big Ten Conference championship, and finished the season ranked fourth in the final AP Poll.

He had only two days of practice before his first game, Indiana's second game of the season, against Northwestern. He scored Indiana's only touchdown in the 7–7 game, when he caught a pass at the Northwestern five-yard line and dragged three defenders with him over the goal line.

He scored the first two touchdowns in Indiana's 26–0 win over Purdue in the final game of the year. Pihos finished the season having carried the ball 92 times for 410 yards and seven touchdowns. He earned first-team All-America honors from *Yank*, the Army weekly magazine, and finished eighth in voting for the Heisman Trophy.

As a senior, Pihos played three positions (fullback, halfback, and quarterback) and was named the most valuable player on the 1946 Indiana Hoosiers football team. In a show of versatility, and despite suffering from illness and injury during the 1946 season, he carried the ball 76 times for 262 rushing yards, completed seven of twelve passes for 84 passing yards, had ten catches for 213 receiving yards, and scored eight touchdowns. He ended his college career by scoring three touchdowns against the Purdue Boilermakers, helping the Hoosiers win the Old Oaken Bucket for the third straight year. Pihos finished third in the voting for the *Chicago Tribune* Silver Football as the most valuable player in the Big Ten Conference.

In four seasons at Indiana, Pihos scored 138 points, which was then the Hoosier's all-time scoring record. He also broke Indiana career records for touchdowns and receptions. Bo McMillin, Indiana's head football coach since 1934, called Pihos "the greatest all around football player our team has known in my time at Indiana."

Pihos was selected by the Philadelphia Eagles in the 1945 NFL draft, but he continued to play for IU in 1945 and 1946. In February 1947, he signed to join the Eagles after his graduation in June. In his first NFL season, he caught 23 passes for 382 yards and seven touchdowns. He also blocked a punt by Sammy Baugh and returned it 26 yards for a touchdown against the Washington Redskins.

In 1947, the Eagles captured its first division championship. In the playoff game against the Pittsburgh Steelers for the Eastern Division title, Pihos blocked a punt to set up the first touchdown in the Eagles' 21–0 win. The Eagles then lost 28–21 to the Chicago Cardinals in the 1947 NFL Championship Game. Pihos caught three passes for 27 yards in that game and intercepted a pass while playing defense. The Eagles then won consecutive NFL championship

games in 1948 and 1949. Pihos scored the only offensive touchdown of the 1949 championship game via a 31-yard reception in the second quarter during a heavy downpour.

Pihos's 766 receiving yards and 11 receiving touchdowns in 1948 were both the second-most in the NFL that season. He earned first-team All-Pro recognition in 1948 from United Press (UP), *New York Daily News*, *Chicago Herald-American*, and *Pro Football Illustrated*, and in 1949 from the International News Service, UP, Associated Press, and *New York Daily News*. He was invited to his first of six-straight Pro Bowls after the 1950 season. In 1951, Pihos led the Eagles in receptions and receiving yards and intercepted two passes as a defensive end.

Pihos trained heavily during the off-season prior to 1953. He went on to have his greatest statistical success over the next three seasons, which were ultimately his final three. He recorded similar statistics over that three-year span (185 receptions, 2,785 yards, and 27 touchdowns) to his first six seasons (188 receptions, 2,834 yards, and 34 touchdowns). Pihos led the NFL in receptions in each of his final three seasons, in receiving yards twice, and in receiving touchdowns once. In 1953, he became the third player to record a "triple crown" in receiving; he led the NFL in receptions (63), receiving yards (1,049), and receiving touchdowns (10) that season.

In November 1955, Pihos announced that the current season would be his last as a player. In his final NFL game, on December 11 against the Chicago Bears, he caught 11 passes for 114 yards. He retired after playing in the Pro Bowl that January, in which he caught four passes and scored the East's first touchdown by out-leaping defender Jack Christiansen to snag a 12-yard pass from Eddie LeBaron. During his nine seasons of play with the Eagles, Pihos missed just one game.

Pihos received numerous honors for his accomplishments as a football player. In October 1961, Pihos was named to the Helms Athletic Foundation's Major League Football Hall of

Fame. In February 1966, he was elected to the College Football Hall of Fame. He was the first Hoosiers football player to receive the honor. In a halftime ceremony during the opening game of Indiana's 1966 season, IU presented Pihos with a special citation for his contribution to the university through football. In August 1969, as part of the NFL's 50th anniversary, the Pro Football Hall of Fame selected all-decade teams for each of the league's first five decades. Pihos was selected as an end on the NFL 1940s All-Decade Team. In February 1970, he was elected to the Pro Football Hall of Fame. At the induction ceremony in August 1970, a telegram was presented from Vice President Spiro Agnew calling Pihos "the golden Greek of football" and "the most durable and versatile football player" of his time.

In 1978, Pihos was inducted into the Indiana Football Hall of Fame. In 1982, he was one of the inaugural inductees into the Indiana Hoosiers Hall of Fame. In November 1987, he was one of the 11 inaugural inductees into the Philadelphia Eagles Honor Roll.

Russ "Mutt" Deal: Undefeated Team Captain

Russ "Mutt" Deal came to IU to play football in 1940 from Bicknell, 60 miles southwest of Bloomington. In high school, he was an All-State tackle.

Just like so many other college athletes during WWII, Deal had to go off to the Army in the middle of his college career. He served in 1943 and 1944 and then returned to IU in 1945. He won football letters in 1941, 1942, 1945, and 1946, and was captain of IU's undefeated Big Ten Championship Team in 1945 and was a third-team All-American as a tackle. He was All–Big Ten in 1946 and played the following year in the College All-Star Game.

After graduating from IU in 1947, Deal was signed by the Baltimore Colts of the AAFC to play for former Purdue and Green Bay coach Cecil Isbell. So, immediately following the college All-Star game at Soldier Field in Chicago, he and his wife prepared to leave

for Baltimore. That is, until he received a call from IU's Bo McMillin, who advised him to drive the short distance over to Hobart, Indiana, and interview for a football coach job at Hobart High School. Bo said that he'd make more money and wouldn't get hurt.

Mutt did go to Hobart, took the job, and became a legend in Indiana high school football. His record was 114–48–7 in 17 seasons. He sent numerous players off to play college and even professional football. Of his football player alumni, 32 have become coaches themselves. He was Hobart Junior High School's principal from 1966 to 1974 and Hobart Senior High School's principal from 1974 until retirement.

Deal is a 1976 Indiana Football Hall of Fame recipient. He won the Z. G. Clevenger Award in 1983 because of his outstanding contributions to IU through service to its athletics program. He was selected for the IU Athletics Hall of Fame in 1993.

After leaving IU, he kept a life-long friendship with Branch McCracken, who was one of his freshman football coaches. Even though McCracken had won the 1940 NCAA Championship for IU, he still helped Bo McMillin coach the football team. Deal, who was affectionately known as Mutt, would phone Branch about the IU basketball season and often be offered free tickets for him and his two sons Mike and Mark (both future IU football players) to attend basketball games.

Bob Ravensberg: 1945 All American

Bob Ravensberg was born in Bellevue, Kentucky, where he was a two-time Kentucky high school pole vault champion and set a state record in the event.

Recruited to IU by Bo McMillin, Ravensberg won varsity letters in football in 1943, 1944, 1945, and 1947. He was a starter on IU's 1945 team, the school's only undefeated and outright Big Ten Conference championship team. In 1945, he was selected as a consensus first-team All-American football player. On that team,

there were three other All–Big Ten players in Ted Kluszewski, Pete Pihos, and George Taliaferro. Ravensberg was the only consensus first-team All-American football player on that team (an end).

After college, Ravensberg played for the powerful Chicago Cardinals NFL teams in 1948–1949. In '48 the Cards beat cross-town rival Chicago Bears to play again in the NFL championship as defending champs.

After two professional seasons, Bob came back to IU as an assistant football coach for the 1950 and 1951 seasons. Then he went into business in St. Louis and lived in Webster Groves, MO.

George Taliaferro: Triple Threat

George Taliaferro's family moved from Tennessee to Indiana when his father took a job with the steel mills. Like many African American kids during that time, Taliaferro grew up admiring Joe Louis and wanting to be a boxer. He even caddied for Louis when the fighter drove from Chicago to play golf in Gary, Indiana. "He said he liked me because I'd always find his golf balls," Taliaferro remembered. But Taliaferro's mother forbade him to box. "My dad insisted that I do something to burn off energy," he said. "Football was that something." He graduated from Gary Roosevelt High School, where he was an outstanding high school athlete. George also grew up a fan of the Chicago Bears NFL team.

After high school, Taliaferro's family insisted that he get a college education. Indiana's coach Bo McMillin recruited him to play for the Hoosiers, who were on the rise in Big Ten football. He came to IU in 1945

When he arrived at Indiana, Taliaferro wasn't happy feeling like a second-class citizen. After being dropped off to stay with a black family, Taliaferro was eager to move onto campus to experience life in the dorms.

As the first day of school approached, Taliaferro was told black students didn't live in dorms. "I called my father and told him I didn't want to be in a place where I couldn't live on campus, where I couldn't swim in the pool, and where I couldn't sit in the bottom section of the movie theater," Taliaferro said. His father told him there were other reasons he was there, and then he hung up the phone. George said, "I was never so hurt because I thought the one person who could understand being discriminated against was him." That tough love stemmed from two things his parents, neither of whom went past sixth grade, told him every day as he grew up. "They'd say, 'We love you,'" he recalled. "And, 'You must be educated.'"

So Taliaferro stayed at IU, and he released that pent-up frustration on the football field. He remembered walking out on the field for his first college game at Michigan on Sept. 22, 1945 and looking at the fans who filled the 85,000-seat stadium—the biggest crowd he had ever seen in his life.

"Every black person from Gary must have come to that game, and when I looked up, I asked God, 'Why am I here?'" Taliaferro said. "And then I said, 'They're going to catch hell catching me.'" And they did. He put on a show.

Taliaferro scored a touchdown (another was called back) in Indiana's 13–7 win. It was the start of the only undefeated season in Indiana history (9–0–1), the Hoosiers' only outright Big Ten title (they shared a championship in 1967), and the highest season-ending school ranking (fourth). It was also the first of three All-America seasons at Indiana for Taliaferro, who led the team twice in rushing (1945 and 1948), three times in punting (1945, 1947, 1948), and once in passing (1948). His 95-yard kickoff return against Minnesota in 1945 still ranks ninth on Indiana's all-time list. As a three-time All-American, Taliaferro led the Hoosiers in rushing twice, punting in 1945, and passing in 1948. Taliaferro helped break the color barrier in sports, playing for the Hoosiers two years before Jackie

Robinson suited up for the Brooklyn Dodgers. He was inducted into the College Football Hall of Fame in 1981.

Since there were no student deferments in those years, George was drafted into the Army after his freshman year and shipped to an Army base in Virginia. He was one of 66 men on the bus from Indiana to Virginia. When he arrived, the other 65 were taken to the barracks; Taliaferro was taken to the office of the commanding officer who said, "I'm happy to have you as a member of our company, and I'm looking forward to having you bring us a championship team in football." Taliaferro recalled "I got hot, right there, and I told him I didn't plan to play."

The commanding officer then leaned forward in his seat, put his elbows on his desk and laid out his two options: play football during his one-year commitment, or go to officer's candidate school with an enlistment of three years.

Taliaferro then said he'd see him on the football field and was the captain of the Army team that won a Mid-Atlantic title before he returned to Indiana.

After graduation from IU, Taliaferro—a halfback, quarterback, and punter—was picked by the Chicago Bears in the thirteenth round of the 1949 NFL Draft, but instead chose to play for the Los Angeles Dons of the All-America Football Conference. This made him the first African American drafted by an NFL team. He played with the Dons in 1949, then moved to the NFL, where he played with the New York Yanks (1950–1951), Dallas Texans (1952), Baltimore Colts (1953–1954), and Philadelphia Eagles (1955). He went to the Pro Bowl in 1951, 1952, and 1953. In seven NFL seasons, Taliaferro played an unheard-of seven positions: quarterback, running back, wide receiver, punter, kick returner, punt returner, and defensive back. During his seven-year professional career, Taliaferro had 15 rushing touchdowns, 1,300 receiving yards, 843 passing yards, and 35 forced fumbles (13 recovered). He averaged 21 yards on kickoff returns, 7.8 yards on punt returns, and 37.7 yards on punts as he

established himself as the most versatile player in NFL history. He was Rookie of the Year in 1949 with the Yanks.

After his career ended, Taliaferro turned down an opportunity to be head coach at Morgan State but served as an unpaid assistant for 13 years and was the dean of students for two years.

He returned to Bloomington in 1972 to become a special assistant to the school president at Indiana University. Both he and his wife, Viola (who became a judge), lived in Bloomington until 2018 when they moved into a retirement home.

Bobby "Slick" Leonard: Cool as a Cucumber

Bobby Leonard—a six-foot, three-inch guard—was recruited to IU from Gerstmeyer High School in Terre Haute, where he was the state champion in tennis and the area's top basketball player.

Known for his long, high, two-handed set-shots, Bobby Leonard could deflate road crowds as much has he exhilarated the Hoosier faithful at IU's fieldhouse. Leonard was the second-leading scorer to Don Schlundt. He was the second Hoosier, after Schlundt, to score 1000 points during his career (1,098). He was a two time All-American for the Hoosiers and captain of IU's 1953 national champions. He hit the game-winning free throws to give Indiana the NCAA championship. He captained two Big Ten championship teams and was the MVP as a sophomore of the East–West college All-Star game in Madison Square Garden.

Jim Enright was a Hall of Fame sports writer for the *Chicago Herald-American* and *The Sporting News,* a college basketball referee with NCAA Final Four and Olympic officiating experience, and Naismith Memorial Basketball Hall of Fame inductee. He wrote in the 1954 Collegiate Basketball Record Book a prediction that Indiana University, 1953 NCAA champion, also would win the 1954 tournament.

He explained, "Anchorman for this Hoosier repeat is Bob Leonard. This fellow, Leonard, is to basketball what Robin Roberts is to baseball, Ben Hogan to golf, and Eddie Arcaro to horse racing. . . . Such a rating covers a lot of ground—but so does Leonard. Pound-for-pound, dribble-for-dribble, pass-for-pass, and shot-for-shot—Bob is, without question, the game's greatest individual player in my book. As the quarterback of the Indiana team, he also reacts to steam-heated pressure with cucumber coolness. Those words describe the man now known as 'Slick' after he hit the free throw to give the Hoosiers a 69–68 victory over Kansas in the intense 1953 title game."

Leonard was selected with the first pick of the second round of the 1954 NBA draft. He spent most of his seven-year professional playing career with the Lakers (four years in Minneapolis, and one year following the team's move to Los Angeles), followed by two years with the Chicago Packers/Zephyrs. In his final season as a player, he also coached the Zephyrs. The next year, the team moved to Baltimore and became the Bullets; Leonard coached them for one more year. Leonard proved to be a fine point guard as a pro, averaging as many as 16.1 points and 5.4 assists in a season.

Five years after coaching the Bullets, Leonard became the coach of the Indiana Pacers in the ABA. He held that position for nearly 12 years. Leonard led the Pacers to three ABA championships before the ABA–NBA merger in June 1976.

Leonard returned to the Pacers in 1985 as a color commentator, first for television with Jerry Baker, then on radio, where he remains alongside Mark Boyle on WFNI 1070 AM. His trademark phrase is "Boom, baby!" for a successful three-point shot by a Pacers player.

On February 14, 2014, Leonard was named as a 2014 inductee to the Naismith Memorial Basketball Hall of Fame; he was formally inducted on August 8 of that year. He was also inducted as a charter member into the IU Athletics Hall of Fame.

Don Schlundt: Three-Time All American

Six-foot, ten-inch Don Schlundt came to IU from Washington Clay High School in South Bend, Indiana, where he once scored 52 points in a basketball game. He was one of America's top recruits and was planning to play basketball for Adolf Rupp at Kentucky University until he met Branch McCracken, whom he later described as one of the finest coaches and men in the country.

The NCAA allowed freshmen to play varsity sports because of the Korean War. Schlundt played as a freshman in 1951 and started slowly competing with Lou Scott who was also six feet, ten inches tall. In his first game, Schlundt only scored six points. But coupled with another freshman star, Bobby Leonard, the Hoosiers began to click and finished 16–6. Schlundt averaged 17.1 points per game, and Leonard averaged 14.5. These were the only players on the team with double-figure scoring averages. From that season forward, Don Schlundt was to become one of the nation's most dominating big men.

The next season, IU won the Big Ten and the NCAA tournament and finished the season 23–3. During that year, Schlundt averaged 25.4 points per game. He shot 310 free throws and made 249 for just over an 80 percent average. He broke his own single-game scoring mark with 39 points in a 91–88 victory over Michigan. In 1954, Schlundt averaged 24.3 points per game and shot field goals at a 50 percent clip and free throws at 77 percent. In 1955, he averaged 26 points a game with a free throw shooting percentage of 79 percent. Schlundt was named an All-American in 1953, '54, and '55. Schlundt's Indiana teams earned consecutive Big Ten championships ('53 and '54) and had a combined 43–7 record.

He left IU as the school's all-time leading scorer with 2,192 points—a mark that stood for 32 years until Steve Alford broke it. He was elected to the Indiana University athletics Hall of Fame in 1982 and is also a member of the Indiana Basketball Hall of Fame. Schlundt was ranked among the nation's leaders in free-throw

percentage in 1953 (7th) and 1955 (40th). He was ranked among the nation's leaders in field-goal percentage in 1952 (20th), 1953 (47th), and 1954 (10th). He was the leading scorer and rebounder for 1953 NCAA Tournament. He was named to 1953 All-NCAA Tournament team and averaged 27 points in six NCAA Tournament games in 1953 and 1954.

After graduating from Indiana University, Schlundt was selected 16th by the first-place Syracuse Nationals in the 1955 NBA draft. He never played in the league and chose a career in business instead.

Walt Bellamy: Mr. Rebound

Walt Bellamy chose to play basketball at Indiana. "In the summer after my junior year of high school, I played with some guys from Indiana", he said. "Indiana at the time was the closest school to the South that would accept African-Americans. It was an easy transition for me to make. Not that I was naive to what was going on in Bloomington in terms of the times, but it didn't translate to the athletic department or the classroom. Every relationship I had at IU was good."

Bellamy graduated from Indiana University with the most rebounds in a career—1,087 in only 70 games (15.5 per game). He also averaged 20.6 points per game and shot 51.7 percent from the floor for his college career. As a senior, Bellamy averaged 17.8 rebounds per game (still Indiana's record). He also holds the school records for most rebounds in a season (649) and most double-doubles in a career (59). In 2000, he was selected to IU's All-Century Team.

Bellamy no longer holds the Indiana record for career rebounds, due largely to the fact his career was limited to a mere 70 games, but it's unlikely his record average of 15.5 per game will ever be broken. In the 54 years since he completed his college career, there have been only a dozen double-figure seasons by Hoosier players, and only IU greats George McGinnis (14.7 in 1971) and Steve Downing

(15.1 in 1972) approached Bellamy's career mark in a single year. In 1960, he led IU to a 20–4 record and a second-place finish in the Big Ten. Unfortunately, that was the season in which a guy named Bob Knight was the sixth man on a national-champ powerhouse team at Ohio State. They won the league by two games and claimed Ohio State's only NCAA championship.

In his final college game, Walt set Indiana and Big-Ten-Conference records that still stand with 33 rebounds (and 28 points) in an 82–67 win over Michigan. Bellamy was named an All-American in both his junior and senior year (1960 and 1961). Bellamy was the first Hoosier taken number one in the NBA draft, and the first Hoosier named NBA Rookie of the Year.

In the 1960 Summer Olympics, Bellamy was the starting center on the gold medal–winning American basketball team. Ten of the 12 college players on the undefeated American squad eventually went on to play professionally in the NBA, including fellow Big Ten player Terry Dischinger and fellow future Hall-of-Famers Jerry West, Oscar Robertson, and Jerry Lucas.

After graduation from IU, Walt Bellamy had a stellar 14-year career in the NBA. He was named the NBA Rookie of the Year in 1962 after having, arguably, one of the three greatest rookie seasons in NBA history (the other two being Wilt Chamberlain and Oscar Robertson). His average of 31.6 points per game that season is second all-time for a rookie to Wilt Chamberlain's 37.6, and the 19 rebounds per game he averaged that season is the third best all-time rookie mark. No NBA rookie has since surpassed Bellamy's 973 field goals during the 1961–62 season.

Bellamy averaged 31.6 points per game and 19.0 rebounds per game during his rookie season. He also led the NBA in field goal percentage in his rookie season and had a 23-point, 17-rebound performance in the 1962 NBA All-Star Game. In the 1964–65 season, Bellamy scored 30 points and 37 rebounds in a win against the St. Louis Hawks. His 37 rebounds was his career-high in rebounds.

Walt played with the Chicago Packers for his first four seasons in the NBA along with two other IU Hall of Fame basketball players: Archie Dees and Bobby "Slick" Leonard. The Packers became the Baltimore Bullets before Bellamy was traded to the New York Knicks for three players and cash a few games into the 1965–66 season. Walt has a record which still stands: he played in 88 regular season games during the 1968–69 season.

Bellamy ended his NBA career with 20,941 points and 14,241 rebounds and is a two-time Naismith Memorial Basketball Hall of Fame inductee, being inducted in 1993 for his individual career, and in 2010 as a member of the 1960 United States men's Olympic basketball team.

Earl Faison: The Tree

On the football field, Earl Faison was an All-Star in high school, college, and the pros. Off the field, he was a civil rights activist, a community leader, a dedicated educator, and a friend to countless people.

Faison, a Newport News, Virginia native, was a highly-recruited star at Huntington High School, where he excelled in football, basketball, and track and field. Earl helped the Huntington Vikings win six Virginia Interscholastic Association state championships before graduating in 1957. During the summer months when he

was in high school, he was a lifeguard at the swimming pool in the East End. He taught many kids how to swim.

He came to IU during a time of great turmoil as rising-star football coach Phil Dickens was forced to sit out a one-year suspension by the Big Ten for recruiting violations. Later, the NCAA gave Indiana the most severe penalty they ever handed down, barring all Hoosier varsity sports from postseason play for four years. The NCAA also vacated all Indiana wins during the 1960 Big Ten football season because of improper recruiting practices. The sanctions were a stain on Indiana's notoriously clean record

and undermined the ability to convince talented athletes to come to Bloomington. Despite these drawbacks Faison stayed at Indiana and was a quality young man and a star athlete.

Faison lettered in 1958, '59, and '60 and was an All–Big Ten pick and third-team All American in 1960. He led the Hoosiers in receptions in 1960 and scoring in 1959. During his sophomore season, Earl blocked a field goal and ran 92 yards for a touchdown against Michigan State. His score on that November afternoon in 1958 gave the Hoosiers a 6–0 victory, their first over their MSU since 1940. Faison, IU's Most Valuable Player in 1960, also played in the East–West Shrine Game, the All-America Bowl, and the Hula Bowl.

Faison was the number-seven overall pick of the 1961 American Football League draft, taken by the San Diego Chargers. The NFL's Detroit Lions also drafted him. He played professionally for many years, most of them with the Chargers. Faison earned AFL Rookie of the Year honors and, two seasons later, helped the Chargers win their only championship. A five-time AFL all-star, the six-foot, five-inch, 270-pound Faison was nicknamed "Tree" because he was so difficult for opponents to move. Injuries derailed his career in 1966, and he was subsequently enshrined in the Chargers' Hall of Fame, Indiana University Hall of Fame, and Virginia Sports Hall of Fame.

After his football career, Faison briefly dabbled in acting, including a pair of appearances in *The Beverly Hillbillies*. He returned to California as an educator and football coach, teaching at Lincoln High School. He served as head coach of Lincoln during the era of future-Pro-Football-Hall-of-Famer Marcus Allen. Faison later served as the school's principal. He then taught physical education at Muirlands Junior High School in La Jolla, California. It was there that he coined the term "grab-asser" for unruly students. From there, Faison went on to become the Vice Principal at University City High School in San Diego.

Earl Faison was a member of The Pigskin Club of Washington, D.C.; the National Intercollegiate All-American Football Players Honor Roll; and, in 1997, he was inducted by the San Diego Hall

of Champions into the Breitbard Hall of Fame which honors San Diego's finest athletes both on and off the playing field.

Jimmy Rayl: The Splendid Splinter

From Kokomo High School to Indiana University to the Indiana Pacers, Jimmy Rayl was one of the state's best examples of Hoosier hysteria. Basketball wasn't just a game to Jimmy, it was a genuine hunger. Once, in front of witnesses, Jimmy hit 532 consecutive free throws in a church gym in Kokomo. But he sealed his legend as a shooter in far more public settings. He averaged nearly 30 points per game his senior season and scored over 40 points five times, including some games that became etched in Indiana basketball lore.

There was the game, for example, against top-ranked Muncie Central, where he played with a 101-degree fever, suffered a gash on his forehead requiring four stitches, and still scored 45 points, going 18–30 from the field in a 79–77 victory.

Rayl also played a lead role in what became known as the Church Street Shootout, the final game played in the Church Street Gymnasium at New Castle High School. Rayl scored 49 points, but New Castle guard Ray Pavy scored 51 to give his team the victory.

Rayl set a North-Central-Conference scoring record by the end of his final regular season. He went on to score 40 points in a state tournament game at the Ft. Wayne Coliseum, hitting 18 of 19 free throws, and sinking a jump shot at the final gun to give Kokomo a 92–90 victory over defending state-champion Fort Wayne South.

He was a first-team all-state selection as a junior and senior and during his final season at Kokomo, when he led a team that filled the high school's 7,500-seat gymnasium for every game. He became one of the most written-about and highly-regarded players in the state's basketball history. He was named the 1959's Indiana Mr. Basketball and the recipient of the Trester Award for the state of Indiana his senior year.

Rayl was an obvious choice for Mr. Basketball in 1959, then came to IU. He didn't become a starter until his junior season, when he set the Big Ten's single-game scoring record of 56 points in an overtime victory over Minnesota. He repeated the feat as a senior against Michigan State. This was without three-point field goals (started in 1986) and timing where the clock continued running when the ball went out of bounds, which shortened games. He was taken out with about 3 1/2 minutes remaining, to the dismay of Hoosier fans.

He averaged 29.8 points as a junior and 25.3 as a senior, the drop-off resulting from improved talent around him, namely the addition of three sophomore scorers. The Van Arsdale twins—Tom and Dick—and Jon McGlocklin all went on to play in the NBA. Rayl shot 41.6 percent from the floor and 83.5 percent from the line in 68 games as a Hoosier.

Rayl wasn't opposed to trash-talking opposing players. He once called Ohio State's six-foot, eight-inch center Gary Bradds a "crybaby" during a game. Bradds took a swing at him, and barely missed his head. Later, in the waning moments of the Hoosier 87–85 overtime victory, to stop the clock, Bradds body-blocked Rayl out of bounds in front of the IU student section. The incensed students were out for blood, Bradds's blood, when the referee ejected the big center from the game. Amid a chorus of boos, as Bradds was escorted from the court, he gave the infamous one finger salute to the IU crowd.

Rayl was selected by the Cincinnati Royals in the third round and 23rd pick of the 1963 NBA draft. He later signed and played two seasons for the Indiana Pacers. He averaged 12 points his first year with the Pacers, scoring 30 or more points three times in the final month, and was voted Most Popular Player by fans.

He was a starter at the beginning of the 1969–1970 season, scoring 21 points in the season-opener and hit five 3-pointers, a

franchise record that stood until Roger Brown hit seven in the final game of the ABA Finals in May of 1970.

He held a career average of 11.1 points per game. Rayl also hit the first three-pointer in Pacer history in their second game, an appropriate distinction for one of the state's greatest shooters.

Tom and Dick Van Arsdale: So Much Alike

The Van Arsdale brothers, Tom and Dick, were as alike as one can imagine. They look exactly alike, sound remarkably similar, and had almost identical playing careers.

The Van Arsdale twins grew up in Greenwood, just south of Indianapolis. Since their dad taught mathematics at Emmerich Manual High School, and their mom worked there on the switchboard, both of the twins attended Manual. The twins were tough basketball players who were very competitive in pick-up games at the "Dust Bowl" at Lockfield Gardens. They played on the team that made it all the way to the state final game against Kokomo. Dick led Manual with 26 points, and Tom tallied 17 points before fouling out with 2:54 left in the game. Manual had Kokomo down by seven points with just over a minute to go, but Kokomo rallied to tie the score at 62–62 with 14 seconds left, sending the game into overtime. In OT, Dick hit a foul shot to tie the score at 66–66 with 26 seconds left, but Ronnie Hughes was fouled with three seconds left. He made both foul shots for Kokomo, who won the game 68–66. The Van Arsdale twins were named co-recipients of the Trester Award for Mental Attitude. Tom and Dick were also co-Mr. Basketballs in '61.

When the twins got to IU, they both pledged Sigma Alpha Epsilon Fraternity and moved into the chapterhouse on Jordan Avenue. Tall, handsome, and blond-haired, they could easily be recognized on campus, but not differentiated from each other. In 1961, no freshmen were eligible to play varsity sports, so Tom and Dick played on the talented freshman team featuring other stars—

Jon McGlocklin and Vick Bender. The team always played an intra-squad game immediately before the Varsity Hoosiers took the court for their game. The freshmen were so good that the fieldhouse was virtually full for every freshman intra-squad game. Even though there were no cheerleaders or public address announcements, the fans roared when Tom or Dick scored or rebounded. That team was so good that, in their one contest for the year against the varsity, they had the game under control until the coach pulled Tom, Dick, John McGlocklin, and Vick Bender out of the game. The students vehemently protested, but coach McCracken couldn't let the varsity be beaten by freshman.

Starting in their sophomore year, both Tom and Dick were starters on the Hoosier varsity for 1963–65. They were co-MVPs in both '64 and '65. Both were All–Big Ten and All-Americans in 1965. Tom ended his IU career with 1,252 points and 723 rebounds. Dick finished IU career with 1,240 points and 719 rebounds.

They went on to have good playing careers in the NBA. Tom was selected by the Detroit Pistons in the second round of the 1965 NBA draft. He was named to the NBA All-Rookie Team in 1966 and played 12 seasons with the Pistons, the Cincinnati Royals, the Kansas City–Omaha Kings, the Philadelphia 76ers, the Atlanta Hawks, and the Phoenix Suns. He was a three-time All-Star and was consistently one of the best free throw shooters in the NBA over his career. He retired from play in 1977. Tom still holds the NBA record for most career games played without a playoff appearance, playing 929 games without making a single playoff appearance. Van Arsdale is also the highest-scoring player (14,232 career points) in NBA history without a playoff appearance.

Dick was selected by the New York Knicks in the second round of the 1965 NBA draft. He was named to the NBA All-Rookie Team in 1966 and played in the NBA for 12 seasons; three with the Knicks and the remainder with the Phoenix Suns (after he was selected in the 1968 expansion draft). Dick, a three-time All-Star,

was also consistently one of the best free throw shooters in the NBA over his career. He retired from play in 1977. He is remembered in Phoenix basketball lore as the "original Sun"

Both Dick and Tom had career peaks between 1968 and '72. In this stretch, although on separate teams, Dick averaged 21 points a game and Tom averaged 21.1.

During the NBA off-seasons, the brothers were stockbrokers. After basketball, they started a real-estate business. Today Tom and Dick own an art studio.

Harry Gonso: IU Board of Trustees

Harry Gonso, an outstanding student athlete from Findlay, Ohio, was recruited to IU by Coach John Pont. Gonso was an honor student, a top football prospect, and one of the nation's top high school swimmers and divers, breaking a swimming record and winning the Ohio diving title. He also competed in track.

Arriving in Bloomington in 1966, Gonso majored in pre-law. At the time, freshmen were not eligible to play varsity sports, so Gonso worked out with a notable group of first-year recruits that melded with veteran Hoosier players to bring glory and fame to IU the next season.

Gonso became one of the finest quarterbacks in the history of Indiana University, he was selected as team MVP for his performance and his leadership twice. Gonso was the starting quarterback for three years and was the school's all-time leader in both passing yardage and passing touchdowns until 1980. He still stands eighth on the all-time yardage list and third in passing scores.

Gonso was the Most Valuable Player on the IU squad that played Southern California in the Rose Bowl following the 1967 season. That year, he completed 67 of 143 passes for 931 yards and nine touchdowns and was an All–Big Ten selection.

Despite missing the better portion of two games as a junior, he still finished the year with 1,109 passing yards and 12 touchdowns and won team MVP honors for the second consecutive season. The five-foot, eleven-inch, 187-pound Gonso finished his career by throwing for 1,336 yards and 11 touchdowns as a senior.

Gonso achieved recognition as Academic All–Big Ten; Academic All-American; National Honor Scholar; and recipient of prestigious Hoosier Award. He was inducted into the IU Athletics Hall of Fame in 1982. He was inducted into the Indiana Football Hall of Fame in 2007.

After graduation, Harry Gonso enrolled in the Indiana University School of Law from which he graduated in 1973. He was Governor Mitch Daniels's Senior Counsel and Chief of Staff from 2005 to 2007, has served on IU Board of Trustees for 18 years, was Vice-President of the Board from 1988 to 1994, and chaired two IU Presidential Search Committees. He eventually became a Partner at Ice Miller, LLP.

John Isenbarger: Punt, John, Punt

All-around athlete John Isenbarger came to IU from Muncie Central, Indiana, where he had been named team MVP in football, basketball, and track 1965–1966. He won three letters in football, three in basketball, and three in track. In football, he was UPI All-State and All-Conference two years as a quarterback. His 1965 team only had two losses in the tough North Central Conference. In basketball, he was All-Conference and All-State as a guard. He finished fourth in pole vault at the state meet.

At Indiana, John joined a talented 1966 freshman class that would join some talented veterans in 1967 to win the Big Ten and a trip to the Rose Bowl to play USC. He became a two-time All–Big Ten selection and led the Big Ten in punting in 1967 and in rushing in 1969. He was a *The Sporting News* All-American and played in the Hula Bowl All-Star Game, Coaches All-American Game, East–West

Game, and College All-Star Game in Chicago in 1970. He won the L. G. Balfour Award for excellence in athletics, school citizenship, and scholastic endeavor. He was inducted into the IU Athletics Hall of Fame in 1991.

In 1967, Isenbarger was a tailback and punter and earned All-American honors. During that season, the Indiana "Cardiac Kids" had close games. One Saturday, as the 3–0 Hoosiers were playing Iowa, John ran from punt formation, by design, on a fourth-and-nine from the IU 18 and gained the first down. It seemed that the Hoosiers had the game in-hand later when, again, John ran from punt formation on fourth down. This time he failed, setting up the Hawkeyes for a go-ahead touchdown. Never daunted, Indiana came back to drive 60 yards for a score with 53 seconds left and win 21–17.

Isenbarger, incredibly, did the same thing against Michigan the next week, instead of punting late in the game, he ran from his own 13-yard line and failed to get the first down. Michigan tied the score, and Pont's team had to drive 85 yards to win 27–20 in the last two minutes. Isenbarger thus became one of the Big Ten's most celebrated backs of the year. That was the third time during the season Isenbarger had decided on his own to run instead of punt and the second time he had failed. "When he did it against Michigan, it was the maddest I've ever been in my life," says Pont, who, in past years, had been with a winner at Miami of Ohio and Yale. Before Pont could say a word to Isenbarger on the bench, however, the big, blond sophomore rushed up to him with his hands on his headgear and yelled something.

"Coach!" Isenbarger shouted. "Why do I do things like that?" It was a question Pont would like to have answered.

The suspense of seeing Isenbarger in punt formation has given the crowd at Indiana home games a new chant that went: "Punt, John, punt!" Her son's missteps even led Mrs. Isenbarger to send a

wire to her boy in Phoenix the day Indiana defeated Arizona 42–7. The wire read: DEAR JOHN. PLEASE PUNT.

Isenbarger was drafted by San Francisco of the NFL 1970 and played for 49ers 1970–1973 and then played with Hawaii of the World Football League in 1974.

Jade Butcher: Hometown Hero

Jade Butcher's trip to IU Memorial Stadium was less than three miles from Bloomington High School. He was All-State Honorable Mention in 1964; All-State First Team 1965-1966; Parade Magazine All-American 1965. BHS had a powerhouse program that went undefeated in 1964. Coach John Pont recruited Jade to play with a handful of top prospects in his freshman class at IU. Butcher and his teammates took the Hoosiers to the Rose Bowl in his sophomore season.

Butcher was one of the greatest receivers in IU history. He held Indiana records for passes received (119) and reception yardage (1,919), touchdowns (30) and points (180) at end of his career. He also held IU season-records for touchdowns (10, all three years) and set a Big-Ten record with 30 career touchdown catches.

Butcher was a letterman in 1967, 1968 and 1969. He was first-team All–Big Ten in 1968 and 1969, and All-American in 1969. He was a member of IU's 1967 Big Ten Co-Championship and Rose Bowl team. He was inducted into the IU Athletics Hall of Fame in 1988 and into the Indiana Football Hall of Fame in 2007.

Mark Spitz: Made the Russians Grow Mustaches

It seems that most top sport-stars started perfecting the skills necessary to excel in their sport early in their lives. Mark Spitz's family moved to Hawaii when he was two years old, enabling him to swim at Waikiki beach every day. "You should have seen that

little boy dash into the ocean. He'd run like he was trying to commit suicide," Lenore Spitz, Mark's mother, told a reporter in 1968.

In 1968, Spitz first gained notoriety as a swimmer at the Summer Olympics in Mexico City, coming home with two gold, one silver, and one bronze medal. He was an 18-year-old high student at Santa Clara High School, in California. The family had moved back to the "mainland" to California 12 years earlier.

Mark Spitz set the Olympic record by winning seven Gold Medals at the 1972 Olympics. This record stood for sixteen years until Michael Phelps won eight in 2008.

Spitz decided to attend Indiana University to train with legendary IU swimming coach Doc Counsilman, who was also his Olympic coach in Mexico City. He called choosing Indiana and Counsilman "the biggest decision of my life [and] the best."

He became the Hoosier's most well-known and successful swimmer ever. He won eight individual NCAA titles and contributed to four school NCAA Championships. He won more NCAA

individual championships in 1969 than any other swimmer or diver ever had. His three titles that year tie with 23 other athletes, including IU's Charlie Hickcox and Gary Hall, as the highest number of individual wins in one season.

Nicknamed "Mark the Shark" by his teammates, Spitz went on to be the star of the 1972 Games, winning seven gold medals. In each event, he set the World Record: gold medal, first place 200 m butterfly, 2:00.70; gold medal, first place 4×100 m freestyle relay, 3:26.42; gold medal, first place 200 m freestyle, 1:52.78; gold medal, first place 100 m butterfly, 54.27 gold medal, first place 4×200 m freestyle relay, 7:35.78; gold medal, first place 100 m freestyle, 51.22; and gold medal, first place 4×100 m medley relay, 3:48.16.

Originally, Spitz was reluctant to swim the 100-meter freestyle, fearing the physical stress on his body would bring him a less-than-gold medal finish. Just before the race, he confessed to ABC's Donna de Varona, "I know I say I don't want to swim before every event, but this time I'm serious. If I swim six and win six, I'll be a hero. If I swim seven and win six, I'll be a failure." Spitz won that seventh event by half a stroke in a world-record time of 51.22 seconds.

Spitz had a moustache in an era when male and female swimmers were shaving body hair. He grew the moustache as a rebellion against the clean-cut look imposed on him in college. Spitz said that it took four months to grow, but he became proud of it and decided the moustache was a "good-luck piece."

Spitz is quoted as saying, "When I went to the Olympics, I had every intention of shaving the moustache off, but I realized I was getting so many comments about it—and everybody was talking about it—that I decided to keep it. I had some fun with a Russian coach who asked me if my moustache slowed me down. I said, 'No. As a matter of fact, it deflects water away from my mouth, allows my rear end to rise, and makes me bullet-shaped in the water, and that's what had allowed me to swim so great.' He's translating as fast as he can for the other coaches, and the following year, every Russian male swimmer had a moustache."

He was inducted into the International Swimming Hall of Fame in 1977, the IU Athletics Hall of Fame in 1982, United States Olympic Hall of Fame in 1983, San Jose Sports Hall of Fame in 2007, Long Beach City College Hall of Fame 2007, and the National Jewish Museum Sports Hall of Fame in 2007. He was ranked number 33 on ESPN Sports Century 50 Greatest Athletes in 1999 (the only aquatic athlete to make the list).

At IU from 1968 to 1972, he was a pre-dental student. *Time* magazine asked him if he wanted to return to dental school after the Olympics. "I always wanted to be a dentist from the time I was in high school, and I was accepted to dental school in the spring of 1972. I was planning to go, but after the Olympics, there were other opportunities."

After Spitz retired from competitive swimming at age 22, he was signed by the William Morris (Talent) Agency, which tried to get him into show business while his name was still familiar due to his athletic success. There was a pin-up poster of Spitz wearing his swimsuit and seven gold medals which sold enough to make him the hottest pin-up since Betty Grable. In Spitz's TV debut, he appeared as himself in a skit as a dentist on a Bob Hope special. Hope was quoted saying, "Mark Spitz makes Superman look like Truman Capote."

He also appeared on *The Tonight Show* starring Johnny Carson, *The Sonny and Cher Comedy Hour*, the TV drama *Emergency*, and *The Dean Martin Celebrity Roast*. Making his debut at the Tribeca Film Festival, he narrated Quentin Tarantino's film *Freedom's Fury*, (2006), a Hungarian documentary about the Olympic water polo team's Blood in the Water match against the Soviet Union during the Revolution of 1956.

Spitz became a multi-millionaire because of endorsements and events following his swimming career. He was probably the first person to capitalize on his Olympic fame and the opportunities it presented. Mark started a successful real estate company in Beverly

Hills, where he became one of the largest residential real estate developers in Southern California and was also involved with an eight figure apartment development in Hawaii. He also became a stock broker and financial manager.

Today Mark travels the country as a highly sought-after motivational speaker for business conferences, sports forums, and other special events.

Spitz worked on many sports presentations for ABC, including coverage of the 1976 Summer Olympics in Montreal and the 1984 Summer Olympics in Los Angeles. In 1985, he appeared as a TV announcer in *Challenge of a Lifetime.* He continued as a broadcaster for some time, but within a few years, he was hardly seen as a public figure except perhaps as a commentator for swimming events like the 2004 Summer Olympics.

Scott May: National Player of the Year

Signed into Bob Knight's second great recruiting class (1972), Scott May, a six-foot, seven-inch forward from Sandusky, Ohio, was to become one of the all-time greats in IU basketball history. May was declared academically ineligible his freshman year because of high school academic scores. As a sophomore, May was doing fine in his studies and joined the basketball team to become the shining star of what many consider the greatest team in college basketball history.

May had the inner drive to do whatever it took to win. He helped to gel the future-championship nucleus of May, Kent Benson, Quinn Buckner, and Bob Wilkerson. As a sophomore, May averaged 12.5 points per game on the Hoosier's Big Ten Championship squad.

In his last two seasons, 1974–75 and 1975–76, the Hoosiers were undefeated in the regular season and won 37 consecutive Big Ten games. The 1974–75 Hoosiers swept the entire Big Ten by an average of 22.8 points per game. However, in an 83–82 win against

Purdue, May broke his left arm. With a cast on his arm, he only played seven minutes as the number one–ranked Hoosiers lost to Kentucky—a team they beat 98–74 earlier in the season—by two in the Mideast Regional (92–90). The next season, the Hoosiers went the entire regular season and 1976 NCAA tournament without a single loss, beating Michigan 86–68 in the title game. Indiana remains the last school to accomplish having and undefeated season.

May was the 1975–76 team's leading scorer and was named NCAA men's basketball National Player of the Year in 1976. He won a gold medal as a member of the United States basketball team in the 1976 Summer Olympics. Scott May graduated from Indiana in the standard four years with a degree in education.

After college, the Chicago Bulls chose May with the second overall pick in the 1976 NBA draft. He made the NBA All-Rookie team after averaging 14.2 points for the Bulls. Injuries kept him to seven seasons in the NBA, scoring 3,690 points and pulling down 1,450 rebounds. He went on to play seven more years in Europe.

During his pro career, May began to buy apartment units around the Indiana University campus. May invested in a couple of projects each off-season and now owns more than two thousand apartments in Bloomington. He is now known as one of the biggest apartment owners in the Bloomington area employing several hundred employees.

May had two sons—Scott Jr. and Sean—who continued his tradition of basketball play. Scott Jr. played for the Indiana basketball team that made the NCAA title game in 2002. His younger son, Sean, helped North Carolina win a national championship in 2005. Scott and Sean May are one duo of four father–son pairs to each win an NCAA basketball championship.

May won the following awards at IU: Naismith College Player of the Year (1976), Adolph Rupp Trophy (1976), Helms Foundation Player of the Year (1976), AP College Player of the Year (1976), NABC Player of the Year (1976), UPI College Player of the Year

(1976), Sporting News College Player of the Year (1976), and two-time consensus first-team All-American (1975, 1976).

Quinn Buckner: The Captain

Quinn Buckner is the only person who ever was named Chicago-area Player of the Year for both football and basketball, playing for Thornridge High School in Dolton, Illinois. His basketball team lost only one game during his junior and senior seasons and won back-to-back state titles. Buckner was also an excellent football player, making all-state in high school.

After considering UCLA, Michigan, and Illinois, the six-foot, three-inch, 190-pound Buckner chose to play football and basketball at his father's alma mater. William Buckner, Quinn's dad, played on Bo McMillin's Hoosiers 1945 undefeated Big Ten–champion football team. Quinn started for John Pont's football team at safety as a freshman, then left the football team after his sophomore year to focus on basketball.

"I was more gifted in football," said Buckner, "but basketball was my favorite sport."

In Buckner's freshman basketball season (1972–73), Indiana reached the Final Four, losing to the eventual–NCAA champion UCLA. In his junior and senior seasons (1974–75 and 1975–76), the Hoosiers were undefeated in the regular season and won 37-consecutive Big Ten games. The 1974–75 Hoosiers swept the entire Big Ten by an average of 22.8 points per game. Buckner, along with three of his teammates, would make the five-man All–Big Ten team.

The following season, 1975–76, Buckner served as a co-captain, and the Hoosiers went the entire season and 1976 NCAA tournament without a single loss, beating Michigan 86–68 in the title game.

He ended his college career as a four-year starter and three-year captain on the Indiana basketball team and played football for one

year. He was selected by the Milwaukee Bucks with the seventh pick of the 1976 NBA draft. He was also selected by the Washington Redskins in the 1976 NFL Draft. He had a ten-year NBA career for three teams (the Bucks, the Boston Celtics, and the Indiana Pacers). In 1984, he won an NBA title with the Celtics.

Buckner is one of only seven players in history to win the trifecta: an NCAA Championship, an NBA Championship, and an Olympic Gold Medal. He also was a State Champion while playing high school basketball in Illinois. He was inducted into the College Basketball Hall of Fame in 2015 and the IU Athletics Hall of Fame in 1986.

In addition to his playing career, Buckner was the head coach of the Dallas Mavericks for one year, from 1993 to 1994. Currently, he is a color analyst for the Indiana Pacers television broadcast team on Fox Sports Indiana. Buckner was also the play-by-play announcer on 989 Sports' line of college basketball games for several years.

In 2006, Buckner was voted as one of the 100 Legends of the IHSA (Illinois) Boys Basketball Tournament—a group of former players and coaches in honor of the 100 anniversary of the IHSA boys basketball tournament.

In July 2004, Buckner became the VP of Communications for Pacers Sports & Entertainment. Buckner was appointed to serve a three-year term on the Indiana University Board of Trustees by then-Indiana governor Mike Pence in June 2016.

Kent Benson: Number One Draft Pick

Kent Benson came to IU as a very highly-recruited player from New Castle, Indiana to play for coach Bobby Knight. He was named Indiana's Mr. Basketball in 1973.

As a freshman, Benson averaged 9.3 points per game, while shooting 50.4 percent. He helped lead IU to a 23–5 record and a Big Ten title. In his sophomore season, Benson helped lead the

Hoosiers to an undefeated conference record (18–0) and on to an Elite Eight appearance. The team had a 31–1 record for the season, and Benson averaged 15 points and 8.9 rebounds a game.

As a junior, Benson helped IU win the NCAA championship along with seniors Quinn Buckner and Scott May. That year, the Hoosiers won every game they played and are still the most recent team to complete an undefeated campaign in Division I. He averaged 17.3 points and 8.8 rebounds a game for the season with his college season-high of 57.8 percent from the field. He scored his career-high of 38 points in a single game against Michigan State during the Big Ten regular season.

In his senior year, Benson became the lone star for Indiana after May and Buckner both graduated. He averaged 19.8 points and 10.4 rebounds a game. He led them to a 16–11 record but received no post-season appearance. He was named the Big Ten's player of the year while being named an All-American for the second straight season.

Benson ended his college career with 1,740 points and 1,031 rebounds and a 72 free throw percentage and a 53.6 field goal percentage. He is currently the third all-time rebounder in school history with 1,031 rebounds.

Benson's career highlights and awards include: J. Walter Kennedy Citizenship Award (1982), NCAA champion (1976), NCAA Final Four Most Outstanding Player (1976), Helms Foundation Player of the Year (1976), two-time consensus first-team All-American (1976, 1977), induction into the Indiana Basketball Hall of Fame (1999), and induction into the IU Athletics Hall of Fame (1989).

After graduating in 1977, he was the number one draft pick of the 1977 NBA Draft by the Milwaukee Bucks. Never to be pushed around, two minutes into his first game as a professional, Benson elbowed Los Angeles Lakers center Kareem Abdul-Jabbar in the abdomen. In retaliation, Abdul-Jabbar broke Benson's jaw with a

punch. Abdul-Jabbar broke his hand in the incident and was out for two months.

Benson spent 11 seasons in the NBA with Milwaukee, Detroit, Utah, and Cleveland. He averaged 9.1 points per game in 680 regular-season games. He wore jersey number 54 for his entire career.

Isiah Thomas: He's Not for Sale

Isiah Thomas grew up impoverished on the crime-ridden west side of Chicago and received a scholarship to attend the private St. Joseph College Preparatory School in Westchester, which was a ninety-minute bus commute from his home. He led St. Joseph to the state finals in his junior year and was considered one of the top college prospects in the country. One recruiter brought a briefcase containing $50,000 to the Thomas house and told Isiah's mother that the briefcase was for the family if Isiah signed the papers to play for his school. Isiah and his brothers were jumping up and down. They had no food and no lights.

Isiah said, "Yes, I'm coming to your school. Yeah dude, I was like where do I sign? My brothers were hugging each other, and we were all so happy." That went on for a couple of minutes before Isiah's mother stepped in and told the man that her son was not for sale.

Later Thomas was recruited by coach Knight, and the only thing he said was, "There's three things I'm going to promise you and your son. He's going to get an education, he'll be a gentleman, and I'll teach him everything I know about the game of basketball." People had written hateful letters to Thomas saying that Knight tied up his players and beat them, but Thomas didn't believe them. Thomas chose Knight and Indiana because he felt that getting away from Chicago would be good. He also thought Knight's discipline would be beneficial.

Isiah said, "You know how some kids announce at a press conference which college they are attending? On the day of the

announcement, my mom tapped the podium, got everybody's attention and said, 'My son has decided that he's going to Indiana University to play for Bob Knight'".

Thomas quickly had to adjust to Knight's disciplinary techniques. Knight picked him to play for the US in the 1979 Pan Am Games, but, because of selfish play, coach threatened to send him home. Knight recalled yelling at the incoming freshman, "You better to go to DePaul, Isiah, because you sure as hell aren't going to be an Indiana player playing like that." In preseason practices before his freshman year (1979–80 season), Knight became so upset with Thomas that he kicked him out of a practice. According to Thomas, Knight made the point that no player, no matter how talented, was bigger than Knight's philosophy.

Thomas was so talented that he soon became a crowd favorite at IU. Fans displayed signs with quotations from the Book of Isaiah ("And a little child shall lead them"). Compared to the other players on the floor, Isiah, at six feet, one inch with his boyish smile, looked the part of a child. He even became a favorite of coach Knight. His superior abilities eventually caused Knight to bend his coaching style. Thomas and Mike Woodson led the Hoosiers to the Big Ten championship and the 1980 Sweet Sixteen.

Thomas was such an exceptional talent that beginning the next year (the 1980–81 season), Knight made him captain and told him to run the show on the floor.

That year, Thomas and the Hoosiers once again won a conference title and the 1981 NCAA tournament, the school's fourth national title. The sophomore earned the tournament's Most Outstanding Player award and made himself eligible for the upcoming NBA draft.

In the 1981 NBA draft, the Detroit Pistons chose Thomas with the number-two pick and signed him to a four-year, $1.6 million contract. Thomas made the All-Rookie team and started for the Eastern Conference in the 1982 NBA All-Star Game. He played for

them his entire career. He led them to two NBA championships in 1988–89 and 1989–90. He was a point guard and made the NBA All-Star team 12 times. He was named one of the 50 Greatest Players in NBA History.

During his playing career, Thomas paid college tuition for more than 75 students. When he was a Piston in 1987, Thomas organized the "No Crime Day" in Detroit. He even had the help of Detroit Mayor Coleman Young to call for a moratorium on crime in the summer of 1986. Also in 1987, Thomas posed for a poster sponsored by the American Library Association with the caption "READ: Isiah Thomas for America's Libraries".

Fulfilling coach Knight's promise to his mother, Thomas finished his college degree at IU during his NBA off seasons and received his Master's in Education from the University of California at Berkeley in 2013. At UC Berkeley, Thomas studied the connection between education and sports, specifically how American society makes education accessible (or inaccessible) to black male college athletes.

After his playing career, he was an executive with the Toronto Raptors, a television commentator, an executive with the Continental Basketball Association, head coach of the Indiana Pacers, and an executive and head coach for the New York Knicks. He was later the men's basketball coach for the Florida International University (FIU) Golden Panthers for three seasons from 2009 to 2012. In early May 2015, amidst controversy, Thomas was named president and part owner of the Knicks' WNBA sister team, the New York Liberty, subsequent to the rehiring of Thomas's former Pistons teammate, Bill Laimbeer, as the team's coach.

As a businessman, Thomas became the founder of business ventures involved in waste removal, recycling, and trying to incubate progress in minority communities. In addition to these business ventures, Thomas is involved in real estate projects in Chicago and the surrounding region, hoping to be a catalyst for change in those

areas to get the population back into those communities and be a catalyst to make a difference. Thomas founded Mary's Court, a foundation that supports economically disadvantaged parents and children in the communities of Garfield Park and Lawndale on the west side of Chicago. The charity is named for Thomas's mother, who he credits with instilling in him the importance of hard work and giving back to the community. Mary's Court has teamed up with another Chicago-based charity, Kids off the Block, to serve meals to Chicago children and families during Thanksgiving.

In April 1999, Thomas became the first African American elected to the Board of Governors of the Chicago Stock Exchange. He served until 2002.

Thomas often speaks to students and professionals around the country about his business experiences.

On February 13, 2017, Thomas was presented the AT&T Humanity of Connection Award during its annual Black History Month celebration in honor of Lewis H. Latimer at the Smithsonian's National Museum of African American History and Culture in Washington, D.C. He was honored for his historic achievements in sports and his countless contributions to the African American community as a leader in the sports, business, and philanthropic industries.

Thomas was elected to the Basketball Hall of Fame in his first year of eligibility. Two years prior, Thomas was inducted into the Michigan Sports Hall of Fame. He was also inducted into the IU Athletics Hall of Fame.

Anthony Thompson

Anthony Thompson (AT) played for Terre Haute North High School, where he was a Parade All-American under Coach Wayne Staley. He was recruited to play at IU by Coach Bill Mallory. AT saw a future with the Hoosier program being built by Mallory and

signed after his senior season in Terra Haute. After the signing, Coach Mallory and an assistant drove back to Bloomington. Coach said about the drive back to Bloomington, "It was tough to keep the car on the road. We were two excited people"! Mallory and IU nation were to experience more excitement from one of the greatest football players in America for the next four years.

During his time with the Hoosiers, AT won the Maxwell Award and Walter Camp Award. He also won the Chicago Tribune Silver Football twice, becoming only the third person to do so at the time (following Paul Giel and Archie Griffin). Thompson finished second in Heisman Trophy voting for the 1989 season. He's the only Hoosier to make consensus All-American twice.

After missing the first few games due to injury, Thompson ran for 806 yards as a freshman. He then went for 1,014 and 12 touchdowns as a sophomore. He exploded for 1,686 yards and 26 TDs as a junior, then tacked on more than 1,700 yards and 24 TDs as a senior.

Thompson grew up a fan of Chicago's Walter Payton and his work ethic. So, AT never let up trying to get to gain stamina and speed. He seemed to get better the more times he touched the ball. That stamina was on display in 1989 when Indiana defeated Wisconsin 45–17 as Thompson ran for a then-NCAA-record 377 yards on an incredible 52 carries. Thompson has always been the type of person to credit those around him. After the game, AT told the Associated Press, "I think if I was a little faster, I could have got maybe five hundred yards the way they were blocking out there today."

When AT came to IU, the Hoosier career-record for touchdowns was 30. With three games left in his senior season, he scored his 65th touchdown. This was the most ever in American collegiate football. He finished his career at IU with 5,299 rushing yards. He rushed for more than 100 yards in 28 games.

After college, AT played in the NFL for four seasons with the Cardinals and Rams. After an injury during his last season, he gave up football for a higher calling and now is a minister and Assistant AD at IU., AT was inducted into the IU Athletic Hall of Fame in 2003, the College Football Hall of Fame in 2007, and the Indiana Football Hall of Fame in 2013.

Calbert Cheaney: The Lefty

Calbert Cheaney played high school ball at Evansville Harrison. Even though he was a high school standout and selected to the 1989 Indiana All-Star team, he suffered a season-ending injury midway through his senior year that took him off the radar and left him a relative unknown to most onlookers as they surveyed Indiana University's number-one ranked recruiting class of 1989.

He was Knight's first left-handed player. Cheaney was known as a smooth player and a good leader all four years at Indiana. During his last three years at Indiana, the team spent all but two of the weeks in the top 10, and 38 of them in the top five. The Hoosiers were 87–16 (84.5 percent) those years and 46–8 (85.2 percent) in the Big Ten Conference. Of the four years that Cheaney played, the Hoosiers went 105–27 and captured two Big Ten crowns ('91 and '93). The 105 games won during Cheaney's four years was the most of any Hoosier to that point.

In 1989–90, Cheaney began his career with a flash, scoring 20 points in the first game of his freshman year. He was the only Indiana freshman to ever do so. The team won ten-straight non-conference games and then ran into much tougher opponents in the Big Ten where they won eight and lost 10. Then they ended with an upset loss (63–65) to California in the NCAA tournament. Cheaney averaged 17 points per game as a freshman.

The next year (1990–91), Cheaney averaged 21.6 points per game, and the Hoosiers ended the regular season with an overall record of 29–5 and 15–3 in the Big Ten. As conference champions, IU gained a two-seed in the NCAA and advanced to the sweet 16.

As a junior (1991–92 season), the Hoosiers added Alan Henderson, and Cheaney wasn't forced to score as much. His average went down to 17.6 points per game. The Hoosiers finished the regular season with an overall record of 27–7 and a second-place conference record of 14–4. The Hoosiers received a two-seed in the1992 NCAA Tournament as well. They advanced to the Final Four but fell to Duke in a foul-plagued game in Minneapolis.

As a senior (1992–93 season), Cheaney's scoring average rose to 22.4 points per game and 6.2 rebounds per game. The Hoosiers finished the regular season with an overall record of 31–4 and a first-place conference record of 17–1. As the Big Ten Conference Champions, the Hoosiers were given a one-seed in the 1993 NCAA Tournament. They advanced to the Elite Eight but were defeated by Kansas.

In his IU career, Cheaney scored 30 or more points thirteen times and averaged 19.8 points per game. With 2,613 career points, he is the all-time leading scorer of both Indiana and the Big Ten. At the conclusion of his collegiate career, Cheaney had captured virtually every post-season honor available. He was the National Player of the Year (winning both the Wooden and Naismith award), a unanimous All-American, and Big Ten Player of the Year.

For National Player of the Year, Cheaney had to beat out Penny Hardaway, Jamal Mashburn, Chris Webber, and Bobby Hurley. Cheaney stands as the career-scoring leader at IU, one of 34 players in Division I history to top 2,600 points.

In 1993, Cheaney was unanimous First-Team All-America and Big Ten Conference MVP.

After graduating from IU, Cheaney was selected sixth overall by the Washington Bullets in the 1993 NBA draft. His strongest showing as a pro came in 1994–1995 when he averaged a career-high 16.6 single-game points for Washington. He spent six years playing for the Bullets/Wizards (including a playoff appearance in 1997). He would go on to play for the Boston Celtics, Denver Nuggets,

and Utah Jazz before closing his career out with three years with the Golden State Warriors, retiring after the 2005–06 season.

Off the court, Cheaney appeared along with many of his 1997 Bullet teammates (Juwan Howard, Ben Wallace, and Ashraf Amaya) in singer Crystal Waters's 1996 music video "Say If You Feel Alright." He also appeared in the 1994 film *Blue Chips* as a player for the Indiana University Hoosiers.

Alan Henderson: NBA or MD?

Alan Henderson attended Brebeuf Jesuit Preparatory School in Indianapolis, where he earned academic high honors and helped the Brebeuf Braves to a state championship game. Due to an upper respiratory infection, Henderson struggled in the final game against Gary Roosevelt, with star player Glenn Robinson. Brebeuf finished runner-up to Roosevelt, and Henderson was runner-up to Robinson for Mr. Basketball, but he was a 1990–91 McDonald's All American

Henderson came to IU in 1991 to play for Bobby Knight and became one of the most multi-talented and valuable players to wear an IU uniform. He produced results in just about every category during his IU career. He scored 1,979 points (sixth), pulled down 1091 rebounds (first), blocked 213 shots (second), made 148 steals (fifth), and made 54 percent of his field goals (ninth). He helped Indiana to the 1992 Final Four as a freshman, averaging 11.6 points and 7.2 rebounds per game and scoring 15 points in a narrow semifinal loss to eventual-champ Duke. Like Scott May, Henderson was at the center of one of those sad stories in which a major injury to a star player impacted the NCAA Tournament. Late in the 1992–93 season, with IU favored to win the title, Henderson injured his knee. He played in all four NCAA Tournament games but went scoreless in three, and the Hoosiers were eliminated by Kansas in the Elite Eight.

He was voted IU's Most Valuable Player in 1994 and 1995 and his 23.5 points-per-game scoring average for the 1995 season is the highest

single-season scoring average for any Indiana player during Bob Knight's 29-year tenure.

An exceptional student, Henderson considered following in his father's footsteps as a cardiologist. He applied and was accepted into medical school at Indiana University and Howard University School of Medicine in 1995. He graduated from college with a degree in biology.

After college in 1995, Henderson was selected with the 16th pick in the NBA draft by the Atlanta Hawks. He has since played for the Hawks, the Dallas Mavericks, Cleveland Cavaliers, and the Philadelphia 76ers.

In his rookie year (1995–96) with the Hawks, he ranked second on the team in total blocked shots (43). During the 1997–98 season, he was the recipient of the NBA Most Improved Player Award after averaging 14.3 points and 6.4 rebounds. He remained a member of Atlanta's team for nine seasons.

He was inducted into the Indiana Basketball Hall of Fame in 2017 and the IU Athletics Hall of Fame in 2008.

Victor Oladipo: Back Home Again In Indiana

Victor Oladipo is one of four children. His mother Joan is from Nigeria and his father Christopher is a native of Sierra Leone. Both parents are in the medical field. Joan is a nurse and Christopher is a public health executive with a PhD in behavioral science. Victor has three sisters.

Oladipo played high school basketball at DeMatha Catholic High School, in Hyattsville, Maryland, which has a rich tradition of producing star athletes like Adrian Dantley (Notre Dame), Danny Ferry (Duke), Keith Bogans (University of Kentucky), James Brown (Harvard), Sidney Lowe (North Carolina State), and Bob Whitmore (University of Kentucky).

As a senior, Oladipo was named to the *Washington Post* 2010 All-Met first team and the first-team All-Washington Catholic Athletic Conference. He was ranked number 144 overall and was the number 41–shooting guard in his class. While Scout.com listed him as the number 39 shooting guard in his class, ESPN listed him at number 53 at his position.

Turning down offers from Notre Dame, Maryland, Xavier, and others, Oladipo chose to play basketball at IU and major in sports communication broadcasting. At his commitment announcement event, he said, "It's like a basketball atmosphere everywhere you go at IU. Bloomington, Indiana is a basketball town. That's perfect."

In his freshman season, Victor played in 32 games (five starts), averaging 7.4 points, 3.7 rebounds, and 1.06 steals for the Hoosiers who ended the season 12–20 and only 3–15 in the Big Ten. Even though the team was struggling, it was becoming evident that Oladipo and other players were building something special.

In Oladipo's sophomore year the Hoosiers knocked off the number-one Kentucky Wildcats 73–72 on a Christian Watford three-point shot at the buzzer. The students stormed the court and America saw that IU was back. That year, Victor was referred to by some commentators as Indiana's most-improved player and he was often cited as the team's best defender. Oladipo scored 10 or more points in 21 games, 11 more games than the previous year. He also increased his free-throw percentage from 61 to 75, shooting four times per game. IU got a four seed in the NCAA tourney and made it to the sweet sixteen.

The next year, in part because of Oladipo's leadership, the Indiana Hoosiers finished the 2012–13 campaign as the outright Big Ten champions. Even though the IU team was loaded with talent, including preseason Player-of-the-Year Cody Zeller, Victor emerged as one of the nation's biggest stars.

Midway through the season, ESPN reporter Eamonn Brenann wrote, "In two and a half seasons in Bloomington, Oladipo has

morphed from a raw athletic specimen to a defensive-specialist, energy-glue guy—he became a hit with IU fans for holding his hand in front of his face after dunks at home, typically after a steal he himself created—into a sudden, stunning, *bona fide* collegiate star."

At the end of the regular season, Oladipo ranked fourth in the country in field goal percentage (61.4), and third in true shooting percentage (68.4) which measures shooting efficiency that considers field goals, three-point field goals, and free throws. He also shot 73.9 percent on offensive rebound put-backs, ranking among the top five in the country. He averaged 13.6 points, 6.3 rebounds, 2.1 assists, and 2.17 steals in 28.4 minutes per game, while shooting 59.9 percent (182–304) from the field and 44.1 percent (30–68) from three-point range.

On defense, Oladipo was even more dominating. Playing number one–ranked Michigan, he guarded four players in 45 possessions, giving up only four points. He had the best net rating of among Wooden Award finalists. Each game, he drew the opponent's top outside shooter and maintained a five-percent steal rate (2.2 per game) ranking 15th in the country. Only Isiah Thomas had more steals in a season (74 during the 1980–81) than Victor's 69 steals in 2012–13.

At the conclusion of his junior year, Oladipo racked up numerous awards. He was named *The Sporting News* Men's College Basketball Player of the Year, the National Co-Defensive Player of the Year, and a first-team All-American by the USBWA and *The Sporting News*. In conference honors, he was named a unanimous pick to the first-team All–Big Ten by both the coaches and media and was named Big Ten Defensive Player of the year.

Victor announced his decision to forgo his senior season at IU and enter the 2013 NBA draft on April 9, 2013, at a press conference with Tom Crean. Everyone (ESPN and CBS Sports) forecasted that he would be a lottery pick. He was selected second overall by the Orlando Magic and signed a multi-million-dollar Rookie Scale contract with the Magic.

Oladipo played three years with Orlando, making the NBA All-Rookie first team (2014). He was traded to the Oklahoma City Thunder for the 2016–2017 season. On July 6, 2017, Oladipo was traded, along with Domantas Sabonis, to the Indiana Pacers in exchange for Paul George.

The Pacer's George had made no secret the previous season of his desire to be traded. George's agent had made it known that his client wasn't going back to Indy but waited until after the NBA Draft to do so. As was later learned, the Lakers had been in contact with George's camp in violation of NBA tampering regulations. The Celtics went back and forth with a rumored package as well. The Pacers declined to wait, and Pacers President Kevin Pritchard pulled the trigger on the deal with Oklahoma City: Paul George for Victor Oladipo and Domantas Sabonis. Victor was back home in Indiana, and all he did was lead the Pacers into the playoffs.

In Game One of the Pacers' first-round playoff series against the Cavaliers, Oladipo scored 32 points in a 98–80 win, becoming only the fourth player in Pacers history with at least 30 points and six three-pointers in a postseason game, joining Reggie Miller, Chuck Person, and Paul George. In Game Six, Oladipo recorded his first career-postseason triple-double with 28 points, 13 rebounds, and 10 assists in a 121–87 win, helping the Pacers force a Game Seven. The Pacers went on to lose Game Seven to bow out of the playoffs, despite Oladipo's 30 points, 12 rebounds, six assists, and three steals.

Victor was named the NBA Most Improved Player for the 2017–18 season, becoming the fifth Pacer player to win the award. He averaged 23.1 points per game (ninth in the NBA), 5.2 rebounds, 4.3 assists, and led the NBA in steals at 2.4 per game.

On January 23, 2019, Victor suffered a ruptured quad tendon in his right knee, which ruled him out for the rest of the season. He underwent successful surgery five days later. Despite the injury-riddled season, Oladipo was selected as an Eastern Conference All-Star reserve.

One of the first things Victor made known upon his return to the state of Indiana was that he was proud of the role he played in helping to bring the Hoosiers back to prominence. He told undefeated.com, "I was a part of something bigger than myself, and there was always something that I remember, always something that I will never forget to be[ing] able to come back and play in front of these fans, try[ing] to do something special again here in Indiana."

Indiana residents apparently love and respect Victor Oladipo even more than their politicos. In the 2018 senatorial election, Victor appeared in a photo with Senator Joe Donnelley running for re-election at a campaign event. A cartoon by conservative Gary Varvel appeared in the *Indianapolis Star* with the caption "Who's that guy with Victor?"

Joining with former teammate Cody Zeller, Victor made a major gift to IU for the building of the Oladipo Zeller Legacy Lounge located in the home locker room complex at Assembly Hall.

He has been featured in TV commercials for milk, Schick razors, PlayStation, Sprint PCS, and GoDaddy.

Coaches We Love

W. H. (Billy) Thom: NCAA Championship

Billy Thom had great teams from 1928 to 1945 as IU's Head Wrestling Coach. He began his coaching career at Wabash High School before moving up to IU in 1927. Thom built the IU wrestling program into a powerhouse, winning eight Big Ten titles and the 1932 NCAA championship during his tenure.

One of Thom's proudest moments came in 1936, when he traveled to Berlin to coach the United States wrestling team in the Olympics. Three of Thom's Indiana students made the squad that summer. Charley McDaniel and Willard Duffy were named alternates, while Dick Voliva, a native of Bloomington and two-time state champion, competed against the world's best. Voliva was a member of Thom's 1932 national championship team. He won an NCAA title of his own in 1934, and, after graduating with his bachelor's degree, he continued to train with Thom while working on his master's degree.

Voliva made it all the way to the gold-medal round, where he finally tasted defeat. He took home the silver, becoming the only Indiana University graduate to medal in wrestling. Thom was thrilled for his student, a young man he had watched over for nearly a decade. "A boy I had seen grow up in Bloomington, had coached

to a Big Ten Championship, an NCAA championship, a National AAU championship, and then the Olympic team . . . if I were to pick one incident as my greatest thrill, that would be it."

Thom's success at the Olympics enabled him to continue recruiting the top wrestlers from across the state.

Thom is a member of the National Wrestling Hall of Fame, the Indiana University Athletics Hall of Fame, and the Indiana Wrestling Hall of Fame. Voliva became an outstanding coach in his own right and joined his mentor in the IU and Indiana Hall of Fame. The Indiana Hall of Fame continues to honor Thom today, presenting the Billy Thom award annually to an individual who has made significant contributions to amateur wrestling in Indiana.

Earl C. "Billy" Hayes: Three NCAA Championships in Five Years

Billy Hayes was born in Southern Indiana near Madison on the Ohio River. For college, Billy traveled north to Michigan to attend Albion College, where he won eight athletic letters, captained the football team, and was president of his class.

Hayes's coaching career started at Mississippi A&M (now known as Mississippi State University), guiding the football team to a 15–8–2 record in three seasons from 1914 to 16 and compiling a 124–54 record in 12 seasons as the basketball coach. Billy came back to Indiana to coach the cross-country and track and field teams from 1924 until his retirement in 1943. Hayes also coached football for the Hoosiers for three years.

Hayes's IU cross-country teams instantly became perennial title contenders, winning eight Big Ten cross country titles during his career, including a stretch of six straight from 1928 to 33. From 1928 until Hayes's retirement, his teams never finished worse than second. His teams also won three NCAA cross-country titles (1938, 1940, and 1942) during his career, as well as five Big Ten track titles, and the 1932 NCAA outdoor track and field title.

Hayes coached four world-record holders and seven Olympians: Roy Cochran, Tom Deckard, Ivan Fuqua, Chuck Hornbostel, Don Lash, and fellow US Track and Field and Cross Country Coaches Association (USTFCCCA) Hall of Famer Fred Wilt; others, such as Archie Harris and Campbell Kane, were National Amateur Athletic Union (AAU) champions. Hayes also coached fellow USTFCCCA Hall of Famers M. E. "Bill" Easton and Bob Timmons.

Hayes was an assistant coach on the 1936 U.S. Olympic Track And Field Team.

Hayes was one of the founders of the National Collegiate Cross-Country Coaches Association (NCCCCA) and was instrumental in organizing the first NCAA Cross Country Championships in 1938. Until the 1970s, the trophy presented to the winner of the NCAA Cross Country Championships was the Billy Hayes Memorial Trophy, in honor of Hayes's achievements. He is recognized for his accomplishments in the Indiana University Athletics Hall of Fame, the Drake Relays Hall of Fame, and the USATF Hall of Fame. The track at Indiana is named in his honor.

Everett Dean: Won in Two Sports

As basketball coach, Dean led IU teams to win one Midwest Conference basketball crown and three Big Ten titles. His record as coach was 162–93 (63.5 percent). As baseball coach, his Hoosier teams won three Big Ten titles and had an overall record of 158—83-–8 (65.9 percent). Perhaps some IU fans feel that one of Everett Dean's greatest achievements was the recruitment of Branch McCracken, a future All-American player and Hall-of-Fame coach for the Hoosiers.

A respected author, Dean wrote two books, Indiana Basketball in 1933 and Progressive Basketball in 1942. Perhaps as a result of all the research necessary for his books, Dean developed a fondness for the local history of his native Washington County, Indiana, which led him to push for the creation of the John Hay Center of Salem,

Indiana. Hay, Lincoln's personal secretary, was from Salem and later became US Secretary of State from 1898–1905.

Branch McCracken: The Sheriff

In 1938, Branch McCracken succeeded Everett Dean as the Hoosier's twentieth Men's Basketball Coach. His IU teams became known as the "Hurrying Hoosiers" because of McCracken replacing the set play offenses of the time with a fast break, which later resulted in some IU scores in excess of 100 points. In later years, other programs copied McCracken's style and it became known as "run and gun" basketball.

Branch had two spans at IU. He coached from 1938 through 1943. Then he served in the Navy for three years rising to the rank of Commander during WWII. After the war, he returned and coached from 1946 through 1965. During McCracken's years coaching IU, he was affectionately called "the Sheriff" by fans and the media. He ran everything for the program like a sheriff in a western movie. Branch occasionally received a technical foul for stomping his polished dress shoe on the raised basketball floor in the fieldhouse. This gunshot-like sound would draw a referee who would then get an earful from Branch.

In 1938, McCracken's first Indiana team went 17–3. The following year, Indiana had unprecedented success with an NCAA championship win over Kansas, 60–42, and a national record of 20 wins. This championship put McCracken, age 31, in the record books as the youngest coach ever to win the NCAA tournament. The 20–3 win record held until 13 years later when McCracken's Hoosiers won 23. During this span, IU had perfect seasons at the 7th Street fieldhouse and posted a 24-game home winning streak between 1938 and 1941.

In 1948, Herman B. Wells and McCracken were responsible for recruiting Bill Garrett, Indiana Mr. Basketball, who became the first African American player in Big Ten-varsity basketball history.

This was one year after Jackie Robinson broke the color barrier in his Rookie of the Year season with the Brooklyn Dodgers.

IU's second NCAA championship was during the 1952–53 season. IU was led by Bobby Leonard, Dick Farley, and three-time All-American Don Schlundt. They went on to win the Big Ten and then the NCAA championship. Once again, IU beat Kansas in the final game, but this time by only one point.

The Hoosiers would again win the Big Ten the following season, and just a few years later, the team won back-to-back conference championships in 1956–57 and 1957–58.

In 1960, first-year football coach Phil Dickens's Indiana Hoosiers football program was hit with four years of NCAA probation for allowing alumni to pay for plane tickets and give stipends to recruits. These sanctions impacted play and recruiting for every varsity sport at the school, including basketball. Although the violations only occurred within the football program, all Hoosier varsity sports were barred from postseason play during the probationary period. The sanctions drastically undermined the ability of coaches to lure talented players to Indiana. Nevertheless, McCracken did manage to successfully recruit the two most sought-after recruits in Indiana, the Van Arsdale twins Dick and Tom, both of whom would earn All-America honors in 1965.

Branch coached IU for 23 years, amassing 364 wins and 210 Big Ten wins. His teams also won four regular-season Big Ten titles and went to the NCAA tournament four times, winning two national titles. Branch's Hoosiers dominated the Boilermakers with a 26–14 record.

McCracken was inducted into the Naismith Memorial Basketball Hall of Fame as a player in 1960. The playing floor at IU's basketball Assembly Hall is named the McCracken Court.

A brilliant coach that won 10 of 13 Bucket games, Bo McMillin always seem to figure out a way for his "po' little boys" to beat Purdue. Here he sends in fullback Joe Bartkiewicz with a play in the 1947, 16–14, Old Oaken Bucket win in his final game coaching for IU.

Bo McMillin: A Football Giant

Arguably, Alvin "Bo" McMillin was IU's greatest football coach ever, with a record of 68–43–11 and an undefeated Big Ten championship. One might even say that he was the greatest football coach in the state of Indiana during his years coaching the Hoosiers. From 1934, when Bo came to IU, through 1947, when he left to coach the Detroit Lions, the best season of his counterpart at Notre Dame Elmer Landry was 8–1. The Purdue Boilermakers suffered through a revolving door of coaches following Noble Kizer with Edward Alley (16–18–6), Elmer Burnham (10–8), Cecil Isbell (14–14–1), and Stu Holcomb (35–42–4).

To be a great IU coach, you must beat Purdue, and Bo McMillin did that very well. His final record against Purdue was 10–3–1. Bo's first game against the Boilermakers was at Purdue. The Hoosiers had lost three straight games against them and only won once in the previous ten matches. The Hoosiers won that game 17–6 (1934). The

next year, IU shut out Purdue 7–0 at 10th Street Memorial Stadium.

Not only did McMillin's teams hold sway over the Boilermakers, but the fans started to turn out in record numbers to Memorial Stadium, which was only designed to hold 22,000. Bo's Hoosiers became the place to be on Saturdays as the Hoosier attendance grew to near 30,000.

Bo was born and raised in Texas and spoke with a distinctive Lone Star drawl. Billy Reed, in a 1968 *Sports Illustrated* article, said, "As a child, Bo was known to pick fights, but was also known all his life as one who never drank nor smoked nor swore. He was a good Irish Catholic."

As a player at Centre College, Bo was the Walter Camp All-America first team at quarterback for three seasons. McMillin scored the only touchdown (32-yard run) against Harvard to break their 25-game winning streak 6–0. MIT students, who have always attended Harvard games to cheer against the Crimson, tore down the goalposts and hoisted Bo on their shoulders.

McMillin began his career as a head coach at Centenary College of Louisiana in 1922. Over a three-year period, he lost only three of 28 games. He then moved to Geneva (Pennsylvania) where his record was 22–5–1. Then he coached Kansas State with a record of 29–21–1 before coming to IU where his teams went 63–48–11.

Historically, Bo's players considered him a great motivator. Elden Auker (McMillin's all-conference quarterback at Kansas State and later a major-league pitcher in three World Series games) wrote in his book, *Sleeper Cars and Flannel Uniforms*, "McMillin was a great psychologist. He really knew how to give us talks that fired us up… The normal routine for McMillin was to bring us out onto the field to loosen up and then take us back into the locker room for a pep talk. By the time he was through talking, we believed we could take on the world."

McMillan endeared himself to success-starved Hoosier fans and alumni by referring to his powerful teams as "My po' little boys"

in pre-game interviews. He gave the impression that the Hoosiers would be up against an almost insurmountable opponent. Then, as the Hoosiers would experience another convincing win, Bo would smile and compliment the players for overcoming adversity.

Bo's obituary in the *Jacksonville Daily Journal* told the story that Indiana had once invaded another Big Ten stadium. McMillin sought entrance several hours before the game, only to find the gates locked and guarded. He coaxed the guards to open one gate so that they could discuss the problem and announced, "This is the Indiana football team. We've been marching around this place long enough, and, suh, we are not wearying ourselves before we get our suits on". The story went on to say that Bo marched the Hoosier team over the guards and, that day, soundly whipped their opponents. Bo died March 31, 1952.

James Edward "Doc" Counsilman: Six NCAA Championships in a Row

Counsilman was born in Alabama but grew up and learned to swim in St. Louis. He swam collegiately for the Ohio State University and set world-bests in the 50- and 300-yard breaststrokes.

Doc was a heavy bomber pilot flying B-24 Liberator aircraft pilot. During World War II, Counsilman served in the United States Army Air Forces in Italy as a pilot with the 455th Bomb Group of the Fifteenth Air Force.

After college at Ohio State, Counsilman went on to earn a master's degree at the University of Illinois, where he also served as an assistant coach, before pursuing doctorate degree in physiology from the University of Iowa. Following award of his doctorate, the newly-dubbed "Doc" began teaching and coaching at Cortland State University, where he would remain from 1952 to 1957 leading into his time at Indiana University.

Doc Counsilman became IU's head swimming coach in 1957 and remained the leader of the program through 1990. To call him

the best in the country could be an understatement because not only did his teams win six consecutive NCAA Men's Swimming and Diving Championships and 23 Big Ten titles, but also served as the Men's Head Coach of the USA's swimming team at the 1964 Olympics (where the USA men won 9 of 11 events) and the 1976 Olympics (USA men won 12-of-13 events).

Counsilman is known as one of the greatest swimming coaches of all time. His innovations include the pioneering of underwater filming—and even watching swimmers underwater as can be seen in Royer Pool at Indiana University today. He also instigated hypoventilation training, where swimmers used reduced breathing frequency to delay the onset of fatigue and would therefore improve performance during competition.

Known for being an innovator, Councilman was able to attract the country's best swimmers to IU. While at IU, Doc coached over 60 Olympic swimmers, including Mark Spitz (seven Olympic gold medals), who chose IU in 1969 because of Doc. He was quoted as saying that choosing IU was, "the biggest and best decision of my life. "

In 1961, he was named Coach of the Year by the American Swimming Coaches Association and inducted as an Honors Coach into the International Swimming Hall of Fame in 1976. He has been inducted into various Hall of Fames, including the IU Athletics Hall of Fame in 2001

In 1979, at the age of 58, he became the then-oldest person to swim the English Channel.

Hobie Billingsley: First-Ever Diving Coach in America

Only a handful of coaches in all of sports are so well regarded that they become the subject of a famous inspirational documentary. Hobie Billingsley is one. He is profiled in the award-winning, widely-televised inspirational documentary *Hobie's Heroes—25th Anniversary*

Edition, which depicts the struggles and successes of young divers training under IU's legendary coach, who was all about challenge, competition, loyalty, faith, and courage.

Hobie's Heroes illuminated these universal themes, as a group of young divers (12–17), strive to improve their skills under the guidance of the famed IU and Olympic diving coach. With toughness and humor, Hobie inspires the divers to meet a challenge with every ounce of their determination. As the young athletes attempt difficult dives from three stories above the pool, the documentary empathizes with their fears and the pressures they face and cheers their triumphs.

In 1959, Hobie Billingsley joined his collegiate teammate (Ohio State) Doc Counsilman as Indiana's (and the nation's) first diving coach. Hobie remained the diving coach at IU through 1989. His divers never lost to Purdue as they won more than 100 national diving titles. He coached Olympic gold medalists and national champions. He founded the World Diving Coaches Association in 1968 and was inducted into the International Swimming Hall of Fame in 1983. He is considered by many to be one of the most influential figures in the history of diving.

Hobie was, himself, an American diving champion and an honoree of the International Swimming Hall of Fame. He considered one of the highlights of his career the 1996 Summer Olympics in Atlanta.

Hobie Billingsley is one of only six diving coaches mentioned in the American Red Cross's Swimming and Water Safety. In the chapter on the history of the sport, Hobie is one of only two diving coaches with multiple mentions. He and Dick Kimball (University of Michigan coach) after admiring women divers in the Olympics were pioneers in encouraging the NCAA to open doors for women in varsity diving programs,' and he is cited as contributing to the sport of diving through analysis based on principles of physical laws of motion.

Following retirement from university coaching, Hobie continues to be active in the sport, training divers and coaches around the world, and is respected as a speaker on diving history, technique, and ethics, and on sports in general. He has recently published the second edition of his *Competitive Diving Illustrated*, a seminal work offering detailed technical support for coaching diving.

John Pont: Brought a Sea of Red

John Pont came to IU with plenty of football and life experience. At Canton's Timken High School, he was All-City and All-County, and third-team All-State Guard. After graduation in 1945, he served in the US Navy as a submariner. After the Navy, Pont went to Miami of Ohio where he played halfback from 1949 to 1951 and became the leading ground-gainer in the program's history with 2,457 rushing yards. His number, 42, is displayed at Miami's Yager Stadium, and he's one of four football players to have his number retired by Miami. After graduation, Pont played professional football in Canada before turning to coaching. His first head-coaching post was at Miami, the cradle of coaches, in 1956. From there, he became the head coach at Yale in 1963 and came to IU in 1965.

In his third season coaching the Hoosiers, John Pont became the most popular man in Indiana and the most famous coach in America as he won the Big Ten and took IU to the 1968 Rose Bowl. He was honored as NCAA Division I-A coach of the year in 1967. That year, it became common at IU and all around the state of Indiana to see signs reading Pont for President.

During Pont's time at IU, men began wearing red flat newsboy caps to the football games. The Memorial Stadium crowds looked like a sea of red compared to other school's mish-mash of colorless fall clothing and hats. Due to the come-from-behind Cinderella story developing at IU, more and more football fans around the country became interested in highlights of Indiana football. People began to notice the red color of the IU section. Indiana became a national

trendsetter. Today, virtually every college football game has fans clad in school colors, team logo hats, and outerwear.

Always a gentleman, Coach John Pont brought a Big Ten Championship and a trip to a Rose Bowl to IU. He treated his players like men and taught us how to wear red.

John Pont was always a gentleman on and off the field and referred to his players as young men. This was refreshing in the college football days of brutal coaches manipulating their "boys." Indiana fans felt their program was something special.

In Pont's first two years at Bloomington, he won a total of three games. But his 1967 team, led by three sophomores—quarterback Harry Gonso, tailback John Isenbarger and flanker Jade Butcher—went 9–1 during the regular season, losing only to Minnesota. IU finished in a three-way tie with Minnesota and Purdue for the Big Ten championship. The Hoosiers became the Big Ten's representative in the Rose Bowl because IU had never been to Pasadena.

During the '67 season, as the victories mounted, thousands of enthusiastic red-clad IU students crowded into the 17th street fieldhouse to watch road games on closed-circuit television. That

was the only place to see an IU game; in those days, there were usually only two college games on TV on any given Saturday. The students would cheer as if the game were at home and they were in the student section at Memorial Stadium.

On New Year's Day 1968, around 15,000 Hoosiers fans wore their red caps and waved red pompoms amid a Rose Bowl crowd of almost 103,000 as Indiana faced a powerful Southern California team. The Hoosiers faced Heisman Trophy winner O. J. Simpson, who ran for two touchdowns and gained 128 yards in Southern California's 14–3 victory. The game was very competitive.

In '67, IU was ranked number four by The Associated Press, and Pont was named the major college coach of the year by the American Football Coaches Association and the Football Writers Association of America. "I think what most of our fans remember is not that we got beat, but that we got there," Pont told the *Evansville Courier & Press* in 2002 of that Rose Bowl appearance.

John Pont was a member of the Cradle of Coaches and the Miami and Indiana Athletic Halls of Fame as well as Mid-American Conference Hall of Fame and the Indiana Football Hall of Fame. At Miami, Pont's teams won two MAC championships (1957–1958). He also won the Imperial Oil Trophy (1952), AFCA Coach of the Year (1967), Eddie Robinson Coach of the Year (1967), Paul "Bear" Bryant Award (1967), *The Sporting News* College Football Coach of the Year, (1967), and Walter Camp Coach of the Year Award (1967).

Bob Knight: The General

Coach Bob Knight was one of only three men who have won an NCAA championship both as a player and coach. The other two were Joe B. Hall of Kentucky and Dean Smith of Kansas/North Carolina. Knight is responsible for IU basketball glory and three of the five NCAA Champion banners hanging in Assembly Hall.

Knight grew up in Orville, Ohio, the home of Smucker's Jam. He attended Ohio State, where he played on the Buckeye's 1960 NCAA championship team with NBA Hall of Fame stars Jerry Lucas and John Havlicek. After he graduated from Ohio State with a degree in history and government, he coached high school basketball in Ohio for one year. He then enlisted in the United States Army and accepted an assistant coaching position with the Army (West Point) in 1963, where, two years later, he was named head coach at the relatively young age of 24. In six seasons at West Point, Knight's Black Knights won 102 games.

At Army, Knight's explosive temper was called "fiery" by the ubiquitous New York media. Perhaps this is where the term "General" became his moniker. He had a zero-tolerance approach to mistakes in coaching and teaching basketball. Knight's uncompromising style led his teams to perfection.

Knight came to IU in 1971 and quickly brought the program back to glory. The Hoosiers once again became a national power just like Branch McCracken's teams of the forties, fifties, and sixties. During his 29 years as head coach, the Hoosiers won 662 games, with 20 or more wins in 22 seasons. Knight's IU teams had 24 NCAA tournament appearances winning 42 of 63 games (66.7 percent), and winning titles in 1976, 1981, and 1987, while losing in the semi-finals in 1973 and 1992.

In 1972–73, Knight's second year as coach, Indiana won the Big Ten championship and reached the Final Four, but lost a close game to UCLA. In the closing minutes of that game, IU's star big-man, Steve Downing (26 points) was standing under the UCLA bucket and seemed to be bumped by Bill Walton. Downing was called for a controversial foul. Both players had four fouls, and IU had to continue without Downing. Minutes later, John Ritter sunk a jumper, and IU was within four points, but if you ask Hoosier fans, the game was decided by the referees. UCLA shot 13 free throws to IU's 6.

The following season, Knight's Hoosiers won the second of four consecutive Big Ten championships. The next two seasons,

the Hoosiers were undefeated in the regular season and won 37 consecutive Big Ten games. The 1974 Hoosiers swept the entire Big Ten season by an average of 22.8 points per game. Sadly, fortunes changed at Purdue's Mackey Arena in an 83–82 win when IU lost All-American forward Scott May to a broken left arm. During that year's NCAA regional, May played only seven minutes with a cast on his arm. The number one Hoosiers lost to Kentucky 92–90, a team they had beaten 98–74 in December.

The next season, the Hoosiers went undefeated and won the 1976 NCAA tournament. After beating Michigan twice in the Big Ten, the Hoosiers dominated them in the NCAA championship game 86–68. The '76 Hoosiers remain the last undefeated NCAA Division I men's basketball team.

In 1981, Knight's Hoosiers won his second national title, featuring the Isiah Thomas dismantling of North Carolina 63–50. Indiana led by only one point at halftime, but the second half opened with two Thomas steals for layup baskets. After that, the game was never close.

Bob Knight's Hoosiers again were NCAA champions in the Louisiana Superdome in 1987 with a 74–73 victory over Syracuse as Keith Smart hit a shot from the corner with only a few seconds remaining. After 30 plus years, videos clearly show that Syracuse never called a timeout, but apparently, and quite mysteriously, the refs at that game called it for them. After the timeout, Syracuse's long lob, inbound pass was intercepted by Smart sending a throng of Hoosier fans onto the streets of New Orleans. The Superdome held almost 70,000 fans, and it seemed like 50,000 of those attending wore IU red. That night, the celebrants mobbed the French quarter and the singing of "Indiana, Our Indiana" could be heard on pianos until the wee hours of the morning. A staff member at the Intercontinental Hotel remarked that the only rowdier crowd they had seen were Chicago Bear fans after their Super Bowl win in 1986.

Knight continued to have great success at IU with All-Americans Damon Bailey, Alan Henderson, and National Player of the Year Calbert Cheaney. Some say IU teams won even more Big Ten championships and reached the top in the polls because of Knight's motion offense. After once being exposed to the Princeton offense, Knight instilled more cutting with the offense he employed, which evolved into the motion offense that he ran for most of his career. Knight continued to develop the offense, instituting different cuts over the years and putting his players in different scenarios.

Defense was also a critical element to his success. On defense Knight was known for emphasizing tenacious "man-to-man" defense where defenders contest every pass and every shot and help teammates when needed.

Knight was well-known for the extreme preparation he put into each game and practice. Kevin Kasakove wrote in The Legacy of Bob Knight that Knight was often quoted as saying, "Most people have the will to win, few have the will to prepare to win." Often during practice, Knight would instruct his players to a certain spot on the floor and give them options of what to do based on how the defense might react. In contrast to set plays, Knight's offense was designed to react according to the defense. In December of 1999, Bernie Miklasz, St. Louis Post Dispatch Hall of Fame sports writer, featured a story of how IU had beaten Mizzou 73–68 by using a disciplined motion offense. He talked about the great discipline of Knight's teams and how, if the world were ending today, Knight would have his team in a gym practicing cutting, screening, and passing.

Knight's US international teams won a Pan-Am Games Gold Medal in 1979, and his Olympic team won the Gold medal in the 1984 Olympics.

Chris Suellentrop wrote in Slate on March 15, 2002 that Knight's academic successes actually rivaled his athletic ones. At Indiana, he graduated nearly 80 percent of his players. The national average for

Division I schools is 42 percent. He endowed two chairs, one in history and one in law, and raised millions for the library.

Knight received several personal honors during and after his coaching career. He was named the National Coach of the Year four times (1975, 1976, 1987, 1989) and Big Ten Coach of the Year eight times (1973, 1975, 1976, 1980, 1981, 1989, 1992, 1993). In 1975, he was a unanimous selection as National Coach of the Year, an honor he was accorded again in 1976 by the Associated Press, United Press International, and Basketball Weekly. In 1987, he was the first person to be honored with the Naismith Coach of the Year Award. In 1989, he garnered National Coach of the Year honors by the AP, UPI, and the United States Basketball Writers Association. Knight was inducted into the Basketball Hall of Fame in 1991.

On November 17, 2006, Knight was recognized for his impact on college basketball as a member of the founding class of the National Collegiate Basketball Hall of Fame. The following year, he was the recipient of the Naismith Award for Men's Outstanding Contribution to Basketball.

Bob Knight must also be recognized for his impact on Indiana basketball. When one enters a shop featuring team apparel most anywhere in Indiana, the IU product display is always larger than that of Purdue, Butler, or Notre Dame thanks to the Bob Knight Hoosiers. It has often been said that if Bob Knight wanted, he could be elected Indiana's governor or senator. His legions of fans and admirers span the small towns and larger cities in Indiana. His teams at IU constantly are the standard to which all Hoosier teams are held.

Jerry Yeagley: The Godfather— Seven NCAA Championships

As an undergraduate athlete at West Chester University (PA), Yeagley was a national champion. He was a player on an NCAA Championship soccer team at West Chester in 1961.

Jerry Yeagley learned quickly that Bloomington wasn't a soccer town when he arrived in 1963 as a physical education instructor and men's soccer coach. IU was a school with a storied basketball tradition and absolutely no soccer history; Yeagley's task was to develop a top-notch soccer program. He learned in his first few months that the future of Hoosier soccer did not look prosperous. He discovered that soccer balls weren't even sold in Bloomington. To make matters worse, some people thought soccer was a sport played on horses.

Yeagley has transformed Indiana soccer from a club sport to a national power, winning seven NCAA Championships and a Division I–record 544 games. He is considered the most successful collegiate soccer coach in the history of the sport. People call him "the Godfather of American Soccer." Yeagley was a six-time NSCAA Coach of the Year and eight-time Big Ten Coach of the Year. He received the NSCAA's Bill Jeffrey Award in 1987 and the Association's Honor Award in 1997. He concluded his tenure at Indiana in 2003 with an 18-match unbeaten streak on the way to his sixth NCAA title. His players earned NSCAA All-America honors 49 times, 65 players went on to play professional soccer, and 20 players have played for the US National Team.

Here are a few of Jerry's accomplishments:
- Big Ten Regular Season Championships (10)—1993, 1994, 1996, 1997, 1998, 1999, 2000, 2001, 2002, 2003.
- Big Ten Tournament Championships (10)—1991, 1992, 1994, 1995, 1996, 1997, 1998, 1999, 2001, 2003.
- College Cup Appearances (16)—1976, 1978, 1980, 1982, 1983, 1984, 1988, 1989, 1991, 1994, 1997, 1998, 1999, 2000, 2001, 2003.
- NCAA Champions (7)—1982, 1983, 1988, 1998, 1999, 2003, 2004.
- Big Ten Coach of the Year (9)—1993, 1994, 1997, 1998, 1999, 2001, 2003.

- NCAA Coach of the Year (6)—1976, 1980, 1994, 1998, 2003.

- NSCAA Coach of the Year—2003.

- Soccer America Coach—2003.

- He has coached 34 players that went on to be All Americans and players that received eight National Player of the Year honors. He is also the NCAA Division I Soccer's All-Time Winningest Coach (544–101–45).

Bill Mallory: A Class Act

Bill Mallory took a circuitous route to IU. He played at Miami University (Ohio) for Ara Parseghian and John Pont. He coached as an assistant under Woody Hayes at Ohio State, Carmen Cozza at Yale, and Doyt Perry at Bowling Green.

As a head coach, Mallory became one of only a handful of coaches in history to guide three different programs to top 20 finishes in national polls. He went 11–0 at Miami, earning an AP fifteenth ranking and a Tangerine Bowl bid. His 24–19 victory that year over Purdue was responsible for the Ohio newspaper headline and common fan slur, "Pur-Who?" At Colorado, he achieved ninth in the polls and an Orange Bowl bid. While at Indiana, Mallory led the Hoosiers to six bowl games including victories in the 1988 Liberty Bowl and the 1991 Copper Bowl. He also led IU to a top 20 ranking in 1987 and 1988.

Coach Mallory's first year coaching IU was of historical significance. The Hoosiers were celebrating history, as it was their 100th year of football. The Hoosiers were to open the season at Duke's historic Wallace Wade Stadium, famous for being the only site of a Rose Bowl (1942) not held in California. Since the Japanese attack on Pearl Harbor less than a month earlier, the government banned all large gatherings on the West Coast. Duke offered their stadium for that Rose Bowl, where they lost to Oregon State 20–16.

Historically, IU has had some losing seasons, but the 1984 schedule proved to be one of the hardest, most trying football seasons ever. The Hoosiers jumped ahead of Duke 14–0 and wound up losing 31–24 to the Blue Devils. That season, the Hoosiers also led Purdue 14–0 before losing, and the team had eight games end with a loss by an average of less than seven points. The Hoosiers went 0–11 in 1984, the worst record in IU history. But IU fans could tell by his stern sideline demeanor that Bill Mallory would be a winner, and they were right. Two years later, their Hoosiers were in a bowl game against the Florida State Seminoles. Then there was a Peach Bowl, a Liberty Bowl, a second Peach Bowl, a Copper Bowl, and an Independence Bowl. Mallory won the Big Ten Coach of the year twice.

It was always about more than just wins or losses for the man that was more than a coach, and he let that show during his life. Whether it was as a coach or a father figure, players knew Mallory would always be there pointing them in the right direction. His wife Ellie, in an interview with the *Indiana Daily Student*, related an event from 1975 in Houston. Mallory, the head coach at Colorado, coached his team to an appearance in the Astro–Bluebonnet Bowl. As Mallory and his team arrived at the hotel, they ran into some trouble. Ellie said that it was a fancy hotel with beautiful artwork, and that, as the team entered, the hotel's manager asked Mallory to have his players wait outside because they hadn't prepared everything yet. He said that the team they had hosted the year before had destroyed their rooms. The manager was expecting nothing less from Mallory's players.

"That's not going to be a problem," Mallory said. "If it becomes a problem, they're walking home." Ellie remembered the players' eyes widening after hearing that statement.

"That's just how it was," Ellie said. "You behaved yourself. . . . It was very important to him to represent the university in a class-fashion, making sure his players knew what he expected from them. He prided himself on creating learning opportunities for his

players. He made sure his players were ready for life beyond the football field, whether it was about being a gentleman and holding the door open, looking somebody in the eye during an interview, or even the difference between a salad and dessert fork at the dinner table. It was very important to him to represent the university in a class-fashion," Ellie said. "He would always make sure his players knew that's what he expected from them."

In 1987, Mallory and the Hoosiers played Michigan State to determine the Big Ten Championship. IU, ranked 16th at the time, had beaten number-nine Ohio State and number-twenty Michigan that season and looked destined for a second Rose Bowl appearance. It wasn't meant to be, however, as the Spartans prevailed, winning 27–3. It would be one of the toughest losses of Mallory's career. With the weight of the loss still on his shoulders, Mallory approached Michigan State Coach George Perles and asked if he could say a few words to the Spartans in their locker room.

In what would turn out to be one of his most famous moments at IU, Mallory commended the Michigan State players on a great effort and gave a rousing rallying speech. As he finished talking, he left them with one final thought. "I'm just going to say this," Mallory said. "By God, go out to the coast and kick their asses because we're all damn tired—" Mallory's voice faded off as the Michigan State players erupted into cheers before he could even finish, even spurring a spirited fist pump out of him as he walked out of the locker room.

Michigan State would go on to defeat the University of Southern California in the Rose Bowl. Maybe, just maybe, Mallory's speech lit the fire inside them the Spartans needed.

Mallory will be remembered as a coach who turned the IU football program around during his stint in Bloomington, which lasted from 1984 to 1996. He ended his coaching career as the program's all-time winningest head coach with 69 total wins, and still owns that record today.

Todd Yeagley: All American— NCAA Championship

Todd Yeagley elected to play for the IU men's soccer team coached by his father Jerry. He earned second-team All-American honors his first three years at Indiana as a forward, midfielder, and defender. His senior year, the team made it to the NCAA championship before losing to Virginia. That year, he earned first-team All-American honors and the Missouri Athletic Club named him player of the year. He graduated in 1994 with a bachelor's degree in sociology.

Todd played seven seasons as a defender in Major League Soccer with the Columbus Crew and one in the USISL with the Richmond Kickers. Yeagley left the pros and joined the Indiana soccer team as an unpaid assistant coach. The team went on to win the NCAA championship. The next year, IU brought Yeagley in as a full-time assistant coach and he had the good fortune to again see his team win the NCAA championship against the University of California, Santa Barbara.

Todd took over the IU program in 2010. In his first season, Indiana captured its first Big Ten regular-season title since 2007. That year and the following season, the Hoosiers advanced to the third round of the NCAA tournament. In 2012, Yeagley's third season as head coach, the Hoosiers advanced to a record-setting 18th College Cup and were the first number sixteen–seed to advance to the title game since the NCAA expanded its seeding to sixteen teams in 2003. The Hoosiers won the 2012 national championship, the school's eighth national title and the first championship for head coach Todd. The win made Todd and his father Jerry the first father-son coaching duo to win college soccer championships.

Yeagley picked up his 100th career win as a head coach on October 3, 2017, when the number one–ranked Hoosiers defeated the Evansville Purple Aces 4–0. The win brought the Hoosiers'

record to 9–0–2. For the season, the Hoosiers had an undefeated record, in which they went 13–0–4.

Year after year, Yeagley's recruiting classes and rankings are among the highest in the nation. Going into 2018, the Hoosiers ranked second in the United Soccer Coaches poll, and the previous year's recruiting class was ranked fourth-best in the NCAA according to *Soccer News* and are ranked among the best in the nation.

Traditions We Love About IU

We Call Ourselves Hoosiers

Being called a Hoosier is not a negative thing. All Indiana University teams, students, alumni, and fans are very proud to be called Hoosiers. What this means is that we know that hard work and honesty will bring a good life. A Hoosier is a person that always has the feeling that he or she can build a future for the next generation that is better than theirs. Being part of the IU family also means honoring past Hoosiers that have built our collective future.

"Chimes of Indiana" was composed by one of those such Hoosiers, IU legend, Hollywood star, and maybe America's most celebrated songwriter Hoagy Carmichael. In 1937, Hoagy presented this song as a gift to IU. The song was proposed as an official Alma Mater song and the Alumni Association officially adopted it as such in 1978.

Sing these chimes of Indiana,
Hail to the crimson hue;
Sing her praise to Gloriana,
Hail to our old IU.
Lift your voices, join in loyal chorus.
Let your heart rejoice in praise of those before us,
Sing these chimes of Indiana,
Ever to her be true!

The oldest account ever in print explaining what it means to be a Hoosier was by John Finley. Finley (1797–1866), who was born in Virginia in 1797, came to Indiana in 1821 and served in various public offices for the rest of his life. He was a Justice of the Peace, legislator, and Enrolling Clerk of the Indiana Senate. He later became the owner and publisher of the *Richmond Palladium* (newspaper).

Finley was also a highly-respected American poet credited with the first ever literary use of the word "Hoosier." He used the name frequently in his poem titled "The Hoosier's Nest."

"The Hoosier's Nest" uses the term Hoosier to explain the good qualities of the people settling Indiana.

In Hoosier life initiated:
Erects a cabin in the woods,
Wherein he stows his household goods.
At first, round logs and clapboard roof,
With puncheon floor, quite carpet proof,
And paper windows, oiled and neat,
His edifice is then complete
Ensconced in this, let those who can
Find out a truly happier man.
The little youngsters rise around him,
So numerous they quite astound him;
Each with an ax or wheel in hand,
And instinct to subdue the land.
Erelong the cabin disappears,
A spacious mansion next he rears;
His fields seem widening by stealth,
An index of increasing wealth;
And when the hives of Hoosiers swarm,
To each is given a noble farm.

As Hoosiers, we build a future for those that come after us, and we honor those that came before us.

Old Oaken Bucket: It Means More Than a Bowl Game

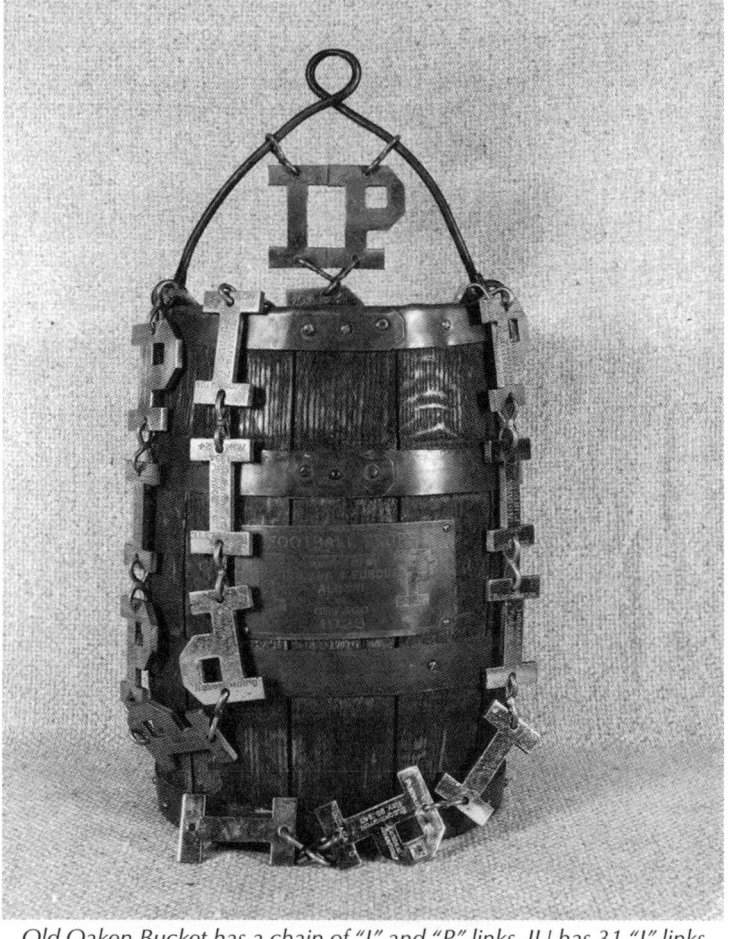

Old Oaken Bucket has a chain of "I" and "P" links. IU has 31 "I" links on the Bucket.

When IU and Purdue moved to separate football divisions in the Big Ten Conference for the 2014 season—the Old Oaken Bucket was the only interdivisional rivalry protected under the new alignment. That's because the Bucket is by far the greatest rivalry trophy in the conference, and maybe even

in the whole country. To explain the importance of the rivalry, it is important to realize the cultural geography of the state and fan base.

The state of Indiana is about 250 miles high and just short of 150 miles wide. The greatest concentrations of population in Indiana are right in the center and around the edges. Save for the Indianapolis metro area, there are more people in the northern half of the state. IU and Purdue are the two largest state universities in Indiana. Purdue, the only agricultural school in Indiana, is located appropriately on flat farm land in the Corn Belt about 60 miles northwest of Indianapolis, while IU is just under 60 miles to the southwest in forested hills amid limestone cliffs. The IU fan base tends to come from Indianapolis and south. The Purdue fan base tends to come from Indianapolis and north to the Chicago area. Fans of both IU and Purdue tend to work in the same businesses and offices together. So, no matter how bad or how good the season is for IU or Purdue, the last game, usually around Thanksgiving, can make or break the year. The winner gets bragging rights that last 365 days. Fans from both schools that meet around the coffeemaker or in lunch rooms and are more than willing to let the other side's grads know who won.

The concept of a trophy for football games played annually between IU and Purdue was first proposed during a joint meeting of the Chicago chapters of the Indiana and Purdue alumni clubs in 1925. They wanted to have a worthy joint-enterprise on behalf of both schools. They appointed IU alumnus Dr. Clarence Jones and Purdue alumnus Russel Gray to come up with a suitable trophy for the IU vs Purdue football game.

Looking back, from 1925 Jones and Gray were both influenced by "The Old Oaken Bucket" song which had been sung by generations of American schoolchildren. It was recorded in 1899 by the Haydn Quartet, the most famous barbershop quartet of the time, and was released on Berliner Gramophone. The first stanza reads:

How dear to this heart are the scenes of my childhood,
When fond recollection presents them to view!
The orchard, the meadow, the deep-tangled wild-wood,
And every loved spot which my infancy knew!
The wide-spreading pond, and the mill that stood by it,
The bridge, and the rock where the cataract fell,
The cot of my father, the dairy-house nigh it,
And e'en the rude bucket that hung in the well—
The old oaken bucket, the iron-bound bucket,
The moss-covered bucket which hung in the well.

With tradition and memories of the poem, Jones and Gray recommended an oaken bucket be that trophy because an old oaken bucket would be a true Hoosier form of trophy. Further, they recommended, the bucket should be taken from some well in Indiana, and a chain made of bronze block "I" and "P" letters should be provided for the bucket. The school winning the traditional football game each year should have possession of the "Old Oaken Bucket" until the next game between the two and should attach the block letter representing the winning school to the bail with the score engraved on the link.

A suitable bucket was found at the Bruner family farm in Jefferson County, just north of the Ohio River, between Kent and Hanover in far southern Indiana. Bruner family lore indicates that the bucket was used by General John Hunt Morgan and his raiders during their jaunt through southeastern Indiana during the Civil War.

In accordance with the Chicago alumni organization's resolution, the winner of the bucket gets a "P" or "I" link added to the chain of the bucket with the score, date, and the city where the game was played engraved on the link. In case of a tie, an "IP" link was added. The inaugural Old Oaken Bucket Game ended in a 0–0 deadlock on November 21, 1925, in Bloomington, resulting in the very first and most visible link, an "IP" link, being added to the handle of the bucket.

The Little 500: America's Greatest College Weekend

The Little 500 was founded in 1951 by Howdy Wilcox Jr., the Executive Director of the Indiana University Foundation, who modeled the race after the Indianapolis 500, which his father had won in 1919. Racers compete in teams of four, racing relay-style for 200 laps (50 miles) along a quarter-mile (440 yard) cinder track. Thirty-three teams are selected in qualification trials to compete in the main race. Money raised by the event goes towards a scholarship fund for working IU students. The race has raised more than $1 million in scholarship money.

Billed as "The World's Greatest College Weekend," the race has expanded into a whole week of activities since its original founding. The Women's Little 500 (100 laps; 25 mi) was first held in 1988 and continues to be run each year. Other events such as the Little Fifty Running Relay Race and Alumni Races add to the festivities. During his run for presidency, then-senator Barack Obama made an unannounced visit to the Little 500.

The events of the Little 500 were dramatized in the 1979 Academy Award-winning movie *Breaking Away*, which depicts a group of Bloomington townies who enter the race as the "Cutters" (a term used by condescending IU students referring to locals, taken from the local Indiana limestone industry's stonecutters) to defeat the favored fraternity teams. Thirty years later, in 2009, Smithville, a communications company, produced a half-hour-long documentary *Ride Fast, Turn Left* that followed four teams preparing for and competing in the race. In February 2015, *One Day in April* was released, which depicts two men's and two women's teams' preparation and dedication preceding the race. A Bollywood movie *Jo Jeeta Wohi Sikandar*, based on the Little 500, was made in 1992, starring Aamir Khan.

Highlights of the 1981 race were shown on ESPN, and the first major coverage was by CBS Sports Saturday for the 1982 race. The

races have also been broadcast live on the Indiana University student radio station WIUX and on television since 2002 on AXS.tv, which is owned by Indiana University alumnus Mark Cuban.

Race weekend often features free concerts and big-name entertainers, singers, and groups from all through the years. In the past, these have been stars like Bob Hope, Hoagy Carmichael, Jerry Lee Lewis, and, in later years, there are always a few popular groups like Sublime with Rome. On the Friday night before the men's race, the streets of campus are like a social parade as thousands of undergrads and young alums walk from event to event.

Don Fischer: The IU Radio Network

Looking at photos of the game-day press box at the old 10th Street Memorial Stadium in Bloomington, one can see 10 or more hanging banners from the larger radio stations and networks covering Hoosier football in the 1940s. They were from Indianapolis, Bloomington, and other Indiana stations, but for big games, like against Notre Dame, there were banners from NBC and Mutual. Back then, listening to IU games was a mish-mash of voices depending on where you had your local radio reception.

In the late 1950s, IU decided to set up its own football–basketball radio network that could be fed to stations around Indiana and neighboring states that wanted to cover the Hoosiers. An ad was placed in the *Daily Student* newspaper to offer auditions for students to do the broadcasts. From that time on, IU broadcasts have been done by some of the all-time greats in the industry. The student chosen from responses to that ad was none other than the late, great, Hall of Fame broadcaster, Dick Enberg. He was at IU working on his master's degree in Health Sciences. He did the play-by-play from 1957 to 1961. Then came John Gutowsky doing play-by-play and Pat Williams doing color for the games. John eventually had a career as the voice of the Minnesota Twins, and Pat became an NBA GM at Philadelphia and Orlando. There were

student announcers that followed until, in the 1967–68 season, Max Skirvin began to do play-by-play.

Don Fischer came to IU as the voice of Indiana basketball and football for the 1973–74 season, and his has become the most recognized voice in Indiana. He is in his 46th year as the "Radio Voice" of Indiana University football and basketball games. Fischer hosts the weekly coaches' talk shows for both football and basketball and does a series of weekly interviews for various radio stations.

Fischer has garnered a huge following of Hoosier fans that actually turn off the television audio and turn on their radios to hear his calls of IU game action. Bob Lee, a Bedford, Indiana businessman, says that every time the game is on TV, he puts on his earphones and listens to the radio to hear Fisch make the call. He says his wife objects because the TV is on a delay and Fisch has the play seconds before the TV, and Bob can't resist cheering or moaning before it comes on TV. He feels like that Fischer gives more detail than the eye can see from his perspective. He says that this is even more important at football games, where the sightline from Lee's seats don't catch all the detail that Fisch and his color team see.

Jim Stawick, a CPA from Indy, feels the same way as Lee. Jim feels that you get used to the delay on TV games. Stawick says, "Fischer's voice on the radio means Indiana sports. Hearing it, you see the Cream and the Crimson in your head. Even if he were to read the stock market reports, you'd still think of Indiana University."

John Ruckelshaus, an Indiana Senator, is also a huge Don Fischer fan. He says, "His [Fischer's] voice is timeless, rich, and deep."

The list of fans could go on and on, but to experience this phenomena, all one needs do is walk into the parking lot at an IU football game. Most radios have Fischer doing the pre-game or post-game loud enough to be heard over the noise of tailgating. If you forget your radio or don't turn on your car radio, you'll still hear Fischer's voice in the air from the hundreds of other cars.

During his work with IU, Fischer has been named Indiana Sportscaster of the Year 30 times total by two different organizations. The National Sportscasters and Sportswriters Association has awarded him 26 times (including 2018), while the Indiana Sportswriters and Sportscasters Association has named him their honoree 4 times. The Indiana Sportswriters and Sportscasters Association inducted Fischer into the ISSA Hall of Fame in 2004. He was inducted into the Indiana Broadcast Hall of Fame in 2010. He was also winner of the first Woody Durham Voice of College Sports Award in 2018 by the National Sports Media Association.

Fischer has broadcast over 1,900 Indiana University games that include eight Bowl games, four NCAA basketball Championship games, and two National Invitation Bracket Championship games. From 1973 through 1987, he worked for ABC Radio, Canada's CBC, and several other major market radio stations, including WIRE, in Indianapolis as their source for reports during the month of May and coverage of the Indianapolis 500. During that 14-year period, he also served Network Indiana, a statewide news network, as their Sports Director.

Fischer grew up in the Illinois town of Rochelle. His favorite baseball team has been the Pittsburgh Pirates since he took a two hour trip, as a youth, to Milwaukee County Stadium where he saw the Milwaukee Braves play the Pirates and their great, Hall-of-Fame right fielder Roberto Clemente. He became a big Roberto Clemente fan.

He took a home correspondence broadcasting course to get a start. His favorite play-by-play voice of all time is the late Dan Kelley, a Canadian-born sportscaster known as the voice of the St. Louis Blues hockey team and nationally televised games for the NHL.

Fischer says that he feels that he has been blessed to be at IU for all these years. Indiana University, her alumni, and her fans feel equally blessed for having Don Fischer at IU.

The William Tell Overture: The Best Timeout in College Basketball

The "William Tell Overture" is the overture to the opera *William Tell* by Gioachino Rossini. It premiered in 1829 and was the last of Rossini's 39 operas. There has been repeated use of parts of this overture in both classical music and popular media. The opera is considered by many to contain some of Rossini's greatest dramatic genius, and yet the opera has never quite held a proper place in the operatic canon.

In some ways, *William Tell* is his most widely-known work, thanks to the famous overture that has made its way into pop culture. Indiana University has an entire time out dedicated to the overture during the third television time out (the time out taken at the eight-minute mark) of the second half of basketball games with the pep band and cheerleading teams performing the piece. This timeout is often referred as the "Best Time Out in College Basketball".

The time out starts the pep band strikes up "William Tell Overture." With the start of the music, spectators begin staccato clapping. A male cheerleader from the Cream squad runs onto the court waving a flag with the words "Go Big Red" on it. This flag is run around the court, followed by the female cheerleaders as they encourage the IU faithful to their feet. The flag bearer runs back to the south end to wave the colors while the other cheerleaders establish a tower in center court. The flag is run to center court, where the cheerleader at the top of the tower takes it and waves it for the crowd. All of the cheerleaders surround the flag in two circles and kneel and wave their pom-poms.

Next, two huge IU Trident flags emerge. One is white, and the other is red. The bearers wave these flags, the fans clap, and the cheer squad circles bow. The whole building is electric. The event culminates with 15 cheerleaders running onto the court with smaller flags spelling I-N-D-I-A-N-A-H-O-O-S-I-E-R-S.

After "William Tell Overture" ends, the band strikes up "Indiana, Our Indiana" with the tuba section and the fans sing the fight song. The words can be heard clearly, even on TV. After the spectators sing the song, the full band plays the fight song loudly. At the end of the song, the fans use their hands to make blades and fists and shout "IU" until the whole building vibrates!

For football games, a similar use of the overture occurs just after the third quarter ends. The band strikes up "William Tell Overture." The huge scoreboards show a black-and-white film of the Lone Ranger riding down a hill and up onto a rise where his horse Silver rears up. Then a similar display of flags, music, clapping, and color occur like in the basketball time out. This time however, at the end of the overture, there are several large aerial bombs that explode above the north end of memorial stadium. Then the Marching Hundred strikes up "Indiana, Our Indiana" as the crowd sings the fight song. After the singing verse, the band plays at full volume, the fans clap, and it all ends with the blades and fists and the audience shouting "IU!"

According to IU Cheerleading Coach Julie Horine, the evolution of the additional flags during the William Tell timeout evolved in series between IU and the University of Kentucky basketball games. She extended the invitation to the UK Cheerleaders to participate the first year, and saw an opportunity to be a little competitive with them by introducing I-N-D-I-A-N-A the next year. The following year, UK brought K-E-N-T-U-C-K-Y flags to follow the Indiana flags, little did they know that Horine was prepared and had H-O-O-S-I-E-R-S ready to run after they brought out Kentucky. The following year, UK brought W-I-L-D-C-A-T-S to follow the Hoosier flags, and IU brought out another BIG flag at the time with the Cam Cameron Logo. The fun continued the following year, when both cheer teams from IU and UK brought their oversized flags to be included in the time out. This eventually evolved into the "Greatest Time out in College Basketball" as described above.

Cream and Crimson: School Colors Have Meaning

Indiana's school colors, cream and crimson, were chosen by the class of 1888. It is also acceptable for IU fans to show the colors of red and white. These colors really symbolize how the Hoosiers feel about IU.

The class of 1988 felt that cream is an elegant color, and crimson represents power.

The Trident

The trident is the official logo of Indiana University. Originating as early as 1898, the current version of the trident, commissioned in 2007, is used institution-wide. The trident, formed from the letters I and U, appears on many structures, from benches in the old quad to buildings and interior walls throughout campus. Many of the early examples of the symbol were used for athletic purposes. IU is one of few NCAA schools that use the same logo for the university and the athletic teams.

Fists and Blades

If an onlooker isn't prepared, the ending of the IU fight song may startle them as the whole Indiana section yells a very loud, "IU." At a Peach Bowl game, when the Hoosiers played Tennessee, the crowd attending the game was about 70 percent fans the Volunteers because the city of Atlanta, which hosted the bowl, is much closer to Tennessee than to IU. For their fans, it was a relatively short one day car trip. For the Hoosier fans, the trip was a very long drive and most likely a four-day event. As always, the Volunteer fans heard and sang "Rocky Top," their usual, many times during the game, trying to intimidate the Hoosiers, but afterwards, all they could talk about was how loud the "IU" was shouted by the Indiana fans after the

fight song. Some Tennessee fans like Jim Cox of Bluefield, Virginia said, "that IU hurt my face, it was so loud"!

The fists and blades come at the conclusion of the lyrics of the fight song "Indiana, Our Indiana," as the musical tune progresses for about six seconds, at which time the crowd performs the fists and blades (forming an IU) to the shout "IU." This tradition is also used when the band, "The Marching Hundred," plays a much-abbreviated version of ending of the fight song on occasions of a long awaited first down or big defensive stop in football, when the entire fight song would be inappropriate.

Candy Stripes

Legendary Indiana coaches James "Doc" Counsilman and Hobie Billingsley outfitted Indiana's swimmers and divers in candy stripes in the 1960s to better spot them at the pool, creating what would become an iconic IU design. Hoosiers, wearing the candy stripes, won six straight NCAA swimming championships.

Bob Knight's 1971–1972 basketball squad was the first to play in Assembly Hall and the first to don the candy-striped warm-ups. There was nothing particularly loud about them in comparison to the fashion at the time, which was dominated by geometric-patterned attire most visibly—and famously—seen on glam rock musicians. They were, however, unique in the college basketball world.

"I just liked them," Knight once told Bob Hammel in classic Bob Knight fashion. "They were different."

The stripes quickly became a fan favorite, growing more popular and more identifiable with Indiana in the 1980s. Since then, even more IU teams have adopted them.

Hep's Rock: the Rock

During Terry Hoeppner's first season as IU's Head Football Coach in 2005, he noticed a limestone boulder adjacent to the

surface of the football practice field. It was removed, placed on a granite slab, and moved to the north end zone inside Memorial Stadium. Nicknamed "The Rock," Hoeppner started the tradition of every coach and team member touching The Rock before running onto the field.

Since limestone is readily available in the Bloomington area, it is not uncommon to see large boulders as well as cliffs of this stone along the roadways. Unproven legend has it that the boulder is from a long-lost stone-quarry buried deep under the Football stadium. Thus, the nickname for memorial stadium has been "The Rock" and "The Quarry."

Terry Hoeppner succumbed to brain cancer on June 19, 2007, and The Rock was re-named "Hep's Rock" during a ceremony with the Hoeppner family on November 6, 2010. Hep's Rock now serves as motivation for the team, as well as a tribute to Hoeppner's influence on the football program.

No Names on Jerseys

Indiana's uniforms are known for the simple, clean, classic look that tradition implies. The most prominent example of this has long been the Men's Basketball uniforms. The absence of players' names on uniforms has been adopted by almost all of Indiana's athletic teams, consistent with the department's Brand and Uniform Guidelines. The classic look is a nod to the notion of "team over self."

Championship Stars

Stars on Hoosier uniforms represent the ultimate intercollegiate athletic accomplishment—a national team championship. The stars may appear in a line, on an arc, or under various sport marks and equal the number of national championships that sport has earned.

The author suggests that Indiana and Purdue carry this a bit further with each school flag. The IU flag would have 24 stars, and the Purdue flag three stars.

Victory Flag

Located in the southeast corner of field, Memorial Stadium's flagpole is the tallest in college football (154.5 feet). Installed in 2013, it is dedicated to all Indiana alumni war veterans.

After every Indiana Football win, the enormous (30 by 50 feet) Victory Flag is raised by members of the Student Athletic Board.

Hoosier Army

Armstrong Stadium is the home for IU soccer. It is named for the late Bill Armstrong, who served as Executive Director and President of the IU Foundation from 1952 to 1983 as a fundraiser and Athletic Department consultant. He was instrumental in starting men's soccer as varsity sport in the 1970s.

Armstrong was nicknamed "Army" by close friends at IU. The Hoosier's first coach called the IU soccer fans his Army. The group name later morphed into Hoosier Army.

When the soccer team plays at Armstrong Stadium, Hoosier goals are celebrated by a cannon shot. People unfamiliar with the huge IU soccer program often are startled by the noise from the stadium and ask, "What was that explosion?" The locals of the northern part of campus and fraternity row generally answer, "It's the Army. The Hoosier Army."

We Love IU's Campus

Campus in General

Whether you like to sit on a cozy bench under the shade of leafy trees, admire a great work of contemporary art, or take photos of stunning architecture built from locally-sourced limestone, there's something for everyone on the beautiful campus of IU in Bloomington.

Out of the "100 Most Beautiful College Campuses in America," Indiana University ranks number 15 on Best College Reviews because of its limestone architecture and natural beauty. It's also ranked number 15 in Best Colleges' "50 Most Amazing College Campuses of 2017" because of its historic buildings and college-town atmosphere.

It was the lush grounds, limestone buildings, and cycling and walking trails that made USA Today readers vote in favor of IU, which placed second on the publication's list of "Top 10 Best Beautiful College Campuses."

The affordability of attending college in such a beautiful setting is what made the IU Bloomington campus rank number two on Great Value Colleges.net/Beautiful Campuses.

The Indiana campus also made the 20 most beautiful list on Condé Nast Traveler's list thanks to the way its limestone buildings and leafy grounds complement the Jordan River, named after IU's first president. *Travel and Leisure* (magazine) also noted the landscaping and limestone in its list of "The Most Beautiful College in Every State."

IU's name can also be found on the BuzzFeed list of the 21 of the most beautiful college campuses in America, and it was USA Today's most Instagrammed place in Indiana.

Beck Chapel and Dunn Cemetery

Almost 80 years ago, Frank Orman Beck and his wife Daisy, gave a gift to IU that was to be used for construction of a nondenominational chapel on campus. Due to the war (WWII), there were a lack of resources available to construct the building, to be completed with wood from southern Indiana forests, Indiana limestone, a slate roof, and a copper spire, so the building had to wait. Groundbreaking finally took place in 1954, and in 1956 the cornerstone was laid. The chapel was officially dedicated as part of the graduation festivities in 1957.

Beck Chapel is nestled in the quiet, wooded area just steps to the east of the Indiana Memorial Union in the heart of Indiana University Bloomington's campus. Over the years, Beck Chapel has seen numerous weddings, christenings, funerals, devotional services, organ recitals, and individual meditations.

Adjacent to the chapel is a tiny cemetery where the Dunn family is laid to rest in the heart of what is now IU's campus. Three Brewster sisters provided resources for the American army toward the end of the Revolutionary War. They lived in Virginia at the time. After the war, they all moved to Bloomington, where they settled and died, according to IU Archives.

They were buried in the Dunn's family cemetery, a plot of land on the Dunn family's farm in what was then east Bloomington. One

of the family grandsons, farmer-turned-US congressman George Grundy Dunn, deeded the 60-by-110 foot plot of land to be a cemetery forever in honor of his grandmother and her two sisters, who were laid to rest there.

But the Brewster–Dunn–Alexander family connections spread far and wide. Many descendants of the Brewster sisters, the Dunns, Alexanders, and Maxwells contributed to the beginnings of the state of Indiana, the city of Bloomington, and Indiana University according to IU Archive records.

David Hervey Maxwell, who helped write the Indiana state constitution, is acknowledged as the father of IU. He passed a bill to make IU a state university in 1820 and served as a founding trustee. Maxwell Hall is named in his honor.

Walking around downtown Bloomington, you see Dunn Street, Dunn Meadow, and Dunn Woods. It all links back this quiet little cemetery plot that often goes unnoticed, untouched, and hardly visited.

Dunn's Woods

Dunn's Woods is the wooded area in the middle of the Old Crescent on the IU campus. The Kirkwood Observatory is in the western edge of the woods and is bounded by Lindley Hall, Maxwell Hall, Bryan Hall, Kirkwood Hall, Owen Hall, Swain Hall, and the School of Law.

Dunn's woods was originally the 20-acre plot purchased from Moses Fell Dunn in 1883 for the "new" campus when IU was located at Seminary Square southwest of the current campus. What is now known as "Dunn's Woods" is what remains of the original 20- acre plot, after the Old Crescent was built. All the buildings in the Old Crescent lay on that original tract of land. In the period when both campuses were still in operation, people usually called the new one the Dunn's Woods campus.

Dunn Meadow

The Dunn Meadow is a grass meadow just northwest of the Indiana Memorial Union. Its north border is 7th Street and its west border is Indiana Avenue. It is often used as a place for concerts, festivals, conventions, protests, camp-outs, as well as just a place to relax. People are often spotted playing with their dogs or throwing a football or Frisbee there.

The Jordan River

The westward-flowing Jordan River is even more beautiful in its winter splendor. A bridge spans the Jordan River north of the student building and Jordan Hall.

The Jordan River isn't really a river as one with a biblical background would think. Visitors or freshmen, upon first arriving at IU, are often surprised when directed to cross the Jordan River

to get to the Memorial Union building. It is only a creek that winds through the Indiana University campus. Over the years was colloquially renamed to "Jordan River" in honor of IU's seventh President, David Starr Jordan, and was formally renamed in 1994.

The Jordan River is a significant natural feature that contributes to IU's natural aesthetic. Sections of the Jordan River, particularly within the historic core, flow through forested areas with naturally vegetated buffer zones.

An IU tradition is for pledges of a fraternity to throw any active member of that chapter that pinned a girl (gave his fraternity pin to a girl) into the Jordan River.

Indiana Memorial Union

Located in what is now the western edge of the IU campus, the Indiana Memorial Union (IMU) building sits just south the Jordan River, Dunn Meadow, and 7th Street. It was dedicated in 1932. At nearly 500,000 square feet, it is one of the world's largest student unions. The IMU contains a hotel, restaurants, a bookstore, a bowling alley, a movie theater, a beauty salon, an electronics store, and gathering spaces for lecturers, meetings, conferences, and performances. The building also houses IU's student government offices within the Student Activities Tower, where as many as 50 campus organizations conduct regular meetings.

The Biddle Hotel and Conference Center was added in 1960 connected to the eastern side of the IMU. This wing contains 189 guest rooms and over 50,000 square feet of meeting space. The IMU hosts more than 17,000 events every year.

On the first floor of the IMU, the Memorial Room pays tribute to members of the Indiana University community that have served in the US military. Contained within this room is the Golden Book, which contains the names of IU's service members going back to the War of 1812.

John Whittenberger, a student, founded the Indiana Union in 1909. Every student at Indiana University's Bloomington campus is a member of the Indiana Memorial Union by default.

IU Auditorium

The Indiana University Auditorium is a large multi-purpose auditorium in the heart of the IU campus. It is used for concerts, theatre shows, speeches, and many other types of performances. Among its many amenities, it has 3,154 seats; a balcony section; orchestra pit; a 4,543-pipe Schantz organ; a 3,700-square-foot stage, hospitality rooms; and a 4;157-square-foot foyer.

The Auditorium was built during the Great Depression as part of the Works Progress Administration program. The Auditorium was the first building designed for Indiana University by New York architectural firm Eggers and Higgins. The Auditorium opened on March 22, 1941.

On permanent display in the Auditorium's Hall of Murals are the highly acclaimed Thomas Hart Benton murals, which depict the industrial and social progress of the state of Indiana. Originally painted by Thomas Hart Benton for display at the 1933 Chicago World's Fair, many of them found new homes in the Auditorium. During the renovation, these murals were delicately cleaned and restored, and now are as vivid as the day they were installed. Also on display is the Daily Family Art collection, which features the work of Indiana artists.

The Auditorium is the primary commercial concert and show venue at Indiana University. The hall has hosted a large variety of performers, including Jerry Seinfeld, Itzhak Perlman, and many touring Broadway musicals.

Lilly Library

The Lilly Library is located on the southern side of a small square in the heart of the IU campus. Showalter Fountain is in the middle of the square. Indiana University Art Museum and Indiana University School of Fine Arts are on the opposite (northern) side of the square. Indiana University Auditorium is on the square's eastern side.

The Lilly Library, dedicated in 1960, has 8.5 million manuscripts; 450,000 books; 60,000 comic books; 16,000 mini books; 35,000 puzzles; and 150,000 sheets of music. It was founded in 1960 with the collection of Josiah K. Lilly, Jr., owner of Lilly Pharmaceuticals in Indianapolis. J. K. Lilly was a collector most of his life. From the mid-1920s until his death, he devoted a great deal of his leisure time to building his collections of books, manuscripts, works of art, coins, stamps, military miniatures, firearms, edged weapons, and nautical models. J. K. Lilly's collections of books and manuscripts, totaling more than 20,000 books and 17,000 manuscripts, together with more than fifty oil paintings and 300 prints, were given by the collector to Indiana University between 1954 and 1957. These materials form the foundation of the rare book and manuscript collections of the Lilly Library.

Here are some of the many notable items in the library's collections: *New Testament of the Gutenberg Bible*; the first printed collection of Shakespeare's works (the *First Folio*); Audubon's *Birds of America*; one of 26 extant copies of the first printing of the Declaration of Independence (also known as the "Dunlap Broadside") that was printed in Philadelphia on July 4, 1776; George Washington's letter accepting the presidency of the United States; Abraham Lincoln's desk from his law office and a leaf from the famous Abraham Lincoln "Sum Book" circa 1824–1826; Lord Chesterfield's letters to his son, the drafts of Robert Burns's "Auld Lang Syne;" the Boxer Codex; a manuscript written circa 1595 which contains illustrations of ethnic groups in the Philippines at the time

of their initial contact with the Spaniards; J. M. Synge's *The Playboy of the Western World*; J. M. Barrie's *Peter Pan*; typescripts of many of Ian Fleming's James Bond novels.

The library also owns the papers of Hollywood directors Orson Welles and John Ford, film critic Pauline Kael, the poets Sylvia Plath and Ezra Pound, and authors Edith Wharton and Upton Sinclair.

The Eskenazi Museum of Art

Inside the Fine Arts Library building, the windows open into the museum's atrium. Designed by I. M. Pei and Partners and completed in 1982, the museum was constructed as a play on angles. It is rumored to have no right angles; however, this is not true. The floors meet the walls at a ninety-degree angle, and there are many square and rectangular windows in the building. The design features two concrete triangles connected by a glass-ceiling atrium. The building was constructed with a weird set of stairs descending to glass doors on the north side. The stair treads were at an angle that required one to focus lest he or she stumble.

The museum is 105,000 square feet: 38,361 square feet are devoted to gallery space; 16,664 square feet are devoted to the Fine Arts Library; and 18,000 square feet comprise the atrium. The other space is used for offices, gift shop, storage, and the outdoor Sculpture Terrace.

The museum has a light totem that was completed in 2007. Artist Robert Shakespeare used LEDs to illuminate both the 70-foot freestanding tower, and the 40-foot tube within the atrium of the museum. The Light Totem also illuminates the wall of the Art Museum with a computerized display of changing colors. Each of the lighted sections can be programmed to project any color and change color up to every tenth of a second. The entire display uses only 3,000 watts of electricity, about the amount used when a hair dryer and toaster are running simultaneously, according to the artist.

Students often can be seen lying on their backs with their feet up on the wall, watching the colors change.

Showalter Fountain

Showalter Fountain is the centerpiece of the Fine Arts Square, around which reside the Auditorium, the School of Fine Arts, and the Lilly Library. Funded by Grace Montgomery Showalter, the sculpture of the goddess Venus being born from a clam shell was designed by former IU faculty member Robert Laurent.

The ledge surrounding the fountain is a favorite spot for students to sit, read, and wait for their next class.

The fountain has an array of dolphins frolicking around Venus, despite their very fish-like tails. One fish stands out from the others in form and appearance. It was originally cast as a spare to have on hand in case one of the regular fish was ever damaged or lost. The odd fish is indeed in place now as the original fish is no longer with us.

A mythical story that has been passed down by students over the years is that Venus will be born the day that a virgin graduates from IU.

Early in the spring, it is common for someone to put laundry detergent in the fountain and let it bubble up. The bubbles usually fill the fountain.

One tradition of graduation from Indiana University is to go over to the fountain, take off your gown and clothes and stand in the water.

Sample Gates

The entrance into the oldest part of the IU campus, known as the Old Crescent, is flanked by the Sample Gates. These Indiana Limestone towers with peaked arches are among the most widely

photographed structures on campus, they are typically surrounded by tulips in the spring. They are located between Franklin Hall and Bryan Hall and serve as a welcoming entryway for students and visitors into IU's beautiful campus. Each gate features a tower flanked with a four-centered arch, through which pedestrians can pass on a sidewalk.

Edson Sample funded construction of the gates in 1987 and dedicated them to his parents, Louise Waite Sample and Kimsey Ownbey Sample Sr.

IU Arboretum

The Indiana University campus has changed so much over the years that it's hard to grasp the full extent of the transformation. What is acutely remarkable is the transformation of the space that is now the Jesse H. and Beulah Chanley Cox Arboretum at IU. Before it was the Arboretum, this site housed IU's first Memorial Stadium. In 1960, a new Memorial Stadium was erected on 17th Street, but the old stadium continued to be used for the Little 500 and other activities. Eventually the old stadium had deteriorated so badly that it had to be demolished.

Structural work on the Arboretum was completed in 1984. It is an ideal place for relaxation and study. The Arboretum is an oasis of beauty, landscaped with hundreds of trees and surrounding greenery. A gazebo overlooks numerous walking/bicycling paths and a pond. The current site of the Arboretum is nestled between the Herman B. Wells Library and the School of Heath, Physical Education and Recreation (HPER).

IU Memorial Stadium

IU's Memorial Stadium is located on the far north edge of campus. It is surrounded by parking areas and other athletic facilities

that are bordered by Indiana highway 46 on the north, Dunn Street on the west, 17th Street on the south, and Fee Lane on the east.

Memorial Stadium is the most beautiful football stadium in the Big Ten. Except for the bleachers and theater seats, all surfaces in the stadium are finished limestone, brick, or concrete. There are no girders or supports visible. The stadium is a complete bowl with seating all the way around.

The field is a bright green FieldTurf Revolution 360 playing surface with red end zones and a red map of the state of Indiana at midfield. The seating bowl is white. Thus, when empty, the football facility is bright and almost Christmassy.

Memorial Stadium opened in 1960 replacing the old Memorial Stadium on 10th Street. It is dedicated as a memorial to IU students who served the US in foreign wars. There are 119 rows of seats from the field to the press box on the west side of the stadium, making it the tallest stadium in America. It is now filled-in on each end, making it a complete bowl. The largest crowd has been 56,223.

Known as The Rock or the Quarry, the stadium has a capacity of more than 50,000. The south end zone is topped by a large

HD scoreboard from Daktronics, one of the largest scoreboards in America. There is also an HD scoreboard in the north end zone.

In 2005, head football coach Terry Hoeppner had a southern Indiana limestone boulder, nicknamed "The Rock," installed in the north end zone as a new campus tradition. This limestone boulder now serves as motivation for the team as well as a tribute to Hoeppner's influence on the football program. As the Hoosiers take the playing field, they touch the rock.

The prow, mainmast, and two guns of the USS Indiana (BB-58) are erected at the western entrance of the stadium. The battleship saw extensive service in the Pacific Theater during World War II, earning nine battle stars and taking part in the invasion of the Gilbert Islands, Marshall Islands, Marianas campaign, and the Battle of Iwo Jima. This truly exemplified the meaning of a true Memorial Stadium, as it is named and dedicated to the memory of members of the IU family that have died in wars.

Acknowledgements

Thanks to the people at Blue River Press for offering me the opportunity to write this book. This author appreciates all who participated in this project by sharing their thoughts, information, opinions, and feelings. Thanks to the Indiana University Athletic Department's J.D. Campbell, Senior Assistant Athletic Director for Men's Basketball Communications; and to Jeff Keag, Senior Assistant Athletic Director for Media Relations (Football). Also, thanks to Mark Deal, Indiana University Assistant Athletic Director for Alumni Relations for his detailed help and stories about Hoosier football history. Thanks to Chuck Crabb, Assistant Athletic Director for Facilities and PA announcer for IU games, for his insight into IU's National Championship Cheerleading program. Also, thanks to Don Fischer, the Hall of Fame broadcast Voice of Indiana Hoosiers, for his recollections of great IU victories.

Thanks to Bill Hicks, Purdue Letterman, John Purdue Club member and brilliant photographer. Also, thanks to the Indiana University photographic archives.

About the Author

Joe Drozda grew up in Northwest Indiana and began to attend both Notre Dame and Purdue college football games at the age of ten. During his senior year of high school, he visited Indiana University and fell in love with the campus, the southern feel of the students, and the athletic teams. He graduated from IU, after a combat tour in Vietnam, in 1970 with a BS in Marketing. He resides in Carmel, Indiana and attends all IU home football and some basketball games. While writing *The Tailgater's Handbook*, he attended every IU football game, both home and away, from Rutgers in the East to Nebraska in the west.

Joe is the author of three sports books and more than 200 articles about both management and tailgating. He has been featured in Sports Illustrated as the father of college football tailgating. He currently writes a column for twelve newspapers.

He and his wife Cynthia have been married for forty-eight years and are the parents of two IU graduates and grandparents of three boys.